eine Zufriedenheit . —

künftig jeden Monath 100 fl: Lehnen 1, würd

nur das Quartal meiner Gage zu

Lindas zurückzustellen werden . —

— nicht noch nicht erhalten /auch gar ,

vom Geld entblößt , so daß ich

und das Wegen mein drohenen

Schuft gänzlich überzeugt bin ; —

— gebüren Nomen nennen Döum

Mozart

Mozart

VOLUME TWO · THE LETTERS

TRANSLATED BY EMILY ANDERSON

EDITED BY
MICHAEL ROSE AND PETER WASHINGTON

EVERYMAN - EMI MUSIC COMPANIONS

GENERAL EDITOR MICHAEL ROSE

Copyright © David Campbell Publishers Ltd.
and EMI Records Ltd., 1997

Music compilation ℗ and © 1997 EMI Classics (USA)

Mozart's letters are reprinted from *The Letters of Mozart and his Family*, edited and translated by Emily Anderson (3rd edition, 1985), by kind permission of Macmillan Press Ltd.

Selection, Music Notes and editorial matter © Michael Rose and Peter Washington, 1997

ISBN 1-85715-603-X

Published by David Campbell Publishers Ltd., 79 Berwick Street, London W1V 3PF

Distributed by Random House (UK) Ltd., 20 Vauxhall Bridge Road, London SW1V 2SA

A CIP catalogue reference for this book is available from the British Library.

Front endpaper: (detail) letter from Mozart to Franz Hofdemel, Vienna, end March 1789 (AKG London)
Back endpaper: (detail) Mozart's postscript to a letter from his mother Maria Anna to his father Leopold in Salzburg, Mannheim, 8 November 1777 (AKG London)
Frontispiece: Wolfgang Amadeus Mozart, wax relief by Leonhard Posch, *c.*1789 (AKG London/Internationale Stiftung Mozarteum, Salzburg)

Design by Anikst Associates
Picture research by Helen Ottaway
Typeset by AccComputing, Castle Cary, Somerset
Printed and bound in Germany by Mohndruck Graphische Betriebe GmbH, Gütersloh

Preface

One of the many extraordinary things about Wolfgang Amadeus Mozart is how he found the time to combine his work as one of the world's most prolific composers – *and* a demanding professional career as a travelling performer – with the production of a large and incomparable correspondence. His letters are probably the most consistently fascinating of any composer's at any period, and he ranks high among letter writers in general, even in an age like the late eighteenth century when the epistolary form was widely cultivated as an art. And the correspondence is made immensely more vivid by the existence of so many letters from his father and other members of his family, which fill out the picture given by Mozart himself and add glimpses of family life and family relationships which would not be possible with only one side of the story.

As Andrew Steptoe observed in the first Mozart volume of the Everyman–EMI Music series, 'the central influence on Mozart's life and development was his father Leopold'. Leopold was a dominant but loving parent, keen to supervise his son's career from a distance even when the boy had grown into a man, and it is to him that most of the composer's surviving letters are addressed. Naturally they are concerned in the main with musical matters, and Mozart used them to give his father a fascinating and amazingly detailed account of his career as performer, teacher and composer. They also provide a lively picture of contemporary musical politics, illuminated by character sketches of the major figures he encountered, especially in the courts and opera houses of Europe. Other letters – to his sister, his mother, his friends and girlfriends – add the delightful social and domestic details which help us to understand what Mozart was like and how he lived. Finally, there are the pathetic begging letters from his last years and the wonderful correspondence with his wife, by turns adoring, arch and admonitory.

In all, nearly 1200 of the letters that passed between Mozart, his family and friends during his lifetime have survived, and of these rather over 600 were translated by Emily Anderson and published in 1938 in an edition which has become one of the classics of musical literature. From this translation we have made a selection which we hope fairly represents the various aspects of Mozart's life (as well as his father's reactions to them), giving complete letters wherever possible but adding extracts where they help to preserve the sense or the flavour of his writing, and providing only such editorial notes and narrative links as seemed necessary to the same end. To reduce footnotes to a minimum an annotated index is included at the back of the book.

In a couple of cases, where we felt there were gaps worth filling in, we have added material from sources outside the letters. At the beginning of Mozart's travels, when he was too young to write himself and his father's letters were largely taken up with the day-to-day details of their journeys, we have included the famous description of Mozart as a boy written by an associate of the Royal Society during his visit to London, and followed it with the reaction of a local contemporary on the Mozart family's return to Salzburg. And at the very end we have included the letter written many years later by Mozart's youngest sister-in-law about the last days of the composer's life.

M. R.
P. W.

(page vi) In spite of his many voyages abroad, Salzburg was Mozart's home and the centre of his family life until his final removal to Vienna. This contemporary engraving (by F. Muller after Franz von Naumann) shows the Residenzplatz with the cathedral and, on the right, the palace of the Archbishop of Salzburg by whom Mozart's father was employed – and Mozart too until his break with the Archbishop in 1781.

The Letters 1762–91

Mozart's father, Leopold, aware that his son was something out of the ordinary as a musical prodigy, was eager to exhibit his amazing abilities to as wide a public as possible. For this purpose it was necessary to get away from the provincial world of Salzburg (where Leopold held an appointment in the Archbishop's Court), and throughout his childhood Wolfgang Mozart was constantly travelling, sometimes with his father and sister, later just with his mother, from one great European city to another. The first journey, to Munich in January 1762, was undertaken without Frau Mozart and has left no documentary record, but the second, to Vienna later in the same year, included the whole family. At this time Mozart was six and a half years old, his sister Nannerl just turned eleven.

Leopold Mozart to Lorenz Hagenauer, Salzburg

Vienna,
16 October 1762

... On the feast of St. Francis we left Linz at half past four in the afternoon by the so-called ordinary boat and reached Mauthausen after nightfall on the same day at half past seven. At noon on the following day, Tuesday, we arrived at Ybbs, where two Minorites and a Benedictine, who were with us on the boat, said Masses, during which our Woferl strummed on the organ and played so well that the Franciscans, who happened to be entertaining some guests at their midday meal, left the table and with their company rushed to the choir and were almost struck dead with

A pencil drawing of the composer's father, probably dating from 1762, the year in which Leopold Mozart decided to take his two brilliant children on a tour of European courts. The drawing is attributed to Franz Lactanz, Count Firmian, high steward to the Archbishop of Salzburg.

amazement. In the evening we reached Stein and on Wednesday at three in the afternoon arrived at Vienna; here at five o'clock we took our midday meal and supper at the same time. On the journey we had continual rain and a lot of wind. Wolfgang had already caught a cold in Linz, but in spite of our irregular life, early rising, eating and drinking at all hours, and wind and rain, he has, thank God, kept well. When we landed, Gilowsky's servant, who was already there, came on board and brought us to our lodgings. But after leaving our luggage safely and tidily there, we soon hurried off to an inn to appease our hunger. Gilowsky himself then came to welcome us. Now we have already been here five days and do not yet know where the sun rises in Vienna, for to this very hour it has done nothing but rain and, with constant wind, has snowed a little now and then, so that we have even seen some snow on the roofs. Moreover it has been and still is very frosty, though not excessively cold. One thing I must make a point of telling you, which is, that we quickly got through the local customs and were let off the chief customs altogether. And for this we have to thank our Master Woferl. For he made friends at once with the customs officer, showed him his clavier, invited him to visit us and played him a minuet on his little fiddle. Thus we got through. The customs officer asked most politely to be allowed to visit us and for this purpose made a note of our lodgings. So far, in spite of the most atrocious weather, we have been to a concert given by Count Collalto. Further, Countess Sinzendorf introduced us to Count Wilschegg and on the 11th to His Excellency the Imperial Vice-Chancellor, Count Colloredo, where we were privileged to see and to speak to the leading ministers and ladies of the Imperial Court, to wit, the Hungarian Chancellor, Count Palffy, and the Bohemian Chancellor, Count Chotek, as well as Bishop Esterházy and a number of persons, all of whom I could not note. All, the ladies especially, were very gracious to us. Count Leopold Kühnburg's fiancée spoke to my wife of her own accord and told her that she is going to be married at Salzburg. She is a pretty, friendly woman, of medium height. She is expecting her betrothed in Vienna very shortly. Countess Sinzendorf is using her influence on our behalf, and all the ladies are in love with my boy. We are already being talked of everywhere: and when on the 10th I was alone at the opera, I heard the Archduke Leopold from his box say a number of things to another box, namely, that there was a boy in Vienna who played the clavier

An oil painting of the child Mozart (left), probably by Pietro Antonio Lorenzoni, painted in Salzburg early in 1763. One of a pair with a portrait of the composer's sister, Nannerl (right), his inseparable companion in childhood.

most excellently and so on. At eleven o'clock that very same evening I received a
command to go to Schönbrunn on the 12th. But the following day there came
a fresh command to go there on the 13th instead (the 12th being the Feast of Maximilian and therefore a very busy gala-day), because, I gather, they want to hear the
children in comfort. Everyone is amazed, especially at the boy, and everyone whom
I have heard says that his genius is incomprehensible. Baron Schell is using his
influence on my behalf and is gratefully acknowledging the kindnesses he enjoyed
at Salzburg. If you have an opportunity, please tell this to Herr Chiusolis with my
respects. Count Daun also has given me a note for Baron Schell and has filled me
with hopes that I shall leave Vienna fully satisfied. And so it seems, since the Court
is asking to hear us before we have announced ourselves. For young Count Palffy

*Johann Lorenz
Hagenauer, Leopold
Mozart's landlord
and banker in
Salzburg, and the
recipient of virtually
all Leopold's
surviving letters from
his travels until the
end of 1768. Copy in
oils (1783) by
Sebastien Stief after
the original painted
on sheet metal in
St. Peter's Cemetery.*

happened to be passing through Linz as our concert was about to begin. He was
calling on the Countess Schlick, who told him about the boy and persuaded him
to stop the mail coach in front of the town hall and attend the concert with her. He
listened with astonishment and spoke later with great excitement of the performance to the Archduke Joseph, who passed it on to the Empress. Thus, as soon as it
was known that we were in Vienna, the command came for us to go to court. That,
you see, is how it happened.

I wrote the above on the 11th, fully intending to tell you on the 12th, after our
return from Schönbrunn, how everything had gone off. But we had to drive from
Schönbrunn straight to Prince von Hildburghausen, and six ducats were more
important to us than the despatch of my letter. I have sufficient confidence in Frau
Hagenauer and trust enough to her kind friendship to know that she will accept
even now our congratulations on her name-day and even in the short form of merely
saying that we shall ask God to keep her and all her loved ones well and strong for
many years to come and to invite us all in due course to play cards in Heaven. Now
all that I have time for is to say in great haste that Their Majesties received us with
such extraordinary graciousness that, when I shall tell of it, people will declare that

I have made it up. Suffice it to say that Woferl jumped up on the Empress's lap, put his arms round her neck and kissed her heartily. In short, we were there from three to six o'clock and the Emperor himself came out of the next room and made me go in there to hear the Infanta play the violin. On the 15th the Empress sent us by the Privy Paymaster, who drove up to our house in state, two dresses, one for the boy and one for the girl. As soon as the command arrives, they are to appear at court and the Privy Paymaster will fetch them. Today at half past two in the afternoon they are to go to the two youngest Archdukes and at four o'clock to the Hungarian Chancellor, Count Palffy. Yesterday we were with Count Kaunitz, and the day before with Countess Kinsky and later with the Count von Ulefeld. And we already have more engagements for the next two days. Please tell everybody that, thank God, we are well and happy. I send greetings and I am your old

Mozart

The Mozarts returned to Salzburg early in January 1763, but in June the whole family were off again – this time on a full European tour, first visiting a number of cities in southern Germany, spending the winter of 1763–4 in Paris, and fetching up in London for the rest of 1764 and a good part of the next year. The following report, received by the Secretary of the Royal Society in London in 1769, describes Mozart

An advertisement for one of Mozart's London concerts, which appeared in the Public Advertiser, *9 May 1764.*

For the Benefit of Sig. GRAZIANI.

HICKFORD's Great Room, in Brewer-Street, Thursday, May 17, will be a Grand Concert of

Vocal and Instrumental MUSIC.

The Vocal Parts by the Signoras Sartori, Cremonini, and Signor Maziotti. First Violin, and a Concerto, by Sig. Giardini. Concerto and Solo on the Violoncello, by Sig. Graziani. Concerto on the German Flute by Sig. Florio. Concerto on the Harpsichord by Master Mozart, who is a real Prodigy of Nature; he is but Seven Years of Age, plays any thing at first Sight, and composes amazingly well. He has had the Honour of exhibiting before their Majesties greatly to their Satisfaction. The Whole to conclude with a Full Piece.
† Tickets, Half a Guinea each, to be had of Sig. Graziani, at the Warwick-street Coffee-house.

towards the end of this London visit, at the age of nine (though his father, ever with
an eye to the main chance, continued to trim his age by a year for the purpose of
public appearances in the city).

Account of a Very Remarkable Young Musician

Sir,

If I was to send you a well attested account of a boy who measured seven feet in height, when he was not more than eight years of age, it might be considered as not undeserving the notice of the Royal Society.

The instance which I now desire you will communicate to that learned body, of as early an exertion of most extraordinary musical talents, seems perhaps equally to claim their attention.

Joannes Chrysostomus Wolfgangus Theophilus Mozart, was born at Saltzbourg in Bavaria, on the 17th of January, 1756.[1]

I have been informed by a most able musician and composer, that he frequently saw him at Vienna, when he was little more than four years old.

By this time he not only was capable of executing lessons on his favourite instrument the harpsichord, but composed some in an easy stile and taste, which were much approved of.

His extraordinary musical talents soon reached the ears of the present empress dowager, who used to place him upon her knees whilst he played on the harpsichord.

This notice taken of him by so great a personage, together with a certain conciousness of his most singular abilities, had much emboldened the little musician. Being therefore the next year at one of the German courts, where the elector encouraged him, by saying, that he had nothing to fear from his august presence; Little Mozart immediately sat down with great confidence to his harpsichord, informing his highness, that he had played before the empress.

In a Letter from the Honourable Daines Barrington, F.R.S. to Mathew Maty, M.D. Sec. R.S. Read Feb. 15, 1770

---

1 I here subjoin a copy of the translation from the register at Saltzbourg, as it was procured from his excellence Count Haslang, envoy extraordinary and minister plenipotentiary of the electors of Bavaria and Palatine:

'I, the under-written, certify, that in the year 1756, the 17th of January, at eight o'clock in the evening, was born Joannes Chrysostomus Wolfgangus Theophilus, son of Mr. Leopold Mozart, organist of his highness the prince of Saltzbourg, and of Maria Ann his lawful wife (whose maiden name was Pertlin), and christened the day following, at ten o'clock in the morning, at the prince's cathedral church here; his godfather being Gottlieb Pergmayr, merchant in this city. In truth whereof, I have taken this certificate from the parochial register of christenings, and under the usual seal, signed the same with my own hand.

Saltzbourg,   Leopald Comprecht,

Jan. 3, 1769.   Chaplain to his Highness in this city.'

An engraved portrait of Mozart as a child, taken from Barrington's Miscellanies (T. Cook after Carmontelle). The existence of this picture reflects the composer's early celebrity.

At seven years of age his father carried him to Paris, where he so distinguished himself by his compositions, that an engraving was made of him.

The father and sister who are introduced in this print, are excessively like their portraits, as is also little Mozart, who, is stiled 'Compositeur et Maitre de Musique, agé de sept ans'.

After the name of the engraver, follows the date, which is in 1764; Mozart was therefore at this time in the eighth year of his age.

Upon leaving Paris, he came over to England, where he continued more than a year. As during this time I was witness of his most extraordinary abilities as a musician, both at some publick concerts, and likewise by having been alone with him for a considerable time at his father's house; I send you the following account, amazing and incredible almost as it may appear.

I carried to him a manuscript duet, which was composed by an English gentleman to some favourite words in Metastasio's opera of Demofoonte.

The whole score was in five parts, viz. accompaniments for a first and second violin, the two vocal parts, and a base. I shall here likewise mention, that the parts for the first and second voice were written in what the Italians stile the *Contralto* cleff; the reason for taking notice of which particular will appear hereafter.

My intention in carrying with me this manuscript composition, was to have an irrefragable proof of his abilities, as a player at sight, it being absolutely impossible that he could have ever seen the music before.

The score was no sooner put upon his desk, than he began to play the symphony in a most masterly manner, as well as in the time and stile which corresponded with the intention of the composer.

I mention this circumstance, because the greatest masters often fail in these particulars on the first trial.

The symphony ended, he took the upper part, leaving the under one to his father.

His voice in the tone of it was thin and infantine, but nothing could exceed the masterly manner in which he sung.

His father, who took the under part in this duet, was once or twice out, though the passages were not more difficult than those in the upper one; on which occasions the son looked back with some anger pointing out to him his mistakes, and setting him right.

He not only however did complete justice to the duet, by singing his own part in the truest taste, and with the greatest precision: he also threw in the accompaniments of the two violins, wherever they were most necessary, and produced the best effects.

It is well known that none but the most capital musicians are capable of accompanying in this superior stile.

As many of those who may be present, when this letter may have the honour of being read before the society, may not possibly be acquainted with the difficulty of playing thus from a musical score, I will endeavour to explain it by the most similar comparison I can think of.

I must at the same time admit, that the illustration will fail in one particular, as the voice in reading cannot comprehend more than what is contained in a single line. I must suppose, however, that the reader's eye, by habit and quickness, may take in other lines, though the voice cannot articulate them, as the musician accompanies the words of an air by his harpsichord.

Let it be imagined, therefore, that a child of eight years old was directed to read five lines[1] at once, in four[2] of which the letters of the alphabet were to have different powers.

For example, in the ·first line A, to have its common powers.

In the second that of B. In the third of C. In the fourth of D.

1 By this I mean, The two parts for the violins. The upper part for the voice. The words set to music. And lastly, the base.

2 By this I mean, The violin parts in the common treble cleff. The upper part for the voice in the contralto cleff as before-mentioned. The words in common characters. And the base in its common cleff.

Let it be conceived also, that the lines so composed of characters, with different powers, are not ranged so as to be read at all times one exactly under the other, but often in a desultory manner.

Suppose then, a capital speech in Shakespeare[1] never seen before, and yet read by a child of eight years old, with all the pathetic energy of a Garrick.

Let it be conceived likewise, that the same child is reading, with a glance of his eye, three different comments on this speech tending to its illustration; and that one comment is written in Greek, the second in Hebrew, and the third in Etruscan characters.

Let it be also supposed, that by different signs he could point out which comment is most material upon every word; and sometimes that perhaps all three are so, at others only two of them.

When all this is conceived, it will convey some idea of what this boy was capable of, in singing such a duet at sight in a masterly manner from the score, throwing in at the same time all its proper accompaniments.

When he had finished the duet, he expressed himself highly in its approbation, asking with some eagerness whether I had brought any more such music.

Having been informed, however, that he was often visited with musical ideas, to which, even in the midst of the night, he would give utterance on his harpsichord; I told his father that I should be glad to hear some of his extemporary compositions.

The father shook his head at this, saying, that it depended entirely upon his being as it were musically inspired, but that I might ask him whether he was in humour for such a composition.

Happening to know that little Mozart was much taken notice of by Manzoli, the famous singer, who came over to England in 1764, I said to the boy, that I should be glad to hear an extemporary *Love Song*, such as his friend Manzoli might choose in an opera.

The boy on this (who continued to sit at his harpsichord) looked back with much archness, and immediately began five or six lines of a jargon recitative proper to introduce a love song.

He then played a symphony which might correspond with an air composed to the single word, *Affetto*.

It had a first and second part, which, together with the symphonies, was of the length that opera songs generally last: if this extemporary composition was not amazingly capital, yet it was really above mediocrity, and shewed most extraordinary readiness of invention.

Finding that he was in humour, and as it were inspired, I then desired him to

1 The words in Metastasio's duet, which Mozart sung, are very pathetic.

compose a *Song of Rage*, such as might be proper for the opera stage.

The boy again looked back with much archness, and began five or six lines of a jargon recitative proper to precede a *Song of Anger*.

This lasted also about the same time with the *Song of Love*; and in the middle of it, he had worked himself up to such a pitch, that he beat his harpsichord like a person possessed, rising sometimes in his chair.

The word he pitched upon for this second extemporary composition was, *Perfido*.

After this he played a difficult lesson, which he had finished a day or two before[1]: his execution was amazing, considering that his little fingers could scarcely reach a fifth on the harpsichord.

His astonishing readiness, however, did not arise merely from great practice; he had a thorough knowledge of the fundamental principles of composition, as, upon producing a treble, he immediately wrote a base under it, which, when tried, had very good effect.

He was also a great master of modulation, and his transitions from one key to another were excessively natural and judicious; he practised in this manner for a considerable time with an handkerchief over the keys of the harpsichord.

The facts which I have been mentioning I was myself an eye witness of; to which I must add, that I have been informed by two or three able musicians, when Bach the celebrated composer had begun a fugue and left off abruptly, that little Mozart hath immediately taken it up, and worked it after a most masterly manner.

Witness as I was myself of most of these extraordinary facts, I must own that I could not help suspecting his father imposed with regard to the real age of the boy, though he had not only a most childish appearance, but likewise had all the actions of that stage of life.

For example, whilst he was playing to me, a favourite cat came in, upon which he immediately left his harpsichord, nor could we bring him back for a considerable time.

He would also sometimes run about the room with a stick between his legs by way of a horse.

I found likewise that most of the London musicians were of the same opinion with regard to his age, not believing it possible that a child of so tender years could

1 He published six sonatas for the harpsichord, with an accompaniment for the violin, or German flute, which are sold by R. Bremner, in the Strand, and are intituled, Oeuvre Trois*me*.

He is said in the title page to have been only eight years of age when he composed these sonatas.

The dedication is to the Queen, and is dated at London, January 8, 1765.

He subscribes himself, 'tres humble, et tres obeissant *petit* serviteur'.

These lessons are composed in a very original stile, and some of them are masterly.

surpass most of the masters in that science.

I have therefore for a considerable time made the best inquiries I was able from some of the German musicians resident in London, but could never receive any further information than he was born near Saltzbourg, till I was so fortunate as to procure an extract from the register of that place, through his excellence count Haslang.

It appears from this extract, that Mozart's father did not impose with regard to his age when he was in England, for it was in June, 1765, that I was witness to what I have above related, when the boy was only eight years and five months old.

I have made frequent inquiries with regard to this very extraordinary genius since he left England, and was told last summer, that he was then at Saltzbourg, where he had composed several oratorios, which were much admired.

I am also informed, that the prince of Saltzbourg, not crediting that such masterly compositions were really those of a child, shut him up for a week, during which he was not permitted to see any one, and was left only with music paper, and the words of an oratorio.

During this short time he composed a very capital oratorio, which was most highly approved of upon being performed ...

His extemporary compositions also, of which I was a witness, prove his genius and invention to have been most astonishing; lest however I should insensibly become too strongly his panegyrist, permit me to subscribe myself, Sir,

Your most faithful

humble servant,

Daines Barrington

Title page of Mozart's Six Sonatas for Violin and Piano (K10–15), composed in London in 1764 and published at Leopold's expense the following year. The alternative flute part was included in deference to the great enthusiasm for the German flute among London amateurs of this period.

Maria Theresa (1717–80), ruler of the Habsburg monarchy from 1740. This portrait dates from about 1760. Mozart and his family had first been presented to the Empress in 1762, when (according to Leopold) the 6-year-old composer had distinguished himself by jumping on to her lap and kissing her. He was received again, with his father, on his second visit to Vienna in 1768, and shown much favour.

The Mozart family arrived home from their European tour at the end of November 1766, a fact noted[1] by Beda Hübner, the Librarian of St. Peter's Abbey, Salzburg, in his 'Diarium'.

... it is easy to imagine the amount of money this Herr Mozart must have made in England, where moreover all presents are given purely and solely in ready cash. In England too they stayed a whole year, and Herr Mozart in particular, who has in any case a very learned head and possesses great knowledge, as well as a very exalted mind and energetic disposition, acquired a complete knowledge of the

1 A little inaccurately: it was Mozart's father, not his mother, who was ill, and Nannerl was by this time fifteen, not thirteen, years old.

English language, having already known Italian and French by reason of his art. From England they went to Holland, and that at the request of the Republic, where again they received very many presents and collected much money. And there again, Herr Mozart, having once learnt the English language, acquired Dutch quite easily.

Joseph II (1741–90), who was co-regent of the Habsburg monarchy with his mother from 1765, when he also became Holy Roman Emperor. He was one of Mozart's earliest patrons, and following Mozart's second presentation at court in 1768, was responsible for commissioning La finta semplice, *though the work did not actually reach performance in Vienna. This portrait was painted in 1770.*

From Holland they went to Switzerland, then to Augsburg, Bavaria, and so on, until at last they once again arrived back at Salzburg in good health, at the keenest desire of the whole town, to the solace, joy and pleasure of everybody of high and low degree, and to their own honour, fame and praise; although nearly all the members of the whole family, especially the wife in England, now and again suffered very dangerous and almost fatal illnesses. The boy is now rather over 10 years of age and the little daughter over 13: the boy Wolfgangl, by the way, has not grown very much during this journey, but Nannerl has become tolerably tall and almost marriageable already. There is a strong rumour that the Mozart family will again not long remain here, but will soon visit the whole of Scandinavia and the whole of Russia, and perhaps even travel to China, which would be a far greater journey and bigger undertaking still.

Russia and China being apparently shelved for the time being, the family's next
undertaking was a second visit to Vienna, where they stayed for sixteen months and
Mozart, having survived smallpox, was presented at court and saw his little opera
Bastien und Bastienne *performed at the private theatre of the famous Dr. Mesmer*
– though another, La finta semplice, *did not achieve performance. They were back*
in Salzburg again for most of 1769, but at the end of that year Mozart and his father
set out on another, more ambitious tour, this time with Italy as the objective. They
travelled down through Verona to Milan and then on via Bologna to Florence, Rome
and Naples, returning over the same ground to Milan where Mozart had been com-
missioned to write an opera (Mitridate, rè di Ponto) *for the carnival season of 1770 –*
71. Mozart was nearly fourteen when they set out, and the first of his own letters date
from this trip.

Mozart to his Mother (a postscript to a letter of his father's)

Dearest Mamma!

My heart is completely enchanted with all these pleasures, because it is so jolly *Wörgl,*
on this journey, because it is so warm in the carriage and because our coachman *14 December 1769*
is a fine fellow who, when the road gives him the slightest chance, drives so fast.
Papa will have already described the journey to Mamma. The reason why I am
writing to Mamma is to show her that I know my duty and that I am with the
deepest respect her devoted son

Wolfgang Mozart

Mozart to his Sister (a second postscript)

My Dearest Sister,

Thank God, we have arrived safely at Wörgl. To tell the truth, I must say that *Wörgl,*
travelling is very jolly, that it is not at all cold and that it is as warm in our carriage *14 December 1769*
as in a room. How is your sore throat? Surely our Signore Seccatore turned up the
very day we left? If you see Herr von Schiedenhofen, tell him that I am always singing
'Tralaliera, Tralaliera' and that I need not put sugar in my soup now that I am no
longer in Salzburg. At Lofer we supped and slept in the house of Herr Helmreich,
who is prefect there. His wife is an excellent lady. She is the sister of Herr Moll. I am
hungry. I am longing to eat something. Meanwhile, farewell. Addio.

PS. – My compliments to all my good friends, to Herr Hagenauer (the merchant),
his wife, his sons and his daughters, to Madame Rosa and her husband, to Herr
Adlgasser and Herr Spitzeder. As for Herr Hornung, ask him from me whether he
has again made the mistake of thinking that I was in bed instead of you.

Wolfgang Mozart

I rejoice with my whole heart that you had such a good time during that sleigh-drive and I wish you a thousand opportunities of amusement so that you may spend your life very merrily. But one thing distresses me, and that is, that you have made Herr von Mölk sigh and suffer so frightfully and that you did not go sleigh-driving with him, so that he might have upset you. How many handkerchiefs will he not have used that day, weeping on your account. No doubt he will have previously taken an ounce of tartar, which will have purged his wretchedly dirty body. I have no news except that Herr Gellert, the poet, has died at Leipzig and since his death has written no more poetry. Just before I began this letter I composed an aria from 'Demetrio', which begins:

Misero tu non sei:
tu spieghi il tuo dolore,
e, se non desti amore,
ritrovi almen pietà.

Misera ben son io
che nel segreto laccio
amo, non spero e taccio,
e l' idol mio nol sa.

The opera at Mantua was charming. They played 'Demetrio'. The prima donna sings well, but very softly; and when you do not see her acting, but only singing, you would think that she is not singing at all. For she cannot open her mouth, but whines out everything. However, we are quite accustomed to that now. The seconda donna looks like a grenadier and has a powerful voice too, and, I must say, does not sing badly, seeing that she is acting for the first time. The primo uomo, il musico, sings beautifully, though his voice is uneven. His name is Caselli. Il secondo uomo is already old and I do not like him. His name is—. As for the tenors, one is called Otini. He does not sing badly, but rather heavily like all Italian tenors, and he is a great friend of ours. I do not know the name of the other one. He is still young, but not particularly good. Primo ballerino – good. Prima ballerina – good, and it is said that she is not hideous, but I have not seen her close to. The rest are quite ordinary. A grotesco was there who jumps well, but cannot write as I do, I mean, as sows piddle. The orchestra was not bad. In Cremona it is good. The first violin is called Spagnoletto. The prima donna is not bad; she is quite old, I should say, and not good-looking; she acts better than she sings and she is the wife of a violinist called Masi, who plays in the orchestra. The opera was: La Clemenza di Tito [by J. A. Hasse]. Seconda donna, young, not at all bad on the stage, but nothing out of the ordinary. Primo uomo, musico, Cicognani – a delightful voice and a beautiful cantabile. The other two castrati, young and passable. The tenor's name is: non lo so. He has a pleasant way with him, and resembles as though he were his natural son, Leroy in Vienna, who came to Geneva.

Ballerino primo, good. Ballerina prima, good but very plain. There was a woman dancer there, who did not dance badly and, what is very remarkable, was not bad-looking on the stage and off it. The others were quite ordinary. A grotesco was there too, who whenever he jumped let off a fart. As for Milan I really cannot tell you very much. We have not yet been to the opera, but we have heard that it has not been a success. Aprile, primo uomo, sings well and has a beautiful even voice. We heard him in a church, when there happened to be a great festival. Madame Piccinelli from Paris, who sang at our concert, is acting in the opera. Monsieur Pick, who danced in Vienna, is dancing here too. The opera is called: 'Didone abban-donata'. This opera will soon come to an end and Signor Piccinni, who is writing the next opera, is here. I have heard that his is called: 'Cesare in Egitto'. Here there are also feste di ballo which begin as soon as the opera is over. The wife of Count von Firmian's steward is a Viennese. Last Friday we dined there and we are dining there again next Sunday. Farewell. Kiss my mother's hands a thousand times in vece mia. I remain, true till death, your brother

Wolfgang de Mozart
The Honourable Highdale,
Friend of the Counting-house

Oh you busy thing!

As I have been idle for so long, I have been thinking that it would not be a bad idea if I did some work again for a short while. Every post-day, when letters arrive from Germany, I enjoy eating and drinking far more than usual. Please write and tell me who is singing in the oratorios and let me know their titles as well. Tell me also how you like [Michael] Haydn's minuets and whether they are better than his earlier ones. I rejoice from my heart that Herr von Amann has recovered. Please tell him to take good care of himself and to avoid violent exercise. Please do not forget this. But tell him also that I often think of him and of how in Triebenbach we used to play at workmen and of how he acted the name Schrattenbach by means of a bag of shot and by making the sound *sh*. Tell him also that I often remember his saying to me: 'Shall we split ourselves up?' and how I always replied: 'Good Gracious, no!' I shall soon send you a minuet which Mr. Pick danced in the theatre and which everyone danced to afterwards at the feste di ballo in Milan, solely in order that you may see how slowly people dance here. The minuet itself is very beautiful. It comes, of course, from Vienna and was most certainly composed by Deller or Starzer. It has plenty of notes. Why? Because it is a stage minuet which is danced slowly. The minuets in Milan, in fact the Italian minuets generally, have

Bologna,
24 March 1770

plenty of notes, are played slowly and have several bars, *e.g.*, the first part has sixteen, the second twenty or twenty-four.

In Parma we got to know a singer and heard her perform very beautifully in her own house – the famous Bastardella [Lucrezia Agujari] who has (1) a beautiful voice, (2) a marvellous throat, (3) an incredible range.

Leopold Mozart to his Wife

Rome,
14 April 1770

... We arrived here safely on the 11th at noon. I could have been more easily persuaded to return to Salzburg than to proceed to Rome, for we had to travel for five days from Florence to Rome in the most horrible rain and cold wind. I am told here that they have had constant rain for four months and indeed we had a taste of it, for we went on Wednesday and Thursday in fine weather to St. Peter's and to the Sistine Chapel to hear the Miserere during the Mass, and on our way home were surprised by such a frightful downpour that our cloaks have never yet been so drenched as they then were. But I will not give you a long description of that dreadful journey. Picture to yourself a more or less uncultivated country and the most horrible, filthy inns, where we got nothing to eat save here and there eggs and broccoli; while on fast-days they sometimes made a fuss about giving us the former. Fortunately we had a good supper at Viterbo and slept well. There we saw St. Rosa of Viterbo, whose body like that of St. Catherine at Bologna can be seen in a well-preserved condition. From the former saint we took away as a remembrance a fever antidote and relics, from the latter a belt. On arriving here on the 11th, we went to St. Peter's after lunch and then to Mass. On the 12th we were present at the Functiones, and when the Pope was serving the poor at table we were quite close to him, as we were standing beside him at the top of the table. This incident was all the more amazing as we had to pass through two doors guarded by Swiss guards in armour and make our way through many hundreds of people. And moreover you must note that we had as yet no acquaintances. But our fine clothes, the German tongue, and my usual freedom of manner which led me to make my servant order the Swiss guards in German to make way for us, soon helped us through everywhere. They took Wolfgang for some German courtier, while some even thought that he was a prince, which my servant allowed them to believe; I myself was taken for his tutor. Thus we made our way to the Cardinals' table. There Wolfgang happened to be standing between the chairs of two Cardinals, one of whom was Cardinal Pallavicini, who made a sign to him and said: '*Will you be so good as to tell me in confidence who you are?*' And Wolfgang told him. The Cardinal showed the greatest astonishment and said: '*Ah, you are the famous boy, about whom so many things have been written to me.*' Whereupon Wolfgang asked him: '*Are you not Cardinal Pallavicini?*'

The Cardinal replied: '*Yes, I am, but why?*' Then Wolfgang told him *that we had letters to deliver to His Eminence and that we were going to pay him our respects.* The Cardinal appeared to be delighted, remarked that Wolfgang spoke Italian very well and among other things added: '*Ik kann auck ein benig deutsch sprecken.*' When we were leaving, Wolfgang kissed his hand and the Cardinal took off his berretta and bowed very politely. You have often heard of the famous Miserere in Rome, which is so greatly prized that the performers in the chapel are forbidden on pain of excommunication to take away a single part of it, to copy it or to give it to anyone. *But we have it already.* Wolfgang has written it down and we would have sent it to Salzburg in this letter, if it were not necessary for us to be there to perform it. But the manner of performance contributes more to its effect than the composition itself. So we shall bring it home with us. Moreover, as it is one of the secrets of Rome, we do not wish to let it fall into other hands, *ut non incurramus mediate vel immediate in censuram Ecclesiae ...*

Mozart to his Mother and Sister (a postscript to his father's letter)

Praise and thanks be to God, I and my wretched pen are well and I kiss Mamma and Nannerl a thousand or 1000 times. I only wish that my sister were in Rome, for this town would certainly please her, as St. Peter's church and many other things in Rome are *regular.* The most beautiful flowers are now being carried past in the street – so Papa has just told me. I am a fool, as everyone knows. Oh, I am having a hard time, for in our rooms there is only one bed and so Mamma can well imagine that I get no sleep with Papa. I am looking forward to our new quarters. I have just now drawn St. Peter with his keys and with him St. Paul with his sword and St. Luke with my sister and so forth. I have had the honour of kissing St. Peter's foot in St. Peter's church and as I have the misfortune to be so small, I, that same old dunce,

Wolfgang Mozart
had to be lifted up.

Leopold Mozart to his Wife

... In Florence we came across a young Englishman, who is a pupil of the famous violinist Nardini. This boy [Thomas Linley], who *plays most beautifully* and who is the same age and the same size as Wolfgang, came to the house of the learned poetess, Signora Corilla, where we happened to be on the introduction of M. De L'Augier. The two boys performed one after the other throughout the whole evening, constantly embracing each other. On the following day the little Englishman, a most charming boy, had his violin brought to our rooms and played the whole afternoon,

Rome,
21 April 1770

Thomas Linley, aged 12, with his sister Elizabeth: oil painting (1768) by Thomas Gainsborough.

Wolfgang accompanying him on his own. On the next day we lunched with M. Gavard, the administrator of the grand ducal finances, and these two boys played in turn the whole afternoon, not like boys, but like men! Little Tommaso accompanied us home and wept bitter tears, because we were leaving on the following day. But when he heard that our departure would not take place until noon, he called on us at nine o'clock in the morning and gave Wolfgang with many embraces the following poem, which Signora Corilla had to compose for him on the previous evening. Then he accompanied our carriage as far as the city gate. I should like you to have witnessed this scene . . .

Mozart to his Sister

My Dear Sister,

I assure you that every post-day I look forward with an incredible eagerness *Rome,*
to receiving some letters from Salzburg. Yesterday we were at San Lorenzo and *25 April 1770*
heard vespers, and this morning the Mass which was sung, and in the evening the
second vespers, because it is the festival of Our Lady of Good Counsel. During the
last few days we have been to the Campidoglio and have seen several fine things. If
I were to write down all that I have seen, this small sheet would not suffice. I have
played at two concerts and tomorrow I am playing at another. This evening we saw
a contralto singer, a castrato, who was very like Signor Meisner, whom by the way
we shall have the honour of meeting at Naples. Immediately after lunch we play
boccia. That is a game which I have learnt in Rome. When I come home, I shall
teach it to you. Tell Signor Mölk that I am delighted and rejoice with him that his
father is in better health and that I ask him to be so kind as to convey my respects
to his father, his mother, his sister, his brother and his cousins and to all his relatives.
Please do what I asked you to do the last time I wrote to you and please send me
a reply about this. When I have finished this letter I shall finish a symphony which
I have begun. The aria is finished [K82]. A symphony is being copied (my father
is the copyist), for we do not wish to give it out to be copied, as it would be stolen.
My greetings to all my friends and please kiss Mamma's hands for me, for I am
(Tra la liera)

Wolfgango in Germania

Roma caput mundi,   and Amadeo Mozart in Italia
  April 25th, 1770,
and next year 1771.
  Behind as in front
  And double in the middle.   I kiss you both.

Mozart to his Mother and Sister (a postscript to a letter of his father's)

Praise and thanks be to God, I am well and kiss Mamma's hand and my sister's *Rome,*
face, nose, mouth, neck and my bad pen and arse, if it is clean. *2 May 1770*

Wolfgango Mozart

Leopold Mozart to his Wife

... We drove yesterday to Portici to call on the minister, Marchese Tanucci, and we *Naples*
shall drive out there again tomorrow. We had dreadful roads and a very cool breeze. *19 May 1770*
We have left our fine cloth suits in Rome and have had to put on our two beautifully
braided summer costumes. Wolfgang's is of rose-coloured moiré, but the colour is

Sir William
Hamilton, British
Ambassador to the
Kingdom of Naples,
and his first wife,
Catherine, with
Vesuvius in the
background. The
Hamiltons were keen
(continued p. 22)

so peculiar that in Italy it is called colore di fuoco or flame-coloured; it is trimmed with silver lace and lined with sky-blue silk. My costume is of the colour of cinnamon and is made of piquéd Florentine cloth with silver lace and is lined with apple green silk. They are two fine costumes, but, before we reach home, they will look like old maids. Yesterday evening we called on the English ambassador, Hamilton, a London acquaintance of ours, whose wife plays the clavier with unusual feeling and is a very pleasant person. She trembled at having to play before Wolfgang. She has a valuable instrument, made in England by Tschudi, which has two manuals and a pedal, so that the two manuals can be disconnected by the action of the foot.

We found at Hamilton's house Mr. Beckford and Mr. Weis, also London acquaintances. We lunched on the 16th with Tschudi, who had been in Salzburg and requested me to convey his greetings to Count Spaur and to all his good friends and very many compliments to you especially and to Nannerl. He embraced us constantly, particularly on our arrival and departure, and offered us his services on all occasions ...

On reading the article about the Miserere, we simply burst out laughing. There is not the slightest cause for anxiety. Everywhere else far more fuss is being made about Wolfgang's feat. All Rome knows and even the Pope himself that he wrote it down. There is nothing whatever to fear; on the contrary, the achievement has done him great credit, as you will shortly hear. You will see to it that the letter is read out everywhere, so that we may be sure that His Grace hears what Wolfgang has done. If the portraits are good likenesses, you may pay the painter whatever you like.

Now I must close, for we are off to the Imperial Ambassador the Count von Kaunitz. Farewell, we kiss you and Nannerl 1000 times and

I am your old

MZT

I trust that your cold left you long ago.

Mozart to his Sister

Cara Sorella Mia,

Vesuvius is smoking furiously today. Thunder and lightning and all the rest. We gorged ourselves today with Herr Doll. He is a German composer and a fine fellow. Now I shall begin to describe my way of life. Alle nove ore, qualche volta anche alle dieci mi sveglio, e poi andiamo fuor di casa, e poi pranziamo da un trattore, e dopo pranzo scriviamo, e poi sortiamo, e indi ceniamo, ma che cosa? Al giorno di grasso, un mezzo pollo, ovvero un piccolo boccone d'arrosto; al giorno di magro, un piccolo pesce; e di poi andiamo a dormire.[1] Est-ce que vous avez compris? Let us talk Salzburgish for a change, for it is more sensible. Thank God, we are well, my father and I.

I hope that you too are well and Mamma also. If Fräulein Aloysia von Schiedenhofen comes to see you again, give her my compliments. Naples and Rome are two sleepy towns. What a beautiful handwriting mine is, is it not?

... The opera here is one of Jommelli's; it is beautiful, but too serious and old-fashioned for the theatre. De Amicis sings amazingly well and so does Aprile, who

(continued from p. 20) *musical amateurs who entertained Mozart and his father when they visited Naples in 1770. Oil painting on copper, 1770, by David Allan (detail).*

Naples,
5 June 1770

---

1 I wake up at nine, sometimes even at ten, and then we go out, and then we lunch at an eating-house, and after lunch we write, and then we go out, and then we have supper, and what do we eat? On ordinary days half a chicken or a small slice of roast meat; on fast-days a little fish; and then we go to bed.

The eruption of Vesuvius in 1774: contemporary oil painting by J. P. Hackert.

sang in Milan. The dances are wretchedly pompous. The theatre is beautiful. The King has had a rough Neapolitan upbringing and in the opera he always stands on a stool so as to look a little taller than the Queen. She is beautiful and gracious, and on the Molo (that is a drive) she bowed to me in a most friendly manner at least six times. Every evening the nobles send us their carriages to drive out with them to the Molo. We were invited on Sunday to the ball given by the French Ambassador. I can't write anything more. My compliments to all our kind friends. Farewell.

Wolfgang Mozart

I kiss Mamma's hand.

Leopold Mozart to his Wife

Rome,
4 July 1770

. . . This very moment a servant of Cardinal Pallavicini has invited us to lunch with

His Eminence tomorrow. We are dining on Friday with His Excellency the Tuscan Ambassador, Baron Sant' Odile. Tomorrow we are to hear a piece of news which, if it is true, will fill you both with amazement. For Cardinal Pallavicini is said to have been commanded by the Pope to hand Wolfgang the cross and diploma of an order.[1] Do not say much about this yet. If it is true, I shall write to you next Saturday. When we were at the Cardinal's house a few days ago he once or twice called Wolfgang 'Signor Cavaliere'. We thought that he was joking, but now I hear that it is true and that this is behind tomorrow's invitation. Addio! Farewell! I must hurry, for the post is going. Wolfgang cannot send you a letter, as he is writing to the son of Field-marshal Pallavicini in Bologna. We kiss you 1000 times.

MZT

Wolfgang grew noticeably in Naples.

Leopold Mozart to his Wife

Rome, 7 July 1770

... What I wrote the other day about the cross of an order is quite correct. It is the same order as Gluck's and is worded as follows: *te creamus auratae militiae equitem.* Wolfgang has to wear a beautiful gold cross, which he has received. You can imagine how I laugh when I hear people calling him 'Signor Cavaliere' all the time. Tomorrow we are to have an audience with the Pope ...

Mozart to his Sister (a postscript to his father's letter)

Cara Sorrella Mia!

I am amazed to find how well you can compose. In a word, the song is beautiful. Try this more often. Send me soon the other six minuets by Haydn, I beg you. Farewell.

Wolfgang Mozart

PS. – My compliments to all my good friends. I kiss Mamma's hand: Mademoiselle, j'ai l'honneur d'être votre très humble serviteur e frère.

Chevalier de Mozart

Rome 7 July 1770 Addio. Keep well, and shit in your bed make a mess of it.

Mozart to his Sister (a postscript to a letter of his father's)

Bologna, 4 August 1770

I am heartily sorry that Jungfrau Martha is so ill and I pray every day that she may recover. Tell her from me that she should not move about too much and that she should eat plenty of salt meats.

---

1 The Order of the Golden Spur, which Pope Clement XIV conferred on Mozart on 8 July 1770.

A propos! Did you give my letter to my dear Sigmund Robinig? You say nothing about it. If you see him, please tell him not to forget me altogether. It is impossible for me to write a better hand, for this pen is for writing music and not for letters. My fiddle has now been restrung and I play every day. But I add this simply because Mamma wanted to know whether I still play the fiddle. More than six times at least I have had the honour of going alone to a church and to some magnificent function. In the meantime I have composed four Italian symphonies, to say nothing of arias, of which I must have composed at least five or six, and also a motet ...

Mozart to his Mother and Sister (a postscript to a letter of his father's)

Bologna,
21 August 1770

I too am still alive and, what is more, as merry as can be. I had a great desire today to ride on a donkey, for it is the custom in Italy, and so I thought that I too should try it. We have the honour to go about with a certain Dominican, who is regarded as a holy man. For my part I do not believe it, for at breakfast he often takes a cup of chocolate and immediately afterwards a good glass of strong Spanish wine; and I myself have had the honour of lunching with this saint who at table drank a whole decanter and finished up with a full glass of strong wine, two large slices of melon, some peaches, pears, five cups of coffee, a whole plate of birds and two full saucers of milk and lemon. He may, of course, be following some sort of diet, but I do not think so, for it would be too much; moreover he takes several little snacks during the afternoon. Addio. Farewell. Kiss Mamma's hands for me. My greetings to all who know me.

Wolfgang Mozart

Mozart to Thomas Linley, Florence

My Dear Friend,

Bologna,
10 September 1770

Here is a letter at last! Indeed I am very late in replying to your charming letter addressed to me at Naples, which, however, I only received two months after you had written it. My father's plan was to travel to Loreto via Bologna, and thence to Milan via Florence, Leghorn and Genoa. We should then have given you a surprise by turning up unexpectedly in Florence. But, as he had the misfortune to gash his leg rather badly when the shaft-horse of our sedia fell on the road, and as this wound not only kept him in bed for three weeks but held us up in Bologna for another seven, this nasty accident has forced us to change our plans and to proceed to Milan via Parma.

Firstly, we have missed the suitable time for such a journey and, secondly, the season is over, for everyone is in the country and therefore we could not earn our expenses. I assure you that this accident has annoyed us very much. I would do

AMADEO WOLFGANGO MOZART ACCAD.FILARMON:DIE
VERONA

(left) In 1770, aged 14, Mozart received the Order of the Golden Spur from the Pope. The oil painting of which this is a copy was commissioned in 1777 by the Academy in Bologna and shows him wearing the cross of the Order.

everything in my power to have the pleasure of embracing my dear friend. Moreover my father and I would very much like to meet again Signor Gavard and his very dear and charming family, and also Signora Corilla and Signor Nardini, and then to return to Bologna. This we would do indeed, if we had the slightest hope of making even the expenses of our journey.

As for the engravings you lost, my father remembered you; and his order arrived in time for two other copies to be kept for you. So please let me know of some means of sending them to you. Keep me in your friendship and believe that my affection for you will endure for ever and that I am your most devoted servant and loving friend

Amadeo Wolfgango Mozart

Mozart to his Mother (a postscript to a letter of his father's)

My Dear Mamma,

Milan, 20 October 1770

I cannot write much, for my fingers are aching from composing so many recitatives. Mamma, I beg you to pray for me, that my opera may go well and that we may be happy together again. I kiss Mamma's hand a thousand times and I have many things to say to my sister, but what? God and I alone know. If it is God's will, I shall soon, I hope, be able to tell them to her myself. Meanwhile I kiss her 1000 times. My greetings to all my good friends ...

Leopold Mozart to his Wife

Milan, 22 December 1770

... Picture to yourselves little Wolfgang in a scarlet suit, trimmed with gold braid and lined with sky-blue satin. The tailor is starting to make it today. Wolfgang will wear this suit during the first three days when he is seated at the clavier. The one which was made for him in Salzburg is too short by half a foot and in any case is too tight and too small ...

Mozart to his Sister (a postscript to a letter of his father's)

Dearest Sister,

Milan, 12 January 1771

I have not written for a long time, for I was busy with my opera, but as I now have time, I will be more attentive to my duty. The opera, God be praised, is a success, for every evening the theatre is full, much to the astonishment of everyone, for several people say that since they have been in Milan they have never seen such crowds at a first opera. Papa and I, thank God, are well, and I hope that at Easter I shall be able to tell you and Mamma everything with my own lips. Addio. I kiss Mamma's hand. A propos! Yesterday the copyist called on us and said that he had orders to transcribe my opera for the court at Lisbon. Meanwhile farewell, my dear Mademoiselle sister. I have the honour to be and to remain from now to all eternity

your faithful brother

Mozart and his father returned to Salzburg in March 1771, but the success of Mitridate *in Milan had been so great that the young composer was invited to return later in the same year, and was asked back yet again to produce an opera,* Lucio Silla, *for the carnival season of 1772–3.*

Leopold Mozart to his Wife

... I am writing this letter today, Friday the 18th, for tomorrow we shall hardly have time to write anything, because we are to have the first rehearsal with all the instruments at half past nine in the morning. During the last few days we have had three rehearsals of the recitatives. The tenor arrived only yesterday evening and Wolfgang composed today two arias for him and has still two more to do. The second rehearsal takes place on Sunday the 20th, the third on Tuesday the 22nd, and the dress rehearsal on Wednesday the 23rd. On Thursday and Friday there will be no rehearsals; but on Saturday the 26th, the very day on which you will receive this letter, we shall have the first performance of the opera. I am writing to you at eleven o'clock at night and Wolfgang has just finished the second aria for the tenor. We shall celebrate Christmas Eve at supper with Herr and Frau von Germani, who send you greetings and who wish that you were here. We are lunching tomorrow with Herr von Mayr and after lunch I shall still be able to write a few words. Addio. Farewell.

Milan,
18 December 1772

Mozart to his Sister (a postscript to his father's letter)

I hope that you are well, my dear sister. When you receive this letter, my dear sister, that very evening my opera will have been performed, my dear sister. Think of me, my dear sister, and try as hard as you can to imagine that you, my dear sister, are hearing and seeing it too, my dear sister. That is hard, I admit, as it is already eleven o'clock. Otherwise I believe and do not doubt at all that during the day it is brighter than at Easter. We are lunching tomorrow, my dear sister, with Herr von Mayr, and why, do you think? Guess! Why, because he has asked us. The rehearsal tomorrow is at the theatre, but Signor Castiglione, the impresario, has begged me not to tell anyone about it; otherwise a whole crowd of people will come running in, and we do not want this. So, my child, I beg you not to mention it to anyone, my child, otherwise too many people will come running in, my child. That reminds me. Have

Anonymous oil painting of Padre Martini (1706–84), an Italian composer, teacher and musical theorist who was said to possess a library of 17,000 books. Besides giving lessons to Mozart, he also taught J. C. Bach, Grétry and Jommelli. In his reply to Mozart's letter of 4 September 1776, sending him the music for La finta giardiniera, *Martini praised it highly, adding that 'it has all the qualities which modern music demands, good harmony, rich modulation, etc.'*

you heard what happened here? I will tell you. We left Count Firmian's today to go home and when we reached our street, we opened the hall door and what do you think we did? Why, we went in. Farewell, my little lung. I kiss you my liver, and remain as always, my stomach, your unworthy

$\left\{\begin{array}{l}\text{frater}\\\text{brother}\end{array}\right.$ Wolfgang

Please, please, my dear sister, something is biting me. Do come and scratch me.

In the summer of 1773 father and son spent two months in Vienna in the hope of obtaining a court appointment for Wolfgang. They had no success, and after a period in Salzburg the young composer accepted a commission for an opera buffa, La finta giardiniera, *in Munich, where he arrived with his father early in December 1774. By now his considerable experience of life in more stimulating foreign cities was making him increasingly aware of the limitations of his Salzburg existence.*

Mozart to his Mother

Thank God! My opera was performed yesterday, the 13th, for the first time and was such a success that it is impossible for me to describe the applause to Mamma. In the first place, the whole theatre was so packed that a great many people were turned away. Then after each aria there was a terrific noise, clapping of hands and cries of 'Viva Maestro'. Her Highness the Electress and the Dowager Electress (who were sitting opposite me) also called out 'Bravo' to me. After the opera was over and during the pause when there is usually silence until the ballet begins, people kept on clapping all the time and shouting 'Bravo'; now stopping, now beginning again and so on. Afterwards I went off with Papa to a certain room through which the Elector and the whole Court had to pass and I kissed the hands of the Elector and Electress and Their Highnesses, who were all very gracious. Early this morning His Grace the Bishop of Chiemsee sent me a message, congratulating me on the extraordinary success of my opera. I fear that we cannot return to Salzburg very soon and Mamma must not wish it, for she knows how much good it is doing me to be able to breathe freely. We shall come home soon enough. One very urgent and necessary reason for our absence is that next Friday my opera is being performed again and it is most essential that I should be present. Otherwise my work would be quite unrecognizable – for very strange things happen here. I kiss Mamma's hands 1000 times. My greetings to all my good friends. My compliments to M. Andretter and I beg him to forgive me for not yet replying, but it has been impossible for me to find the time. However, I shall do so very soon. Adieu. 1000 kisses to Bimberl.

Munich,
14 January 1775

Mozart to Padre Martini, Bologna

Most reverend Padre Maestro, my esteemed Patron,

The regard, the esteem and the respect which I cherish for your illustrious person have prompted me to trouble you with this letter and to send you a humble specimen of my music, which I submit to your masterly judgment. I composed for last year's carnival at Munich an opera buffa, 'La finta giardiniera'. A few days before

Salzburg,
4 September 1776

my departure the Elector expressed a desire to hear some of my contrapuntal compositions. I was therefore obliged to write this motet in a great hurry, in order to have time to have the score copied for His Highness and to have the parts written out and thus enable it to be performed during the Offertory at High Mass on the following Sunday. Most beloved and esteemed Signor Padre Maestro! I beg you most earnestly to tell me, frankly and without reserve, what you think of it. We live in this world in order to learn industriously and, by interchanging our ideas, to enlighten one another and thus endeavour to promote the sciences and the fine arts. Oh, how often have I longed to be near you, most Reverend Father, so that I might be able to talk to and have discussion with you. For I live in a country where music leads a struggling existence, though indeed apart from those who have left us, we still have excellent teachers and particularly composers of great wisdom, learning and taste. As for the theatre, we are in a bad way for lack of singers. We have no castrati, and we shall never have them, because they insist on being handsomely paid; and generosity is not one of our faults. Meanwhile I am amusing myself by writing chamber music and music for the church, in which branches of composition we have two other excellent masters of counterpoint, Signori Haydn and Adlgasser. My father is in the service of the Cathedral and this gives me an opportunity of writing as much church music as I like. He has already served this court for thirty-six years and as he knows that the present Archbishop cannot and will not have anything to do with people who are getting on in years, he no longer puts his whole heart into his work, but has taken up literature, which was always a favourite study of his. Our church music is very different from that of Italy, since a mass with the whole Kyrie, the Gloria, the Credo, the Epistle sonata, the Offertory or Motet, the Sanctus and the Agnus Dei must not last longer than three quarters of an hour. This applies even to the most Solemn Mass said by the Archbishop himself. So you see that a special study is required for this kind of composition. At the same time, the mass must have all the instruments – trumpets, drums and so forth. Alas, that we are so far apart, my very dear Signor Padre Maestro! If we were together, I should have so many things to tell you! I send my devoted remembrances to all the members of the Accademia Filarmonica. I long to win your favour and I never cease to grieve that I am far away from that one person in the world whom I love, revere and esteem most of all and whose most humble and devoted servant, most

Reverend Father, I shall always be.

Wolfgango Amadeo Mozart

If you condescend to write to me, please address your letter to Salzburg via Trento.

Mozart to Archbishop Hieronymus Colloredo

Your Grace, Most Worthy Prince of the Holy Roman Empire!

    I will not presume to trouble Your Grace with a full description of our unhappy circumstances, which my father has set forth most accurately in his very humble petition which was handed to you on March 14th, 1777. As, however, your most gracious decision was never conveyed to him, my father intended last June once more most respectfully to beg Your Grace to allow us to travel for a few months in order to enable us to make some money; and he would have done so, if you had not given orders that in view of the imminent visit of His Majesty the Emperor your orchestra should practise various works with a view to their performance. Later my father again applied for leave of absence, which Your Grace refused to grant, though you permitted me, who am in any case only a half-time servant, to travel alone. Our situation is pressing and my father has therefore decided to let me go alone. But to this course also Your Grace has been pleased to raise certain objections. Most Gracious Prince and Lord! Parents endeavour to place their children in a position to earn their own bread; and in this they follow alike their own interest and that of the State. The greater the talents which children have received from God, the more are they bound to use them for the improvement of their own and their parents' circumstances, so that they may at the same time assist them and take thought for their own future progress. The Gospel teaches us to use our talents in this way. My conscience tells me that I owe it to God to be grateful to my father, who has spent his time unwearyingly upon my education, so that I may lighten his burden, look after myself and later on be able to support my sister. For I should be sorry to think that she should have spent so many hours at the harpsichord and not be able to make good use of her training.

    Your Grace will therefore be so good as to allow me to ask you most humbly for my discharge, of which I should like to take advantage before the autumn, so that I may not be obliged to face the bad weather during the ensuing winter months. Your Grace will not misunderstand this petition, seeing that when I asked you for permission to travel to Vienna three years ago, you graciously declared that I had nothing to hope for in Salzburg and would do better to seek my fortune elsewhere. I thank Your Grace for all the favours I have received from you and, in the hope of being able to serve you later on with greater success, I am

Salzburg,
1 August 1777

your most humble and obedient servant

Wolfgang Amade Mozart

A note from the Archbishop of Salzburg to his Court Chamberlain on 28 August 1777
communicated his decision that 'in the name of the Gospel father and son have my

permission to seek their fortune elsewhere'. Leopold Mozart in fact stayed on in his Court appointment, but in less than a month Wolfgang was off again, this time with his mother only, on what was intended to be a tour of the musical centres of southern Germany in search of a permanent job. After a couple of unfruitful weeks in Munich they moved on to Augsburg (Leopold's birthplace) and thence to Mannheim where they stayed for four and a half months. In spite of the many new friends he made there, and the stimulation provided by the artistic life of one of the liveliest musical cities in Europe, Mozart made no headway in his attempts to get a Court appointment. As his financial situation became more and more precarious, it became clear that the tour of southern Germany had to be abandoned in favour of something more radical.

Mozart to his Father

Mon trés cher Pére,[1]

Munich,
26 September 1777

We arrived here on the 24th at half past four in the afternoon. The first piece of news we heard was that we had to drive to the customs house accompanied by a grenadier with a fixed bayonet ...

... I was at Count Seeau's today, Friday the 26th, at half past eight in the morning. This is what happened. I walked into the house and Madame Niesser, the actress, who was just coming out, asked me: 'I suppose you want to see the Count?' 'Yes,' I replied. 'Well, he is still in his garden and goodness knows when he will return.' I asked her where the garden was. 'Well,' she said, 'I too want to see him, so let us go together.' We had hardly passed the lodge gates before the Count came towards us; and when he was about twelve paces from us, he recognized me, addressed me by name, and was extremely polite. He was already acquainted with my story. As we mounted the steps together very slowly, I disclosed to him very briefly the object of my visit. He said that I should ask immediately for an audience with His Highness the Elector and that if for any reason I was unable to see him, I should put my case before him in writing. I begged him to keep the whole thing secret and he promised me to do so. When I remarked that a first-rate composer was badly needed here, he said: 'I am well aware of it.' After this I called on the Bishop of Chiemsee and was with him for half an hour. I told him everything and he promised me to do his best in the matter. He was going to Nymphenburg at one o'clock and promised to speak to Her Highness the Electress without fail. The Court returns to Munich on Sunday evening ...

Munich,
29–30 September 1777

... I was with Count Seeau yesterday morning at half past ten and found him much more serious and not so frank as he was the first time. But it was only in appearance.

1 Mozart's French spelling has been retained.

Then today I called on Prince Zeill, who said to me in the most polite manner: 'I am afraid that we shall not accomplish very much here. When we were at table at Nymphenburg I had a few words in private with the Elector. He said: "It is too early yet. He ought to go off; travel to Italy and make a name for himself. I am not refusing him, but it is too soon."' So there we are! Most of these great lords are downright infatuated with Italy. Zeill advised me, however, to go to the Elector and put my case before him all the same. I had a private talk at table today with Woschitka, who told me to call at nine o'clock tomorrow morning, when he will certainly procure an audience for me. We are good friends now. He wanted absolûment to know who the person was, but I just said: 'Rest assured that I am your friend and ever will be, and that I too am convinced of your friendship. That must suffice.' Now to return to my story. The Bishop of Chiemsee also had a word in private with the Electress, who, however, shrugged her shoulders and said that she would do her best, but was very doubtful. Now to go back to Count Seeau. When Prince Zeill had told him the whole story, he said: 'Do you know whether Mozart gets enough money from home to enable him with a small subsidy to remain on here? I should very much like to keep him.' 'I do not know,' replied the Bishop, 'but I very much doubt it. However, you have only to ask him.' So that was why on the following day he was so thoughtful. I like Munich and I am inclined to think, as many of my friends do, that if only I could stay here for a year or two, I could win both profit and honour by my work and therefore would be sought after by the Court instead of having to canvass them. Since my arrival Herr Albert has thought out a scheme, which, I believe, would not be impossible of execution. It amounts to this. He wants to collect ten good friends, each of whom would fork out one ducat a month, thus making ten ducats or fifty gulden a month, or 600 gulden a year. Then if I could get 200 gulden a year from Count Seeau, I should have 800 gulden. Now what does Papa think of this idea? Is it not a proof of friendship? And should I not accept it, provided, of course, that the proposal is serious? It seems perfectly satisfactory to me. I should be near Salzburg, and if you, my dearest Papa, should feel inclined (as I heartily wish that you may) to leave Salzburg and end your days in Munich, the plan would be delightful and quite simple. For if we have had to live in Salzburg on 504 gulden, surely we could manage in Munich on 600 or 800? ...

... At nine o'clock today, the 30th, I went as arranged with M. Woschitka to Court. Everyone was in hunting dress. Baron Kern was acting chamberlain. I might have gone there yesterday evening, but I did not want to tread on the toes of M. Woschitka, who of his own accord had offered to procure me an audience with the Elector. At ten o'clock he showed me into a little narrow room through which His Highness was to pass on his way to hear Mass before going to hunt. Count Seeau went by and greeted me in the most friendly fashion, saying: 'How do you do, my very dear Mozart!' When the Elector came up to me, I said: 'Your Highness will allow me to throw myself most humbly at your feet and offer you my services.' 'So you have left Salzburg for good?' 'Yes, Your Highness, for good.' 'How is that? Have you had a row with him?' 'Not at all, Your Highness. I only asked him for permission to travel, which he refused. So I was compelled to take this step, though indeed I had long been intending to clear out. For Salzburg is no place for me, I can assure you.' 'Good Heavens! There's a young man for you! But your father is still in Salzburg?' 'Yes, Your Highness. He too throws himself most humbly at your feet, and so forth. I have been three times to Italy already, I have written three operas, I am a member of the Bologna Academy, where I had to pass a test, at which many maestri have laboured and sweated for four or five hours, but which I finished in an hour. Let that be a proof that I am competent to serve at any Court. My sole wish, however, is to serve Your Highness, who himself is such a great—' 'Yes, my dear boy, but I have no vacancy. I am sorry. If only there were a vacancy—' 'I assure Your Highness that I should not fail to do credit to Munich.' 'I know. But it is no good, for there is no vacancy here.' This he said as he walked away. Whereupon I commended myself to his good graces. Herr Woschitka has advised me to put in an appearance at Court as often as I can. This afternoon I went to see Count Salern. The Countess, his daughter, is now a maid of honour. She had gone out hunting with the rest. Ravani and I were in the street when the whole company passed by. The Elector and the Electress greeted me in a most friendly manner. Countess Salern recognized me at once and waved her hand to me repeatedly. Baron Rumling, whom I saw beforehand in the antechamber, has never been so *civil* to me as he was on this occasion. How I got on with Salern I shall tell you in my next letter. It was quite satisfactory. He was very polite – and frank. I do beg you to take great care of your health. I kiss Papa's hands 100000 times and always remain your most obedient son

Wolfgang Amadé Mozart

Maria Anna Mozart to her Husband

Munich,
2–3 October 1777

Wolfgang is lunching today with Madame Branca and I have lunched at home; but as soon as three o'clock strikes I am going to Frau von Tosson, who is sending someone to fetch me. Herr von Krimmel turned up again yesterday with Herr von Unhold. He is a good friend of ours and is trying hard to persuade us to go to Memmingen and to give a first-class concert, as he assures us that we shall make more there than at a court. I quite believe it, for, as hardly anybody goes to such a place, the people there are glad when they can get anyone at all. Now how is your health? I am not really satisfied with your letters. I don't like that cough, which is lasting far too long. You ought not to have anything wrong with you at all. I beg

you to use the sago soon, and the sooner the better, so that you may regain your
strength as quickly as possible. We received the parcel by the mail coach and the
other one too by the ordinary post. I send greetings to Nannerl. Please tell her not
to get cross with you and to take good care that you have no worries and to help
you to pass the time so that you do not get melancholy. Bimperl, I trust, is doing
her duty and making up to you, for she is a good and faithful fox terrier. I send
greetings to Tresel also and should like you to tell her that it is all one whether

Mozart continues

I shit the muck or she eats it. But now for something more sensible ... At four
o'clock I went to Frau von Tosson, where I found Mamma and Frau von Hepp. I
played there until eight o'clock and then we went home. About half past nine in the
evening a small orchestra of five players, two clarinets, two horns and one bassoon,
came up to the house. Herr Albert (whose name-day is tomorrow) had ordered this
music in his and my honour. They did not play at all badly together. They were the
same people who play in Albert's dining-hall during the meals. But you can tell at
once that Fiala has trained them. They played some of his compositions and I must
say that they were very pretty and that he has some very good ideas.

Tomorrow we are going to have a little scratch-concert among ourselves, but, I
should add, on that wretched clavier. Oh! Oh! Oh! Well, I wish you a very restful
night and I improve on this good wish by hearing to hope soon that Papa is well
quite. I forgiveness your crave for my disgraceful handwriting, but ink, haste, sleep,
dreams and all the rest ... I Papa your, my hands kiss, a thousand times dearest,
and my embrace, the heart, sister I with all my brute of a, and remain, now and
for ever, amen,

Wolfgang most obedient your
Amadé Mozart son

Leopold Mozart to his Son

Mon très cher Fils!

I have no great hopes of anything happening in Munich. Unless there is a vacancy, *Salzburg,*
the Elector is bound to refuse to take anyone and, moreover, there are always secret *4 October 1777*
enemies about, whose fears would prevent your getting an appointment. Herr
Albert's scheme is indeed a proof of the greatest friendship imaginable. Yet, however
possible it may seem to you to find ten persons, each of whom will give you a ducat
a month, to me it is quite inconceivable. For who are these philanthropists or these
music-lovers? And what sort of undertaking or what kind of service will they require
from you in return? To me it seems far more likely that Count Seeau may contribute

something. But unless he does, what you may expect from Albert would only be a mere trifle. If he could make the arrangement even for a year – that is all I will say for the moment – then you could accept an offer from Count Seeau. But what would he demand! – perhaps all the work which Herr Michl has been doing? Running about and training singers! That would be a dog's life and quite out of the question! In short, I cannot see where these ten charming friends are to come from. Further, Albert may not be able to see them at once, as some of them are perhaps out of town. Moreover, I should prefer merchants or other honest persons to these courtiers, for a great deal would depend on whether they would keep their word and for how long. *If the arrangement is immediately practicable, well and good, and you ought to accept it.* But if it cannot be made at once, then you simply must not lounge about, use up your money and waste your time. For in spite of all the compliments and shows of friendship which you are receiving, you cannot hope to make a farthing in Munich! ...

... I have just been to see the Chief Steward, who is paying me a special visit one of these days in order that I may tell him everything in detail. For there is no peace at his house; someone is always being announced or else his Countess comes rushing in. He loves you with his whole heart. Before he heard our story, he had already bought four horses and was looking forward to the pleasure he would give you by turning up with one of them for you to ride on. When, however, he heard about our affair, he simply could not express his annoyance. He was paying his respects one day to the Archbishop, who said to him: '*Now we have one man less in the orchestra.*' Firmian replied: '*Your Grace has lost a great virtuoso.*' '*Why?*' asked the Prince. The reply was: '*Mozart is the greatest player on the clavier whom I have ever heard in my life; on the violin he rendered very good services to Your Grace; and he is a first-rate composer.*' The Archbishop was silent, for he had nothing to say. Now I must close because I have no more room. When writing you should at least mention *whether you have had such and such a letter.* You must surely have received by now the parcel containing the roll with the diplomas and Padre Martini's testimonial. We kiss you millions of times and I am your old

Mozart

Be careful not to lose Padre Martini's testimonial.

Mozart to his Father

Mon trés cher Pére!

Munich,
11 October 1777

Why have I said nothing so far about Mysliwecek? Because it was a relief not to have to think of him for a while. For whenever he was mentioned, I was obliged to hear how highly he has been praising me and what a good and true friend of mine he is! At the same time I felt pity and sympathy for him. People described his

appearance to me and I was nearly distracted. Was I to know that Mysliwecek, so good a friend of mine, was in a town, even in a corner of the world where I was and was I not to see him, to speak to him? Impossible! So I resolved to go and see him. But on the previous day I went to the Governor of the Ducal Hospital and asked him whether he could not arrange for me to talk to Mysliwecek in the garden, since, although everyone, even the doctors had assured me that there was no longer any danger of infection, I did not want to go to his room, as it was very small and smelt rather strongly. The Governor said that I was perfectly right and told me that Mysliwecek usually took a walk in the garden between eleven and twelve and that if I did not find him there, I was to ask whether he would not come down. I went therefore on the following day with Herr von Hamm, Secretary for War (about whom I shall have something to say later on), and with Mamma to the hospital. Mamma went into the church and we walked into the garden. Mysliwecek was not there; so we sent him a message. I saw him coming across the garden towards us and recognized him at once by his walk. I should say here that he had already sent me his compliments through Herr Heller, the cellist, and had begged me to be so kind as to visit him before my departure. When he came up to me, we shook hands in the most friendly fashion. 'You see,' he said, 'how unfortunate I am!' These words and his appearance, which Papa already knows about, as it has been described to him, so wrung my heart that all I could say half sobbing was: 'With my whole heart I pity you.' *'My dear friend,'* he said, for he saw that I was moved and began at once to speak more cheerfully, *'do tell me what you are doing. I was told that you were here, but I could hardly believe it. Was it possible that Mozart was in Munich and had not visited me all this time?'* I replied: 'Indeed I must crave your forgiveness. I have had so many calls to pay. I have so many true friends here.' *'I am sure that you have very true friends here, but none so true as I, that I can assure you.'* He asked me whether I had not heard from Papa about a letter –'Yes,' I interrupted, 'he wrote to me (I was so distracted and trembled so in every limb that I could hardly speak), but not in detail.' Mysliwecek then told me that Signor Gaetano Santoro, the Naples impresario, had been obliged owing to *impegni* and *protectione* to give the carnival opera this season to a certain Maestro Valentini, but that next year he would have three to distribute, one of which would be at his disposal. *'So,'* said Mysliwecek, *'as I have already composed six times for Naples, I have not the slightest objection to taking on the less important opera and giving you the better one, I mean, the one for the carnival. God knows whether I shall be able to travel. If I cannot, then I shall just return the scrittura. The cast for next year is excellent; they are all singers whom I have recommended. My credit in Naples, you see, is so high that when I say, "Engage this man", they engage him at once.'* The primo uomo is Marchesi, whom he praises very highly and so does the whole of Munich. Then there is Marchiani, a good prima donna, and, further, a tenor, whose name I have forgotten, but who, as Mysliwecek says, is now the best tenor in Italy. *'I implore you,'* he urged, *'go to Italy. There one is really esteemed and valued.'* And I am sure he is right. When I think it over carefully, I have to admit that in no country have I received so many honours, nowhere have I been so esteemed as in Italy; and certainly it is a real distinction to have written operas in Italy, especially for Naples ...

I have an inexpressible longing to write another opera. It is a long way to go, it is true, but it would be a long time before I should have to write it. Many things may happen before then. But I think that I ought to accept it. If in the meantime I fail to secure an appointment, eh bien, then I can fall back on Italy. I shall still have my certain 100 ducats at the carnival and once I have composed for Naples, I shall be in demand everywhere. Moreover, as Papa is well aware, there are also opere buffe here and there in the spring, summer and autumn, which one can write for practice and for something to do. I should not make very much, it is true, but, all the same, it would be something; and they would bring me more honour and credit than if I were to give a hundred concerts in Germany. And I am happier when I have something to compose, for that, after all, is my sole delight and passion. And if I secure an appointment or if I have hopes of settling down somewhere, then the *scrittura* will be an excellent recommendation, will give me prestige and greatly enhance my value. But all this is only talk – talk out of the fulness of my heart. If Papa can prove conclusively that I am wrong, well, then I shall acquiesce, although unwillingly. For I have only to hear an opera discussed, I have only to sit in a theatre, hear the orchestra tuning their instruments – oh, I am quite beside myself at once.

Tomorrow Mamma and I are taking leave of Mysliwecek in the garden. For only the other day, when he heard me say that I had to fetch my mother in the church, he said: 'If only I were not such a sight, I should very much like to meet the mother of such a great virtuoso.' I implore you, my dearest Papa, to reply to Mysliwecek. Write to him as often as you have time. You can give him no greater pleasure. For the man is completely deserted and often no one goes to see him for a whole week. 'I assure you,' he said, 'it seems very strange that so few people come to see me. In Italy I had company every day.' If it were not for his face, he would be the same old Mysliwecek, full of fire, spirit and life, a little thin, of course, but otherwise the same excellent, cheerful fellow. All Munich is talking about his oratorio 'Abramo ed Isacco', which he produced here. He has now finished, except for a few arias, a cantata or serenata for Lent. When his illness was at its worst he composed an opera for Padua. But nothing can help him. Even here they all say that the Munich doctors and surgeons have done for him. He has a fearful cancer of the bone. The surgeon Caco, that ass, burnt away his nose. Imagine what agony he must have suffered, Herr Heller has just been to see him. When I wrote that letter to him yesterday, I sent him my serenata which I composed in Salzburg for Archduke Maximilian;[1] and Heller gave it to him with the letter.

Now for something else ...

Immediately after lunch yesterday I went with Mamma to a coffee party at the two Fräulein Freysingers'. Mamma, however, drank no coffee, but had two bottles of Tyrolese wine instead. She went home at three o'clock to put a few things together for our journey. I went with the two young ladies to the said Herr von Hamm, where the three ladies each played a concerto and I played one of Eichner's at sight and then went on improvising. Miss Simplicity von Hamm's teacher is a certain clergyman of the name of Schreier. He is a good organist, but no cembalist. He kept on staring at me through his spectacles the whole time. He is a dry sort of fellow, who does not say much: but he tapped me on the shoulder, sighed and said: 'Yes – you are – you know – yes – that is true – you are first-rate.' A propos. Does Papa not

---

1 *Il rè pastore*, composed in 1775 on the occasion of a visit of the Archduke Maximilian, Maria Theresa's youngest son.

recall the name Freysinger? The Papa of the two beautiful young ladies whom I have mentioned says that he knows Papa quite well, and was a student with him. He still remembers particularly Wessobrunn, where Papa (this was news to me) played on the organ amazingly well. *'It was quite terrifying,'* he said, *'to see how rapid your Papa was with his feet and hands. Indeed he was absolutely amazing. Ah, he was a great fellow. My father thought the world of him. And how he fooled the clerics to the top of their bent about becoming a priest! You are the very image of him, as he then was, absolutely the very image. But when I knew him, he was just a little shorter.'* A propos. Now for something else. A certain Court Councillor, Öfele by name, who is one of the best Court Councillors here, sends his most humble greetings to Papa. He could have been Chancellor long ago, but for one thing – his love of the bottle. When I first saw him at Albert's, I thought, and so did Mamma, 'Goodness me, what a superlative idiot!' Just picture him, a very tall fellow, strongly built, rather corpulent, with a perfectly absurd face. When he crosses the room to go to another table, he places both hands on his stomach, bends over them and hoists his belly aloft, nods his head and then draws back his right foot with great rapidity. And he performs the same trick afresh for every person in turn. He says he knows Papa infinitely well. I am now off to the theatre for a while. Later on I shall write more. I simply cannot do so now, for my fingers are aching horribly ...

Maria Anna Mozart continues

And I am sweating so that the water is pouring down my face, simply from the fag of packing. The devil take all travelling. I feel that I could shove my feet into my mug, I am so exhausted. I hope that you and Nannerl are well. I send most cordial greetings to my dear Sallerl and Monsieur Bullinger. Please tell Nannerl not to give Bimperl too much to eat, lest she should get too fat. I send greetings to Thresel. Addio. I kiss you both millions of times.

Maria Anna Mozart

Maria Anna Mozart to her Husband

Augsburg,
14 October 1777

We left Munich on the 11th at noon and arrived safely in Augsburg at nine in the evening; and this journey we did in nine hours with a hired coachman who, moreover, fed his horses for an hour.

Mozart continues

So we did not make a mistake about the date; for we wrote in the morning; and we shall be off again, I think, next Friday, that is, the day after tomorrow. For just hear how kind and generous these good Augsburg gentlemen have been! In no place have I been overwhelmed with so many marks of honour as here. My first visit was to the magistrate, Longotabarro. My uncle, a most excellent and lovable man and an honourable townsman, accompanied me and had the honour of waiting upstairs on the landing like a lackey until I should come out of the Arch-Magistrate's room. I did not forget to deliver at once my Papa's most humble respects. He was so good as to remember our whole history and asked me: *'How has he fared all this time?'* Whereupon I at once replied: 'Very well, thanks and praise be to God. And I trust that you too have fared very well?' After that he began to unbend, and addressed me in the second person, while I continued to address him as 'Your Highness', as I had done from the very first. He would not let me go and I had to follow him upstairs to his son-in-law (on the second floor); and meanwhile my uncle had the honour of waiting, seated on a stool in the lobby. I had to restrain myself, most manfully, otherwise I should have said something quite politely, of course. Upstairs I had the honour of playing for about three quarters of an hour upon a good clavichord by Stein in the presence of the dressed-up son and the long-legged young wife and the stupid old lady. I improvised and finally I played off at sight all the music he had, including some very pretty pieces by a certain Edelmann. They were all exceedingly polite and I too was very polite. For it is my custom to treat people as I find them; it pays best in the end. I told them that after lunch I was going to see Stein. The young gentleman of his own accord offered to take me there. I thanked him for his kindness and promised to call again at two o'clock, which I did. We all set off together, accompanied by his brother-in-law, who looked the perfect student. Although I had asked them to keep my identity a secret, yet Herr von Langenmantel was so thoughtless as to say to Herr Stein: 'I have the honour of introducing to you a virtuoso on the clavier', and began to snigger. I at once protested and said that I was only an unworthy pupil of Herr Siegl in Munich, who had asked me to deliver 1000 compliments to him. He shook his head – and said finally: 'Is it possible that I have the honour of seeing Herr Mozart before me?' 'Oh, no,' I replied, 'my name is Trazom and I have a letter for you.' He took the letter and wanted to break the seal at once. But I did not give him time to do so and asked: 'Surely you do not want to read that letter now? Open the door, and let us go into your room. I am most anxious to see your pianofortes.' 'All right,' he said, 'just as you wish. But I feel sure that I am not mistaken.' He opened the door and I ran straight to one of the three claviers which stood in the room. I began to play. He could scarcely open

The piano maker Johann Andreas Stein (1728–92): miniature on ivory (1753) by J. E. Nilson. The Mozarts had already made the acquaintance of Stein (and presumably of his instruments) when Leopold bought a portable clavier from him on a visit to Augsburg in 1763. Mozart was greatly impressed by the new piano that Stein showed him in 1777, and gave two concerts with him on Stein instruments.

the letter in his eagerness to make sure. He only read the signature: 'Oh,' he cried and embraced me. He kept crossing himself and making faces and was as pleased as Punch. I shall tell you later on all about his claviers. He then took me straight to a coffee-house. When I entered I thought that I should drop down, overcome by the stink and fumes of tobacco. But with God's help I had to stand it for an hour; and I pretended to enjoy it all, though to me it seemed as if we were in Turkey...

Mozart to his Father

Mon trés cher Pére!

Augsburg,
17 October 1777

This time I shall begin at once with Stein's pianofortes. Before I had seen any of his make, Späth's claviers had always been my favourites. But now I much prefer Stein's, for they damp ever so much better than the Regensburg instruments. When I strike hard, I can keep my finger on the note or raise it, but the sound ceases the moment I have produced it. In whatever way I touch the keys, the tone is always even. It never jars, it is never stronger or weaker or entirely absent; in a word, it is always even. It is true that he does not sell a pianoforte of this kind for less than

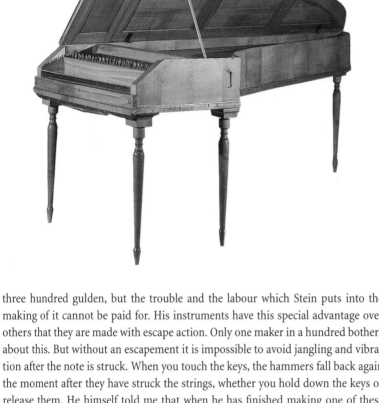

Pianoforte by Johann Andreas Stein, Augsburg, 1788. It was in this period that the piano emerged as the dominant keyboard instrument, relegating harpsichord and organ to the musical peripheries. This change is reflected in the power and complexity of Mozart's late concertos – though Stein's instruments themselves were renowned for a delicacy of touch particularly suited to Mozart's own technical style.

three hundred gulden, but the trouble and the labour which Stein puts into the making of it cannot be paid for. His instruments have this special advantage over others that they are made with escape action. Only one maker in a hundred bothers about this. But without an escapement it is impossible to avoid jangling and vibration after the note is struck. When you touch the keys, the hammers fall back again the moment after they have struck the strings, whether you hold down the keys or release them. He himself told me that when he has finished making one of these claviers, he sits down to it and tries all kinds of passages, runs and jumps, and he shaves and works away until it can do anything. For he labours solely in the interest of music and not for his own profit; otherwise he would soon finish his work. He often says: 'If I were not myself such a passionate lover of music and had not myself some slight skill on the clavier, I should certainly long ago have lost patience with my work. But I do like an instrument which never lets the player down and which is durable.' And his claviers certainly do last. He guarantees that the sounding-board will neither break nor split. When he has finished making one for a clavier, he places it in the open air, exposing it to rain, snow, the heat of the sun and all the devils in order that it may crack. Then he inserts wedges and glues them in to make the instrument very strong and firm. He is delighted when it cracks, for he can then be sure that nothing more can happen to it. Indeed he often cuts into it himself and then glues it together again and strengthens it in this way. He has finished making three pianofortes of this kind. Today I played on one again ...

... Here and at Munich I have played all my six sonatas by heart several times [K279–84]. I played the fifth, in G, at that grand concert in the Stube. The last one in D, sounds exquisite on Stein's pianoforte. The device too which you work with your knee is better on his than on other instruments. I have only to touch it and it works; and when you shift your knee the slightest bit, you do not hear the least reverberation. Well, tomorrow perhaps I shall come to his organs – I mean, I shall come *to write about them*; and I am saving up his little daughter for the very last. When I told Herr Stein that I should very much like to play on his organ, as that instrument was my passion, he was greatly surprised and said: 'What? A man like you, so fine a clavier-player, wants to play on an instrument which has no douceur, no expression, no piano, no forte, but is always the same?' 'That does not matter,' I replied. 'In my eyes and ears the organ is the king of instruments.'

'Well,' he said, 'as you like.' So off we went together. I noticed at once from what he said that he thought that I would not do much on his organ; that I would play, for instance, in a thoroughly pianistic style. He told me that he had taken Schubart at his own request to this same organ. 'I was rather nervous,' he said, 'for Schubart had told everyone and the church was pretty full. For I thought of course that this fellow would be all spirit, fire and rapid execution, qualities which are not at all suited to the organ. But as soon as he began I changed my opinion.' All I said to Stein was: 'Well, Herr Stein, do you think that I am going to canter about on your organ?' 'Ah, you,' he replied, 'that is quite another matter.' We reached the choir and I began to improvise, when he started to laugh; then I played a fugue. 'I can well believe,' he said, 'that you like to play the organ, when you play so well.' At first the pedal seemed a bit strange to me, as it was not divided. It started with C, and then D and E followed in the same row. But with us D and E are above, as E♭ and F♯ are here. But I soon got the hang of it. I have also been to St. Ulrich to play on the old organ there. The staircase there is perfectly dreadful. I begged them to get someone to play on the organ, saying that I should like to go down and listen, for up above it produces no effect whatever. But I could form no opinion, for the young choirmaster, a priest, rushed up and down the keyboard in such a fashion that one could not get the least idea of anything. And when he wanted to play a few chords, the result was simply discords, for the notes did not harmonize. Afterwards we had to go off to a wine-shop, as my Mamma, my little cousin and Herr Stein were with us. A certain Father Emilian, a conceited ass and a sorry wit of his profession, was very sweet on my little cousin and wanted to jest with her, but she made fun of him – finally when he was a bit tipsy, which soon happened, he began to talk about music and sang a canon, saying: 'In my life I have never heard anything more beautiful.' I said: 'I am sorry that I cannot join in, but nature has not bestowed on me the gift of intoning.' 'That does not matter,' he said. He began. I took the third voice, but I invented quite a different text, i.e. 'Pater Emilian, oh, you idiot, you, lick my arse. I beg you.' All this, *sotto voce*, to my cousin. Then we laughed together for another half-hour. He said to me: 'If only we could be together longer, I should like to discuss composition with you.' 'Then,' I replied, 'we should soon have dried up.' *On the scent, Towser.* To be continued in my next.

W. A. Mozart

Leopold Mozart to his Wife and Son

My Dear Wife!

Tell Wolfgang that the Court Baker's saucer-eyed daughter who danced with him at the Stern, who often paid him friendly compliments and who ended by entering the convent at Loreto, has returned to her father's house. She heard that Wolfgang was going to leave Salzburg and probably hoped to see him again and to prevent him from doing so. Will Wolfgang be so kind as to refund to her father the money which the pomp and all the fine preparation for entering her convent cost him! You are still in Augsburg? Bravissimo! ... Of course, if you want to give a concert, you must make it known several days in advance. I only hope that it may be profitable! Though I doubt whether it will bring in much. Everyone who comes will probably pay one gulden, twelve kreuzer; but will a great many turn up? *I am very curious to hear all about it* ...

Salzburg,
23 October 1777

Mon très cher Fils!

I am to wish you happiness on your name-day! But what can I now wish you that I do not always wish you? And that is, the grace of God, that it may follow you everywhere, that it may never leave you. And this it will never do, if you are diligent in fulfilling the duties of a true Catholic Christian. You know me. I am no pedant and no praying Peter and still less am I a hypocrite. But surely you will not refuse the request of a father, that you should take thought for your soul's welfare so that in the hour of his death you may cause him no anxiety, and that in that dread moment he may have no reason to reproach himself for not having watched over your soul's salvation. Farewell! Be happy! Be sensible! Honour and care for your mother, who in her old age is having much anxiety. Love me as I love you. Your truly affectionate father

Leop. Mozart

Maria Anna Mozart to her Husband

Today, the 23rd, Wolfgang is lunching again at the Holy Cross Monastery and I too was invited, but as the cold has given me pains in my belly, I have stayed at home. Is it as cold at Salzburg as it is here, where everything is frozen hard just as if it were midwinter? If nothing prevents us, we intend to leave for Wallerstein on the day after tomorrow Saturday. The concert here was an amazing success. The papers will tell you more. Herr Stein took infinite trouble and rendered us many kindnesses. You must write him a letter and thank him. I hope that you and Nannerl are in good health, but somehow I am dreadfully anxious lest you should be unwell, as we have not had a line from you this week. Do write to me soon and relieve me of my anxiety. I am very much surprised that you have not received the Schuster duets—

Mozart continues

Why, of course he has received them.
Mamma. Not at all, he has kept on writing that he has not yet received them.
Wolfgang. I detest arguing. He has certainly got them and that's an end of it.
Mamma. You are wrong, Wolfgang.
Wolfgang. No, I am right. I will show it to Mamma in black and white.
Mamma. Where then?
Wolfgang. There, read that.
    Mamma is reading your letter now. Last Sunday I attended Mass in the Church of the Holy Cross and at ten o'clock I went to Herr Stein. That was on the 19th. We rehearsed a few symphonies for the concert. Afterwards I lunched with my uncle at the Holy Cross Monastery. During the meal we had some music. In spite of their poor fiddling I prefer the monastery players to the Augsburg orchestra. I performed a symphony and played Vanhal's violin concerto in B♭, which was unanimously applauded. The Dean, who is a cousin of Eberlin, by name Zeschinger, is a fine, jolly fellow and knows Papa quite well. In the evening at supper I played my Strassburg concerto [K218], which went like oil. Everyone praised my beautiful, pure tone. Afterwards they brought in a small clavichord and I improvised and then played a sonata and the Fischer variations [K179]. Then the others whispered to the Dean that he should just hear me play something in the organ style. I asked him to give me a theme. He declined, but one of the monks gave me one. I put it through its paces and in the middle (the fugue was in G minor) I started off in the major key and played something quite lively, though in the same tempo; and after that the theme over again, but this time arseways. Finally it occurred to me, could I not use my lively tune as the theme for a fugue? I did not waste much time in asking, but

did so at once, and it went as neatly as if Daser [a tailor] had fitted it. The Dean was absolutely staggered. 'Why, it's simply phenomenal, that's all I can say,' he said. 'I should never have believed what I have heard. You are a first-rate fellow. My Abbot told me, it is true, that he had never in his life heard anyone play the organ so smoothly and so soundly.' (For he had heard me a few days before, when the Dean was away.) At last someone produced a sonata in fugal style and wanted me to play it. But I said: 'Gentlemen, this is too much. Let me tell you, I shall certainly not be able to play that sonata at sight.' 'Yes, that I can well believe,' said the Dean very pressingly, for he was my strong supporter. 'It is too much to expect. No one could tackle that.' 'However,' I said, 'I should like to try it.' I heard the Dean muttering behind me all the time: 'Oh, you little villain, oh, you rascal, oh, you — !' I played until eleven o'clock, for I was bombarded and besieged with themes for fugues. When I was at Stein's house the other day he put before me a sonata by Beecke – I think that I have told you that already. That reminds me, now for his little daughter. Anyone who sees and hears her play and can keep from laughing, must, like her father, be made of stone. For instead of sitting in the middle of the clavier, she sits right up opposite the treble, as it gives her more chance of flopping about and making grimaces. She rolls her eyes and smirks. When a passage is repeated, she plays it more slowly the second time. If it has to be played a third time, then she plays it even more slowly. When a passage is being played, the arm must be raised as high as possible, and according as the notes in the passage are stressed, the arm, not the fingers, must do this, and that too with great emphasis in a heavy and clumsy manner. But the best joke of all is that when she comes to a passage which ought to flow like oil and which necessitates a change of finger, she does not bother her head about it, but when the moment arrives, she just leaves out the notes, raises her hand and starts off again quite comfortably – a method by which she is much more likely to strike a wrong note, which often produces a curious effect. I am simply writing this in order to give Papa some idea of clavier-playing and clavier-teaching, so that he may derive some profit from it later on. Herr Stein is quite crazy about his daughter, who is eight and a half and who now learns everything by heart. She may succeed, for she has great talent for music. But she will not make progress by this method – for she will never acquire great rapidity, since she definitely does all she can to make her hands heavy. Further, she will never acquire the most essential, the most difficult and the chief requisite in music, which is, time, because from her earliest years she has done her utmost not to play in time. Herr Stein and I discussed this point for two hours at least and I have almost converted him, for he now asks my advice on everything. He used to be quite crazy about Beecke; but now he sees and hears that I am the better player, that I do not make grimaces, and yet play with such expression that, as he himself confesses, no one up to the present has been able to get such good results out of his pianofortes. Everyone is amazed that I can always keep strict time. What these people cannot grasp is that in tempo rubato in an Adagio, the left hand should go on playing in strict time. With them the left hand always follows suit. Count Wolfegg and several other passionate admirers of Beecke, publicly admitted at a concert the other day that I had wiped the floor with him. The Count kept running about in the hall, exclaiming: 'I have never heard anything like this in my life.' And he said to me: 'I really must tell you, I have never heard you play as you played today. I shall tell your father so too as soon as I return to Salzburg.' Now what does Papa think that we played immediately after the symphony? Why, the concerto for three claviers [K242]. Herr Demmler played the first, I the second and Herr Stein the third. Then I gave a solo, my last sonata in D, written for Baron Dürnitz [K284], and after my concerto in B♭ [K238]. I then played another solo, quite in the style of the organ, a fugue in C minor and then all of a sudden a magnificent sonata in C major, out of my head, and a Rondo to finish up with. There was a regular din of applause. Herr Stein was so amazed that he could only make faces and grimaces. As for Herr Demmler, he couldn't stop laughing. He is a quaint fellow, for when he likes anything very much, all he does is to burst into fits of laughter. In my case he even started to curse. Addio. I kiss Papa's hands and embrace my sister with my whole heart. I am your most obedient son

Wolfgang Amadé Mozart

24 October, 1777. Augusta Vindelicorum.

Mozart to his Father

Augsburg,
25 October 1777

The concert, before expenses were deducted, brought in ninety gulden. So, adding the two ducats I was given in the Stube, we have now taken in one hundred gulden. The expenses of the concert amounted to about sixteen gulden, thirty kreuzer. I had the hall for nothing; and many of the performers, I think, will have given their services *free. Altogether* we are now twenty-six or twenty-seven gulden out of pocket; which is not too bad. I am writing this letter on Saturday, the 25th. I received this morning your letter containing the sad news of the death of the wife of the Chief Purveyor. Fräulein Tonerl can now point her snout – and perhaps she will have to open it very wide – and then close it without having snatched *anything*. As for the Court Baker's daughter, I have no objection whatever to raise. I saw all this coming long ago and that was the reason why I was so reluctant to leave home and why I felt our departure so keenly. But I hope the story is not known all over Salzburg? I implore Papa most earnestly to keep it quiet as long as possible and for Heaven's sake to refund on my behalf the expenses which her father incurred in connection with her magnificent entry into the convent; pending my return to Salzburg when (like Father Gassner in his little monastery) quite naturally and without any sorcery I shall make the poor girl first ill and then well again and restore her to her convent for life ...

... This is my second letter from Mannheim. I am with Cannabich every day. Mamma too came with me today to his house. He is quite a different person from what he used to be and the whole orchestra say the same thing. He has taken a great fancy to me. He has a daughter who plays the clavier quite nicely; and in order to make a real friend of him I am now working at a sonata for her, which is almost finished save for the Rondo [K309]. When I had composed the opening Allegro and the Andante I took them to their house and played both to them. Papa cannot imagine the applause which this sonata won. It so happened that some members of the orchestra were there, young Danner, a horn-player called Lang, and the oboist [Friedrich Ramm] whose name I have forgotten, but who plays very well and has a delightfully pure tone. I have made him a present of my oboe concerto [K314], which is being copied in a room at Cannabich's, and the fellow is quite crazy with delight. I played this concerto to him today on the pianoforte at Cannabich's, and, although *everybody knew that I was the composer*, it was very well received. Nobody said that it was not *well composed*, because the people here do not understand such matters – they had better consult the Archbishop, who will at once put them right. I played all my six sonatas today at Cannabich's. Herr Kapellmeister Holzbauer himself took me today to Count Savioli, the Intendant, and Cannabich happened to be there. Herr Holzbauer spoke to the Count in Italian, suggesting that the Elector ought to grant me the favour of a hearing. He added that I had been here fifteen years ago, when I was seven, but that now I was older and more developed in music as well as in body. 'Ah,' said the Count, 'that is — ' Goodness knows who he thought I was. But Cannabich stepped in at once, and I pretended not to hear and fell into conversation with some other people. I noticed, however, that he was speaking to the Count about me with an earnest expression. The latter then said to me: 'I hear that you play the clavier quite passably.' I bowed ...

Mannheim,
4 November 1777

Mozart to his Cousin, Maria Anna Thekla Mozart, Augsburg

Dearest Coz Fuzz!

I have received reprieved your dear letter, telling selling me that my uncle carbuncle, my aunt can't and you too are very well hell. Thank God, we too are in excellent health wealth. Today the letter setter from my Papa Ha! Ha! dropped safely into my claws paws. I hope that you too have got shot the note dote which I wrote

Mannheim,
5 November 1777

Christian Cannabich (1731–98) was one of the most distinguished composers of the highly regarded Mannheim court orchestra, generally recognized as the best in Europe, during its most important years. Cannabich and his family were a tower of strength and hospitality to Mozart during his visits to Mannheim, and later Munich. Engraving by Egid Verhelst, 1779.

to you from Mannheim. If so, so much the better, better the much so. Now for some sense. I am very sorry to hear that the Abbot rabbit has had another stroke so soon moon. But I trust that with God's cod's help it will have no serious consequences excrescences. You say lay that you will keep the compromise which you made me before I left Augsburg and that you will do so soon boon. Well, that will certainly be a shock to me. You write further, you pour out, disclose, divulge, notify, declare, signify, inform, acquaint me with the fact, make it quite clear, request, demand, desire, wish, would like, order me to send lend you my portrait. Eh bien, I shall certainly despatch scratch it to you. Oui, par ma foi. I shit on your nose and it will run down your chin. A propos. Have you got that Spuni Cuni business? Do tell me! Do you still love me? I am sure you do! If so, so much the better, better the much so! ...

Mozart to his Father

... Now for some news from Mannheim. Yesterday I had to go with Cannabich to Count Savioli, the Intendant, to fetch my present. It was just as I had expected. No money, but a fine gold watch. At the moment ten carolins would have suited me better than the watch, which including the chains and the mottoes has been valued at twenty. What one needs on a journey is money; and, let me tell you, I now have five watches. I am therefore seriously thinking of having an additional watch pocket on each leg of my trousers so that when I visit some great lord, I shall wear both watches (which, moreover, is now the 'mode') so that it will not occur to him to present me with another one. I see from Papa's letter that he has not seen Vogler's book. I have just read it, as I borrowed it from Cannabich. Let me give you a short history of Vogler. He came here, absolutely down and out, performed on the clavier and composed a ballet. People took pity on him and the Elector sent him to Italy. When the Elector happened to be in Bologna, he asked Padre Vallotti about him and received this reply: 'O altezza, questo è un gran uomo!' He also asked Padre Martini, who informed him: 'Altezza, è buono; ma a poco a poco, quando sarà un poco più vecchio, più sodo, si farà, si farà, ma bisogna che si cangi molto.'[1] When Vogler returned to Mannheim, he took orders and was immediately made Court chaplain. He produced a Miserere which, everyone tells me, simply cannot be listened to, for it sounds all wrong. Hearing that his composition was not receiving much praise, Vogler went to the Elector and complained that the orchestra were playing it badly on purpose. In a word, he was so clever at pulling strings (he had had more than one naughty little affair with women, who were useful to him) that he was appointed Deputy-Kapellmeister. But he is a fool, who imagines that he is the very pitch of perfection. The whole orchestra, from A to Z, detest him. He has caused Holzbauer a great deal of annoyance. His book is more useful for teaching arithmetic than for teaching composition. He says he can turn out a composer in three weeks and a singer in six months, but so far no one has seen him do it. He disparages the great masters. Why, he even belittled Bach to me. Bach has written two operas here, the first of which was more popular than the second, 'Lucio Silla'. Now, as I too had composed a 'Lucio Silla' in Milan, I wanted to see Bach's opera and I had heard from Holzbauer that Vogler possessed a copy. So I asked him for it. 'Delighted,' he said. 'I shall send it to you tomorrow. But you will not make head or tail of it.' When he saw me a few days later, he asked me with an obvious sneer: 'Well, do you find it beautiful? Have you learnt anything from it? – It has one fine

Mannheim,
13 November 1777

---

1 Your Highness, he is good; and gradually, as he becomes older and surer of himself, he will improve. But he will have to change considerably.

aria. Let me see, what are the words?' He turned to somebody who happened to be standing beside him. 'What sort of aria?' asked his companion. 'Why, of course, that hideous aria by Bach, that filthy stuff – yes, yes, *Pupille amate*, which he certainly wrote in his cups.' I thought I should have to seize his front hair and pull it hard, but I pretended not to hear him, said nothing and walked off. He has had his day with the Elector. My sonata for Mlle Rosa Cannabich is now finished. Last Sunday I tried the organ in the chapel for fun. I came in during the Kyrie and played the end of it, and, when the priest had finished intoning the Gloria, I played a cadenza. As my performance was so different from what they are accustomed to here, they all looked round, especially Holzbauer. He said to me: 'If I had known this I should have put on another mass.' 'Yes,' I replied, 'so that you could have caught me out!' The elder Toeschi and Wendling were standing beside me all the time. The people were splitting with laughter. Now and then the music was marked pizzicato and each time I just touched the keys very lightly. I was in my very best spirits. Instead of a Benedictus the organist has to play here the whole time. So I took the theme of the Sanctus and developed it as a fugue. Whereupon they all stood gaping. Finally, after the *Ita missa est*, I played a fugue. The pedal there is different from ours, which put me out a bit at first; but I soon got the hang of it. Now I must close . . .

Mannheim,
14 November 1777

I, Johannes Chrysostomus Amadeus Wolfgangus Sigismundus Mozart, hereby plead guilty and confess that yesterday and the day before (not to mention on several other occasions) I did not get home until midnight; and that from ten o'clock until the said hour at Cannabich's house and in the presence and company of the said Cannabich, his wife and daughter, the Treasurer, Ramm and Lang I did frequently, without any difficulty, but quite easily, perpetrate – rhymes, the same being, moreover, sheer garbage, that is, on such subjects as muck, shitting and arse-licking – and that too in thoughts, words – but not in deeds. I should not have behaved so godlessly, however, if our ringleader, known under the name of Lisel (Elisabetha Cannabich), had not egged me on and incited me; at the same time I must admit that I thoroughly enjoyed it. I confess all these sins and transgressions of mine from the bottom of my heart and in the hope of having to confess them very often, I firmly resolve to go on with the sinful life which I have begun. Wherefore I beg for the holy dispensation, if it can be easily obtained; if not, it's all one to me, for the game will go on all the same. *Lusus enim suum habet ambitum*, as the late Meisner, the singer, says (chap. 9, p.24); so does Saint Ascenditor too, patron of burnt soup coffee, musty lemonade, almondless milk of almonds and, more particularly, of strawberry ice full of bits of ice, as he himself is a great connoisseur and artist in ices. As soon as I can, I shall have the sonata which I have written for Mlle Cannabich

copied out on small paper and shall send it to my sister. I began to teach it to Mlle
Rosa three days ago. We finished the opening Allegro today. The Andante will give
us most trouble, for it is full of expression and must be played accurately and with
the exact shade of forte and piano, precisely as they are marked. She is very smart
and learns very easily. Her right hand is very good, but her left, unfortunately, is
completely ruined. I can honestly say that I often feel quite sorry for her when I
see her struggling, as she so often does, until she really gets quite out of breath, not
from lack of skill but simply because she cannot help it. For she has got into the
habit of doing what she does, because no one has ever shown her any other way. I
have told her mother and I have told her too that if I were her regular teacher, I
would lock up all her music, cover the keys with a handkerchief and make her
practise, first with the right hand and then with the left, nothing but passages, trills,
mordants and so forth, very slowly at first, until each hand should be thoroughly
trained. I would then undertake to turn her into a first-rate clavierist. For it's a great
pity. She has so much talent, reads quite passably, possesses so much natural facility
and plays with plenty of feeling. They both said that I was right. Now for the opera
[*Günther von Schwarzburg*], but quite briefly. Holzbauer's music is very beautiful.
The poetry doesn't deserve such music. What surprises me most of all is that a man
as old as Holzbauer should still possess so much spirit; for you can't imagine what
fire there is in that music. The prima donna was Mme Elizabeth Wendling, not the
flautist's wife, but the fiddler's. She is always indisposed and, what is more, the
opera was not written for her, but for a certain Danzi, who is at present in England;
consequently it is not suited to her voice but is too high for her. On one occasion
Raaff sang four arias, about 450 bars in all, in such a fashion as to call forth the
remark that his voice was the strongest reason why he sang so badly. Anyone who
hears him begin an aria without at once reminding himself that it is Raaff, the once
famous tenor, who is singing, is bound to burst out laughing. It's a fact. I thought
to myself: 'If I didn't know that this was Raaff, I should double up with laughing.'
As it is, I just pull out my handkerchief and hide a smile. Moreover, he has never
been, so people here tell me, anything of an actor; you'd only have had to hear him,
without even looking at him; nor has he by any means a good presence. In the opera
he had to die, and while dying sing a very very very long aria in slow time; well, he
died with a grin on his face, and towards the end of the aria his voice gave out so
badly that one really couldn't stand it any longer. I was sitting in the orchestra
beside Wendling the flautist. He had objected beforehand that it was unnatural for
a man to keep on singing until he died, as it was too long to wait. Whereupon I
remarked: 'Have a little patience. He'll soon be gone, for I hear it.' 'So do I,' he said
and laughed ...

Monsieur mon trés cher Pére,

I can still write nothing definite about my position here. Last Monday, after going for three days in succession, morning and afternoon, to his natural children, I had at last the good fortune to meet the Elector. We all thought indeed that once more our efforts were to be in vain, as it was then quite late. But at last we saw him coming. The governess at once told the Countess to seat herself at the clavier and I placed myself beside her and gave her a lesson; and that was how the Elector found us when he came into the room. We stood up but he told us to go on. When the Countess had finished playing, the governess was the first to speak and said that I had composed a very fine Rondo. I played it and he liked it very much. At length he asked: 'But will she be able to learn it?' 'Oh yes,' I replied. 'I only wish that I might have the good fortune to teach it to her myself.' He smiled and said: 'I should like it too. But would not her playing be spoilt if she had two different masters?' 'Oh no, Your Highness,' I replied. 'All that matters is whether she has a good one or a bad. I hope Your Highness will not doubt – and will have confidence in me.' 'Oh, most certainly,' he replied. The governess then said: 'See, Herr Mozart has also written some variations on Fischer's minuet for the young Count.' I played them and he liked them very much. He then began to jest with the Countess. I thanked him for his present. He said: 'Well, I shall think it over. How long are you going to stay here?' *My reply*: 'As long as Your Highness commands. I have no engagements whatsoever: I can stay as long as Your Highness requires.' That was all ...

Maria Anna Mozart adds a postscript

My dear Husband,

You see that I can't write very much to you, as Wolfgang has left me no room. In any case he has told you all there is to tell, so that I have no more news for you about our affairs. Often I just wish that I could spend at least one day with you, so that I could talk to you about all the things we cannot write about. To do so is quite impossible, for the letters would be far too long. We write to you twice every week, so you ought to get as many letters as we do. Addio. Keep well. I kiss you both many 100000 times and remain your faithful wife

Maria Anna Mozart

All sorts of messages to all our acquaintances.

Maria Anna Mozart to her Husband

My dear Husband,

You insist on knowing how much we have spent on our journey. We told you about Albert's account and that our bill in Augsburg was 300 gulden. Wolfgang told you that we were 24 gulden on the wrong side; but he forgot to include the expenses of the concert, which were 16 gulden, and also our landlord's account. Thus by the time we got to Mannheim we had only about 60 gulden in all. So if we had gone off again after a fortnight, we should not have had much left. For travelling expenses have gone up a lot since everything has become so dear. It is not anything like what it used to be, you would be surprised. As for Wolfgang's journey to Paris, you must think it over and let us know if you approve. At this time of the year Paris is the only place where there is anything doing. Monsieur Wendling is an honest fellow, as everybody knows. He has travelled far and wide and has been to Paris thirteen times already. He knows every stick and stone there; and then our friend Herr Grimm is his best friend and has done a lot for him. So make up your mind and whatever you decide will suit me. Herr Wendling has assured me that he will be a father to Wolfgang, whom he loves as if he were his own son; and Wolfgang will be looked after as well as if he were with me. As you may imagine, I myself do not like to let him go, nor do I like to have to travel home alone, it is such an awful distance. I can't bear to think of it. But what can we do? I am too old to undertake such a long journey to Paris and besides it would cost too much. To travel à quatre is much cheaper than to meet all one's expenses oneself. I shall write more next post-day. Today I have a headache and I think I am in for a cold. It is bitterly cold here. I am so frozen that I can hardly hold my pen. Wolfgang has gone out to look at lodgings. The cheap ones are very scarce here, but there are plenty of expensive ones. Tell Nannerl that people do not wear jackets here except indoors. Out-of-doors they wear chiefly cloaks and capes. The caps they wear are much prettier than what we wear in Salzburg and quite different – their frisure is quite wonderful, nothing piled up at all. The women are very smartly dressed. If it were not such a distance, I would send Nannerl a cap and a Palatine. Addio. Keep well, both of you. I kiss you many 1000000 times and remain your faithful wife

Maria Anna Mozart

Mozart to his Father

Next Wednesday I am going for a few days to Kirchheim-Bolanden to visit the Princess of Orange. People here have said such nice things to me about her that I have at last decided to go. A Dutch officer, a good friend of mine, got a terrible scolding from her for not bringing me with him when he went to offer her his New Year wishes. I shall get eight louis d'or at least, for, as she is passionately fond of singing, I have had four arias copied for her and, as she has a nice little orchestra and gives a concert every day, I shall also present her with a symphony. Moreover the copying of the arias will not cost me much, for it has been done by a certain Herr Weber, who is accompanying me there. I don't know whether I have already

*Mannheim,
17 January 1778*

written about his daughter or not – She sings indeed most admirably and has a lovely, pure voice. The only thing she lacks is dramatic action; were it not for that, she might be the prima donna on any stage. She is only sixteen. Her father is a thoroughly honest German who is bringing up his children well, and for that very reason the girl is persecuted with attentions here. He has six children, five girls and one son. He and his wife and children have been obliged to live for fourteen years on an income of 200 gulden and because he has always attended carefully to his duties and has provided the Elector with a very talented singer, who is only sixteen, he now gets in all – 400 gulden. She sings most excellently my aria written for De Amicis with those horribly difficult passages and she is to sing it at Kirchheim-Bolanden. She is quite well able to teach herself. She accompanies herself very well and she also plays galanterie quite respectably. What is most fortunate for her at Mannheim is that she has won the praise of all honest people of good will. Even the Elector and the Electress are only too glad to receive her, provided it doesn't cost them anything. She can go to the Electress whenever she likes, even daily; and this is due to her good behaviour ...

Monsieur
   Mon trés cher Pére!

Mannheim,
4 February 1778

   I simply cannot wait as I usually do until Saturday, because it is too long already since I have had the pleasure of talking to you in a letter. The first thing I want to tell you about is how I and my good friends got on at Kirchheim-Bolanden. Well, it was just a holiday trip – nothing more. We set off from here at eight o'clock on Friday morning, after I had breakfasted with Herr Weber. We had a smart covered coach which held four and we reached Kirchheim-Bolanden at four o'clock. We had to send a list of our names at once to the castle. Early next morning Herr Konzertmeister Rothfischer called on us. He had already been described to me in Mannheim as a most honest fellow; and I found him so. In the evening, Saturday evening, we went to Court, where Mlle Weber sang three arias. I say nothing about her singing – only one word, excellent! I wrote to you the other day about her merits; but I shall not be able to close this letter without telling you something more about her, for only now have I got to know her properly and as a result to discover her great powers. We had to dine afterwards at the officers' table. We were obliged to walk a good distance to church next day, for the Catholic church is rather far off. That was Sunday. We lunched again with the officers, but they had no concert in the evening, as it was Sunday. So they have only 300 concerts in the year. We could have dined at Court in the evening, but we did not wish to do so, preferring to remain in the inn by ourselves. We would have unanimously and with heartfelt gladness done without the meals at Court, for we never enjoyed ourselves better than when we were alone. But we had to think a little about economy – for, as it was, we had quite enough to pay for. The following day, Monday, we again had a concert, and also on Tuesday and Wednesday. Mlle Weber sang thirteen times in all and played the clavier twice, for she does not play at all badly. What surprises me most is her excellent sight-reading. Would you believe it, she played my difficult sonatas at sight, *slowly* but without missing a single note! On my honour I would rather hear my sonatas played by her than by Vogler! I played a dozen times in all, and once by request on the organ in the Lutheran church. I presented four symphonies to the Princess and received only seven louis d'or in silver, mark you, and my poor dear Mlle Weber only five. Really it was the last thing I expected. I was not hoping for much, but at least I thought that each of us would receive eight louis d'or. Basta! We have lost nothing by it, however, for I still have a profit of 42 gulden and moreover the inexpressible pleasure of making the acquaintance of a thoroughly honest, good Catholic Christian family. I am truly sorry that I did not get to know them long ago . . .

. . . I propose to remain here and finish entirely at my leisure that music for De Jean, for which I am to get 200 gulden. I can stay here as long as I like and neither board nor lodging costs me anything. In the meantime Herr Weber will endeavour to get engagements here and there for concerts with me, and we shall then travel together. When I am with him, it is just as if I were travelling with you. The very reason why I am so fond of him is because, apart from his personal appearance, he is just like you and has exactly your character and way of thinking. If my mother were not, as you know, too *comfortably lazy* to write, she would tell you the very same thing! I must confess that I much enjoyed travelling with them. We were happy and merry; I was hearing a man talk like you; I had nothing to worry about; I found my torn clothes mended; in short, I was waited on like a prince.

I have become so fond of this unfortunate family that my dearest wish is to make them happy; and perhaps I may be able to do so. My advice is that they should go to Italy. So now I should like you to write to our good friend Lugiati, and the sooner the better, and enquire what are the highest terms given to a prima donna in Verona – the more the better, one can always climb down – perhaps too it would be possible to obtain the Ascensa in Venice. As far as her singing is concerned, I would wager my life that she will bring me renown. Even in a short time she has greatly profited by my instruction, and how much greater will the improvement be by then! I am not anxious either about her acting. If our plan succeeds, we, M. Weber, his two daughters and I will have the honour of visiting my dear Papa and my dear sister for a fortnight on our way through Salzburg. My sister will find a friend and a companion in Mlle Weber, for, like my sister in Salzburg, she has a reputation for good behaviour, her father resembles my father and the whole family resemble the

Mozarts. True, there are envious folk, as there are in Salzburg, but when it comes to the point, they have to speak the truth. Honesty is the best policy. I can say that I shall look forward immensely to going to Salzburg with them, if only that you may hear her sing. She sings superbly the arias which I wrote for De Amicis, both the bravura aria and 'Parto, m'affretto' and 'Dalla sponda tenebrosa'. I beg you to do your best to get us to Italy. You know my greatest desire is – to write operas.

I will gladly write an opera for Verona for 50 zecchini, if only in order that she may make her name; for if I do not compose it, I fear that she may be victimized. By that time I shall have made so much money on the other journeys we propose to undertake together, that I shall not be the loser. I think we shall go to Switzerland and perhaps also to Holland. Do write to me soon about this. If we stay anywhere for long, the eldest daughter will be very useful to us; for we could have our own ménage, as she can cook . . .

. . . Well, it is time for me to stop. If I were to write all I think, I should have no paper left. Send me an answer soon, I beg you. Do not forget how much I desire to write operas. I envy anyone who is composing one. I could really weep for vexation when I hear or see an aria. But Italian, not German; seriosa, not buffa . . .

Maria Anna Mozart to her Husband

My dear Husband!

Mannheim,
5 February 1778

You will have seen from this letter that when Wolfgang makes new acquaintances, he immediately wants to give his life and property for them.

True, she sings exceedingly well; still, we must not lose sight of our own interests. I never liked his being in the company of Wendling and Ramm, but I never ventured to raise any objections, nor would he ever have listened to me.

But as soon as he got to know the Webers, he immediately changed his mind. In short, he prefers other people to me, for I remonstrate with him about this and that, and about things which I do not like; and he objects to this. So you yourself will have to think over what ought to be done. I do not consider his journey to Paris with Wendling at all advisable. I would rather accompany him myself later on. It would not cost so very much in the mail coach. Perhaps you will still get a reply from Herr Grimm. Meanwhile we are not losing anything here. I am writing this quite secretly, while he is at dinner, and I shall close, for I do not want to be caught. Addio.

I remain your faithful wife

Maria Anna Mozart

Mozart to his Father

... In my last letter I forgot to mention Mlle Weber's greatest merit, which is her superb cantabile singing. Please do not forget about Italy. I commend this poor, but excellent little Mlle Weber to your interest with all my heart, *caldamente*, as the Italians say. I have given her three of De Amicis's arias, the scena I wrote for Madame Duschek (to whom I shall be writing soon) and four arias from 'Il Rè pastore'. I have also promised her to have some arias sent from home. I hope you will be kind enough to send them to me, but send them *gratis*, I beg you, and you will really be doing a good work! You will find the list of them on the French song which her father has copied out, and the paper is part of a present from him; but indeed he has given me much more. Now I must close ...

Mannheim,
7 February 1778

Leopold Mozart to his Son

My dear Son!

I have read your letter of the 4th with amazement and horror. I am beginning to answer it today, the 11th, for the whole night long I was unable to sleep and am so exhausted that I can only write quite slowly, word by word, and so gradually finish what I have to say by tomorrow. Up to the present, thank God, I have been in good health; but this letter, in which I only recognize my son by that failing of his which makes him believe everyone at the first word spoken, open his kind heart to every plausible flatterer and let others sway him as they like, so that he is led by whimsical ideas and ill-considered and impracticable projects to sacrifice his own name and interests, and even the interests and the claims of his aged and honourable parents to those of strangers – this letter, I say, depressed me exceedingly, the more so as I was cherishing the reasonable hope that certain circumstances which you had had to face already, as well as my own reminders, both spoken and written, could not have failed to convince you that not only for the sake of your happiness but in order that you may be able to gain a livelihood and attain at length the desired goal in a world of men in varying degrees good and bad, fortunate and unfortunate, it was imperative for you to guard your warm heart by the strictest reserve, undertake nothing without full consideration and never let yourself be carried away by enthusiastic notions and blind fancies. My dear son, I implore you to read this letter carefully – and take time to reflect upon it. Merciful God! those happy moments are gone when, as child and boy, you never went to bed without standing on a chair and singing to me *Oragna fiagata fa*, and ending by kissing me again and again on the tip of my nose and telling me that when I grew old you would put me in a glass case and protect me from every breath of air, so that you might always have me with you and honour me. Listen to me, therefore, in patience! You are fully

Salzburg,
11–12 February 1778

acquainted with our difficulties in Salzburg – you know my wretched income, why I kept my promise to let you go away, and all my various troubles. The purpose of your journey was twofold – either to get a good permanent appointment, or, if this should fail, to go off to some big city where large sums of money can be earned. Both plans were designed to assist your parents and to help on your dear sister, but above all to build up your own name and reputation in the world . . .

. . . You took that journey to Munich – with what purpose you know – but nothing could be done. Well-meaning friends wanted to keep you there and you wished to remain . . .

. . . At that time you were quite amazingly taken up with the little singer at the theatre and your dearest wish was to forward the cause of the German stage; now you declare that you would not even care to write a comic opera! No sooner had you left the gates of Munich behind you than (as I prophesied) your whole company of subscribers had forgotten you. What would be your lot were you in Munich now? – In the end one can always see the providence of God. In Augsburg too you had your little romance, you amused yourself with my brother's daughter, who now must needs send you her portrait . . . When you were in Mannheim you did well to win the good graces of Herr *Cannabich*. But you would have gained nothing, had he not been seeking a double advantage therefrom. I have already written to you about the rest. Next, Herr Cannabich's daughter was smothered in praises, her temperament was recorded in the Adagio of a sonata, in short, *she* was now the reigning favourite. Then you made the acquaintance of Herr Wendling. *He* was now the most honourable friend – and what happened next, I need not repeat. Suddenly you strike up a new acquaintanceship – with Herr Weber; all your other friends are forgotten; now *this family* is the most honourable, the most Christian family and the daughter is to have the leading role in the tragedy to be enacted between your own family and hers! In the transports into which your kind and too open heart has thrown you, you think all your ill-considered fancies as reasonable and practicable as if they were bound to be accomplished in the normal course of nature. You are thinking of taking her to Italy as a prima donna. Tell me, do you know of any prima donna who, without having first appeared many times in Germany, has walked on to the stage in Italy as prima donna? . . . What impresario would not laugh, were one to recommend him a girl of sixteen or seventeen, who has never yet appeared on a stage! As for your proposal (I can hardly write when I think of it), your proposal to travel about with Herr Weber and, be it noted, his two daughters – it has nearly made me lose my reason! My dearest son! How can you have allowed yourself to be bewitched even for an hour by such a horrible idea, which must have been suggested to you by someone or other! Your letter reads like a romance. For could you really make up your mind to go trailing about the world with strangers? Quite apart from your reputation – what of your old parents and your dear sister? To expose me to the mockery and ridicule of the Prince and of *the whole town which loves you?* Yes, to expose me to mockery and yourself to contempt, for in reply to repeated questions, I have had to tell everyone that you were going to Paris. And now, after all, you want to roam about with strangers and take your chance? Surely, after a little reflection you will give up all idea of doing so! But that I may convince you of your rash precipitancy, let me tell you that the time is now coming when no man in his senses could think of such a thing. Conditions are now such that it is impossible to guess where war may break out, for everywhere regiments are either on the march or under marching orders. – To Switzerland? – To Holland? Why, there is not a soul there the whole summer; and at Berne and Zürich in winter one can just make enough not to die of starvation, but nothing more. As for Holland they have things to think of there besides music; and in any case half one's takings are eaten up by Herr Hummel and concert expenses. Besides, what will become of your reputation? Those are places for lesser lights, for second-rate composers, for scribblers, for a Schwindel, a Zappa, a Ricci and the like. Name any one great composer to me who would deign to take such an abject step! *Off with you to Paris!* and that soon! Find your place among great people. *Aut Caesar aut nihil.* The mere thought of seeing Paris ought to have preserved you from all these flighty ideas. *From Paris the name and fame of a man of great talent resounds throughout the whole world. There the nobility treat men of genius with the greatest deference, esteem and courtesy; there you will see a refined manner of life, which forms an astonishing contrast to the coarseness of our German courtiers and their ladies; and there you may become proficient in the French tongue . . .* Your desire to help the oppressed you have inherited from your father. But you really must consider first of all the welfare of your parents, or else your soul will go to the devil. Think of me as you saw me when you left us, *standing beside the carriage in a state of utter wretchedness.* Ill as I was, I had been packing for you until two o'clock in the morning, and there I was at the carriage again at six o'clock, seeing to everything for you. Hurt me now, if you can be so cruel! Win fame and *make money* in Paris; then, *when you have money to spend,* go off to Italy and get commissions for operas. This cannot be done by writing letters to impresarios, though I am prepared to do so. Then you could put forward Mlle Weber's name, which can be the more easily done if you do so personally. Write to me by the next post without fail. We kiss you both a million times and I remain your old honest husband and father

MZT

Bullinger sends his greetings.
Nannerl has wept her full share during these last two days. Addio.

Mozart to his Father

Monsieur

Mon trés cher Pére!

Mannheim,
19 February 1778

I hope you received my last two letters safely. In the last one I discussed my mother's journey home, but I now see from your letter of the 12th that this was quite unnecessary. I always thought that you would disapprove of my undertaking a journey with the Webers, but I never had any such intention – I mean, of course, *in our present circumstances*. I gave them my word of honour, however, to write to you about it. Herr Weber does not know how we stand – and I shall certainly never tell anyone. I wish my position were such that I had no cause to consider anyone else and that we were all comfortably off. In the intoxication of the moment I forgot how impossible it is at present to carry out my plan, and therefore also – to tell you what I have now done. The reasons why I have not gone off to Paris must be sufficiently evident to you from my last two letters. If my mother had not first raised the point, I should certainly have gone with my friends; but when I saw that she did not like the scheme, then I began to dislike it myself. For as soon as people lose confidence in me, I am apt to lose confidence in myself. Those days when, standing on a chair, I used to sing to you *Oragna fiagata fa* and finish by kissing you on the tip of your nose, are gone indeed; but do I honour, love and obey you any the less on that account? I will say no more. As for your reproach about the little singer in Munich, I must confess that I was an ass to tell you such a palpable lie. Why, she does not yet know what *singing* means. It is true that for a person who had only been studying for three months she sang surprisingly well, and she had, in addition, a very pleasing and pure voice. Why I praised her so much may well have been because I was hearing people say from morning to night 'There is no better singer in all Europe' and 'Who has not heard her, has heard nothing'. I did not dare to contradict them, partly because I wanted to make some good friends, and partly because I had come straight from Salzburg, where we are not in the habit of contradicting anyone; but as soon as I was alone, I never could help laughing. Why then did I not laugh at her when writing to you? I really cannot tell.

What you say so cuttingly about my merry intercourse with your brother's daughter has hurt me very much; but since matters are not as you think, it is not necessary for me to reply. I don't know what to say about Wallerstein. I was very grave and reserved at Beecke's; and at the officers' table also I maintained a very serious demeanour and did not say a word to anyone. Let us forget all that; you only wrote it in a temper.

What you say about Mlle Weber is all perfectly true; and at the time I wrote that letter I knew quite as well as you do that she is still too young and that she must first learn how to act and make frequent appearances on the stage. But with some people one must proceed – by degrees. These good people are as tired of being here as – you know whom and where; and they think that every scheme is practicable. I promised them to write everything to my father; but when the letter was on its way to Salzburg, I kept on telling them: 'She must be patient a little longer, she is a bit too young yet, etc.' They do not mind what I say to them, for they have a high opinion of me. On my advice the father has engaged Madame Toscani (an actress) to give his daughter lessons in acting. Everything you say about Mlle Weber is true, except one thing – that 'she sings like a Gabrielli'; for I should not at all like her to sing in that style. Those who have heard Gabrielli are forced to admit that she was an adept only at runs and roulades; she adopted, however, such an unusual inter-pretation that she won admiration; but it never survived the fourth time of hearing. In the long run she could not please, for people soon get tired of coloratura passages. Moreover she had the misfortune of not being able to sing. She was not capable of *sustaining* a breve properly, and, as she had no *messa di voce*, she could not dwell on her notes; in short, she sang with skill but without understanding. Mlle Weber's singing, on the other hand, goes to the heart, and she prefers to sing cantabile. Lately I have made her practise the passages in my grand aria, because, if she goes to Italy, she will have to sing bravura arias. Undoubtedly she will never forget how to sing cantabile, for that is her natural bent. Raaff himself (who is certainly no flatterer), when asked to give his candid opinion, said 'She sang, not like a student, but like a master.' So now you know all. I still commend her to your interest with all my heart; and please don't forget about the arias, cadenzas and the rest. Farewell. I kiss your hands 100000 times and remain your most obedient son

Wolfgang Amadé Mozart

(right) The manuscript of a letter Mozart wrote to his cousin Maria Anna Thekla on 10 May 1779.

I can't write any more for sheer hunger. My mother will display the contents of our large cash-box. I embrace my sister with all my heart. Tell her she must not cry over every silly trifle, or I shall never go home again. My greetings to all our good friends, especially to Herr Bullinger.

Mozart to his Cousin, Maria Anna Thekla Mozart, Augsburg

Mademoiselle ma trés chére Cousine!

Perhaps you think or are even convinced that I am dead? That I have pegged out? Or hopped a twig? Not at all. Don't believe it, I implore you. For believing and shitting are two very different things! Now how could I be writing such a beautiful hand if I were dead? How could that be possible? I shan't apologize for my very long silence, for you would never believe me. Yet what is true is true. I have had so many things to do that I had time indeed to think of my little cousin, but not to

Mannheim, 28 February 1778

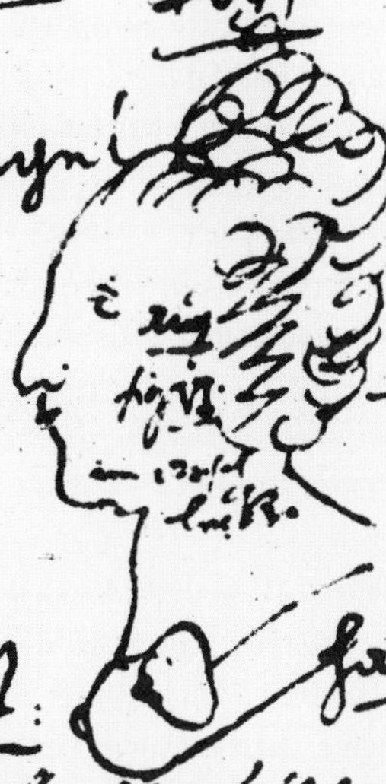

fig. I Kopf

fig. III Nasen.   fig. II

fig. IV   fig. V

Adieu — Adieu — Adieu.

write, you see. So I just had to let things be. But now I have the honour to inquire how you are and whether you perspire? Whether your stomach is still in good order? Whether indeed you have no disorder? Whether you still can like me at all? Whether with chalk you often scrawl? Whether now and then you have me in mind? Whether to hang yourself you sometimes feel inclined? Whether you have been wild? With this poor foolish child? Whether to make peace with me you'll be so kind? If not, I swear I'll let off one behind! Ah, you're laughing! Victoria! Our arses shall be the symbol of our peacemaking! I knew that you wouldn't be able to resist me much longer. Why, of course, I'm sure of success, even if today I should make a mess, though to Paris I go in a fortnight or less. So if you want to send a reply to me from that town of Augsburg yonder, you see, then write at once, the sooner the better, so that I may be sure to receive your letter, or else if I'm gone I'll have the bad luck, instead of a letter to get some muck. Muck! – Muck! – Ah, muck! Sweet word! Muck! chuck! That too is fine. Muck, chuck! – muck! – suck – o charmante! muck, suck! That's what I like! Muck, chuck and suck! Chuck muck and suck muck! . . .

Mozart to his Father

Mon trés cher Pére,

Yesterday, Monday the 23rd, at four o'clock in the afternoon we arrived here, thank God, both safe and sound, having been nine and a half days on our journey. *Paris, 24 March 1778* We really thought that we should not be able to hold out; for never in all my life have I been so bored. You can easily imagine what it meant for us to leave Mannheim and so many dear, kind friends and then to have to spend nine and a half days, not only without these good friends, but without anyone, without a single soul with whom we could associate or converse. Well, thank Heaven! we are at our journey's end and I trust that with the help of God all will go well . . .

The Paris visit was not a happy one for Mozart. He missed the many friends he had left behind in Mannheim, he didn't like the Parisians, and in spite of a promising start no commissions were forthcoming. His one achievement was the 'Paris' Symphony. And then, after only a few months in this unfamiliar city, Mozart's mother suddenly became ill and died on the night of 3 July. Few things in this correspondence are more touching than the innocent deception Wolfgang practised on his father in order to soften the unexpected blow, writing a letter within a couple of hours of her death pretending that she was still only seriously ill, and immediately after it, in the small hours of 4 July, another to a close friend in Salzburg telling him the truth and begging him to go in person to prepare his father for the news.

I have so much to do already, that I wonder what it will be like in winter! I think I told you in my last letter that the Duc de Guines, whose daughter is my pupil in composition, plays the flute extremely well, and that she plays the harp magnifique. She has a great deal of talent and even genius, and in particular a marvellous memory, so that she can play all her pieces, actually about two hundred, by heart. She is, however, extremely doubtful as to whether she has any talent for composition, especially as regards invention or ideas. But her father who, between ourselves, is somewhat too infatuated with her, declares that she certainly has ideas and that it is only that she is too bashful and has too little self-confidence. Well, we shall see. If she gets no inspirations or ideas (for at present she really has none whatever), then it is to no purpose, for – God knows – I can't give her any. Her father's intention is not to make a great composer of her. 'She is not,' he said, 'to compose operas, arias, concertos, symphonies, but only grand sonatas for her instrument and mine.' I gave her her fourth lesson today and, so far as the rules of composition and harmony are concerned, I am fairly well satisfied with her. She filled in quite a good bass for the first minuet, the melody of which I had given her, and she has already begun to write in three parts. But she very soon gets bored, and I am unable to help her; for as yet I cannot proceed more quickly. It is too soon, even if there really were genius there, but unfortunately there is none. Everything has to be done by rule. She has no ideas whatever – nothing comes. I have tried her in every possible way. Among other things I hit on the idea of writing down a very simple minuet, in order to see whether she could not compose a variation on it. It was useless. 'Well,' I thought, 'she probably does not know how she ought to begin.' So I started to write a variation on the first bar and told her to go on in the same way and to keep to the idea. In the end it went fairly well. When it was finished, I told her to begin something of her own, – only the treble part, the melody. Well, she thought and thought for a whole quarter of an hour and nothing came. So I wrote down four bars of a minuet and said to her: 'See what an ass I am! I have begun a minuet and cannot even finish the melody. Please be so kind as to finish it for me.' She was positive she couldn't, but at last with great difficulty – something came, and indeed I was only too glad to see something for once. I then told her to finish the minuet, I mean, the treble only. But for *home work* all I asked her to do was to alter my four bars and compose something of her own. She was to find a new beginning, use, if necessary, the same harmony, provided that the melody should be different. Well, I shall see tomorrow what she has done . . .

Leopold Mozart: a detail from the family portrait by Johann Nepomuk della Croce, for whom the Mozarts sat in Salzburg in the winter of 1780–81.

Maria Anna Mozart to her Husband

My dear Husband,

We received on June 9th your letter of May 28th and were delighted to hear that you were both in good health. Thank God, Wolfgang and I are quite well. I was bled yesterday, so I shan't be able to write much today. Wolfgang is not at home, as he is lunching with Herr Raaff at Count Sickingen's, where they go at least once a week, for Sickingen is devoted to Wolfgang and is himself a great connoisseur of music and composes too. Herr Raaff comes to see us almost every day. He calls me 'Mother', is very fond of us and often spends two or three hours with us. One day he came especially to sing to me and sang three arias, which gave me great pleasure. And now whenever he comes to see us he always sings something to me, for I am quite in love with his singing. He is a most honourable man and sincerity itself; if you

Paris,
12 June 1778

knew him, you would love him with all your heart. You want to know where we are lodging? First of all, find the rue Montmartre and then the rue Cléry. It is the first street on the left, if you enter the rue Cléry from the rue Montmartre. It is a fine street, inhabited almost entirely by the upper classes, very clean, fairly near the Boulevards, and the air is healthy. The owners of the house are good, honest folk and not out to make money, which is unusual in Paris ...

Leopold Mozart to his Wife and Son

My dear Wife, my dear Son!

Salzburg,
29 June 1778

We trust that you are well. We are both in excellent health! You will have received my letter of June 11th. On Holy Trinity Sunday I lunched, as usual, at the priests' house. In the afternoon Haydn played the organ during the Litany and the Te Deum, the Archbishop being present, and he played so abominably that we were all terrified and thought he was going the way of Adlgasser of pious memory. But it was only a slight tipsiness, which made his head and his hands refuse to agree. Since Adlgasser's accident I have never heard anything like it ...

Mozart to his Father

Monsieur

Mon trés cher Pére!

Paris,
3 July 1778

I have very sad and distressing news to give you, which is, indeed, the reason why I have been unable to reply sooner to your letter of June 11th. My dear mother is very ill. She has been bled, as in the past, and it was very necessary too. She felt quite well afterwards, but a few days later she complained of shivering and feverishness, accompanied by diarrhoea and headache. At first we only used home remedies – antispasmodic powders; we would gladly have tried the black powder too, but we had none and could not get it here, where it is not known even by the name of *pulvis epilepticus*. As she got worse and worse (she could hardly speak and had lost her hearing, so that one had to shout to make oneself understood), Baron Grimm sent us his doctor. But she is still very weak and is feverish and delirious. They give me hope – but I have not much. For a long time now I have been hovering day and night between hope and fear – but I have resigned myself wholly to the will of God – and trust that you and my dear sister will do the same. How else can we manage to be calm or, I should say, calmer, for we cannot be perfectly calm! Come what may, I am resigned – for I know that God, Who orders all things for our good, however strange they may seem to us, wills it thus. Moreover I believe (and no one will persuade me to the contrary) that no doctor, no man living, no misfortune and no chance can give a man his life or take it away. None can do so but God alone. These are only the instruments which He usually employs, though not always. For we see people around us swoon, fall down and die. Once our hour has come, all means are useless; they rather hasten death than delay it. This we saw in the case of our late friend Hefner. I do not mean to say that my mother will and must die, or that all hope is lost. She may recover health and strength, but only if God wills it. After praying to Him with all my might for health and life for my dear mother, I like to indulge in these consoling thoughts, because they hearten, soothe and comfort me; and you may easily imagine that I need comfort! Now let us turn to something else. Let us banish these sad thoughts; let us hope, but not too much; let us put our trust in God and console ourselves with the thought that all is well, if it is in accordance with the will of the Almighty, as He knows best what is profitable and beneficial to our temporal happiness and our eternal salvation ...

Mozart to the Abbé Bullinger, Salzburg

Most beloved Friend!

For you alone.

    Mourn with me, my friend! This has been the saddest day of my life – I am writing this at two o'clock in the morning. I have to tell you that my mother, my dear mother, is no more! God has called her to Himself. It was His will to take her, that I saw clearly – so I resigned myself to His will. He gave her to me, so He was able to take her away from me. Only think of all my anxiety, the fears and sorrows I have had to endure for the last fortnight. She was quite unconscious at the time of her death – her life flickered out like a candle. Three days before her death she made her confession, partook of the Sacrament and received Extreme Unction. During the last three days, however, she was constantly delirious, and today at twenty-one minutes past five the death agony began and she at once lost all sensation and consciousness. I pressed her hand and spoke to her – but she did not see me, she did not hear me, and all feeling was gone. She lay thus until she expired five hours later at twenty-one minutes past ten. No one was present but myself, Herr Heina (a kind friend whom my father knows) and the nurse. It is quite impossible for me to describe today the whole course of her illness, but I am firmly convinced that she was bound to die and that God had so ordained it. All I ask of you at present is to act the part of a true friend, by preparing my poor father very gently for this sad news. I have written to him by this post, but only to say that she is seriously ill; and now I shall wait for his answer and be guided by it. May God give him strength and courage! ...

Paris,
3 [actually 4] July
1778

(right) The opening page of Mozart's letter to the Abbé Bullinger, dated 3 July 1778, in which the composer announces the death of his mother and begs Bullinger's assistance in preparing his father for the news.

Allerbester freünd!   Paris ce 3 jullied
                                                          1778

für sie ganz allein.

Trauern sie mit mir, mein freünd! — dies war der traurigste tag in meinem
leben — dies schreibe ich um 2 uhr nachts — ich muß es ihnen doch sagen, meine Mutter,
Meine liebe Mutter ist nicht mehr! — gott hat sie zu sich berufen — er wollte sie
Er hatte sie mir Klar — mithin habe ich mich in willen gottes gegeben —
nur alle meine einsicht, ängsten und sorgen vor die ich sie nun 14 täge nach
geschrieben haben. — sie starb ohne daß sie etwas von sich wuste — löschte
worden, und hat die heiligen ölung bekommen — die lezten 3 täge aber
phatasirte sie beständig, und heüt aber um 5 uhr 21 minuten geng sie
in Zügen, verlohr selbgleich derbey alle empfindung und alle ihre
ich drückte ihr die Hand, redete sie an — sie sahe mich aber nicht, hörte
mich nicht, und aumerkung nicht — so lag sie bis sie verschied, namlich
in 5 stunden um 10 uhr 21 minuten verband — als aber niemand derbey,
selb ich, ein güter freünd von uns, den mein Vatter kent, H. Haina, und
die wärterin — die ganze krankheit kan ich ihnen heüt ohnmöglich
schreiben — ich bin der Mainung daß sie hat sterben müßen — gott
hat es so haben wollen. ich bitte sie unterdeßen um nichts als um
das freünd=stück, daß sie meinen armen vatter ganz sachte
Zu dieser traurigen nachricht bereiten — ich habe ihm mit der
nehmlichen fost geschrieben — aber nur daß sie schwer kranck ist —
warten auf nur euch eine antwort — darmit ich mich darnach richten
kan. gott gebe ihm stärcke und muth! — mein freünd! — ich
bin nicht izt, sondern schon lange her getröstet! — ich habe euch be=
sonderer gnade gottes alles mit standhaftigkeit und gelaßenheit
überstanden. wie es so gefährlich würde, so batt ich gott nur um

Mozart to his Father

Monsieur mon trés cher Pére!

    I hope that you are now prepared to hear with fortitude one of the saddest and   *Paris,*
most painful stories; indeed my last letter of the 3rd will have told you that no good   *9 July 1778*
news could be hoped for. On that very same day, the 3rd, at twenty-one minutes
past ten at night my mother fell asleep peacefully in the Lord; indeed, when I wrote
to you, she was already enjoying the blessings of Heaven – for all was then over. I
wrote to you during that night and I hope that you and my dear sister will forgive
me for this slight but very necessary deception; for as I judged from my own grief
and sorrow what yours would be, I could not indeed bring myself suddenly to shock
you with this dreadful news! But I hope that you have now summoned up courage
to hear the worst, and that after you have at first given way to natural, and only too
well justified tears and anguish, you will eventually resign yourself to the will of
God and worship His unsearchable, unfathomable and all-wise providence. You will
easily conceive what I have had to bear – what courage and fortitude I have needed
to endure calmly as things grew gradually and steadily worse. And yet God in His
goodness gave me grace to do so. I have, indeed, suffered and wept enough – but
what did it avail? So I have tried to console myself: and please do so too, my dear
father, my dear sister! Weep, weep your fill, but take comfort at last. Remember
that Almighty God willed it thus – and how can we rebel against Him? Let us rather
pray to Him, and thank Him for His goodness, for she died a very happy death. In
those distressing moments, there were three things that consoled me – my entire
and steadfast submission to the will of God, and the sight of her very easy and
beautiful death which made me feel that in a moment she had become so happy;
for how much happier is she now than we are! Indeed I wished at that moment to
depart with her. From this wish and longing proceeded finally my third source of
consolation – the thought that she is not lost to us for ever – that we shall see her
again – that we shall live together far more happily and blissfully than ever in this
world. We do not yet know when it will be – but that does not disturb me; when
God wills it, I am ready. Well, His heavenly and most holy will has been fulfilled.
Let us therefore say a devout Paternoster for her soul and turn our thoughts to other
matters, for all things have their appropriate time. I am writing this in the house
of Madame d'Épinay and M. Grimm, with whom I am now living. I have a pretty
little room with a very pleasant view and, so far as my condition permits, I am
happy. It will be a great help to restoring my tranquillity to hear that my dear father
and sister are submitting wholly and with calmness and fortitude to the will of God
– are trusting Him with their whole heart in the firm belief that He orders all things
for the best. My dearest father! Do not give way! Dearest sister! Be firm! You do not
yet know your brother's good heart – for he has not yet been able to prove it. My

two loved ones! Take care of your health. Remember that you have a son, a brother, who is doing his utmost to make you happy – knowing well that one day you will not refuse to grant him his desire and his happiness – which certainly does him honour, and that you also will do everything in your power to make him happy. Oh, then we shall live together as peacefully, honourably and contentedly as is possible in this world – and in the end, when God wills it, we shall all meet again in Heaven – for which purpose we were destined and created.

I have received your last letter of the 29th and see with pleasure that you are both, thank God, in good health. I had to laugh heartily about Haydn's tipsy fit. If I had been there, I should certainly have whispered in his ear '*Adlgasser!*' It is really disgraceful that such an able man should through his own fault render himself incapable of performing his duties – at a service instituted in honour of God – in the presence of the Archbishop too and the whole Court – and with the church full of people. How disgusting! That is one of my chief reasons for detesting Salzburg – those coarse, slovenly, dissolute court musicians. Why, no honest man, of good breeding, could possibly live with them! Indeed, instead of wanting to associate with them, he would feel ashamed of them. It is probably for this very reason that musicians are neither popular nor respected among us. Ah, if only the orchestra were organized as they are at Mannheim. Indeed I would like you to see the discipline which prevails there and the authority which Cannabich wields. There everything is done seriously. Cannabich, who is the best conductor I have ever seen, is both beloved and feared by his subordinates. Moreover he is respected by the whole town and so are his soldiers. But certainly they behave quite differently from ours. They have good manners, are well dressed and do not go to public houses and swill. This can never be the case in Salzburg, unless the Prince will trust you or me and give us full authority *as far as the music is concerned* – otherwise it's no good. In Salzburg everyone – or rather no one – bothers about the music. If I were to undertake it, I should have to have complete freedom of action. The Chief Steward should have nothing to say to me in musical matters, or on any point relating to music. For a courtier can't do the work of a Kapellmeister, but a Kapellmeister can well be a courtier ...

Leopold Mozart to his Wife and Son

My dear Wife and my dear Son!

I am writing today so that my letter may reach you a few days before my dear wife's name-day. I wish her millions of happinesses and congratulate her on being able to celebrate it once more, and I pray to Almighty God that He may send her many happy returns with good health and as much good fortune as is possible on this changeable stage of the world. I am absolutely convinced that if she is to be really happy she must have her husband and her daughter. God in His unsearchable wisdom and His most holy providence will order all things for our good. Would you have thought a year ago that you would be spending your next name-day in Paris? However incredible this would then have seemed to many, though indeed not to ourselves, it is just as possible that before we expect it, we may all with God's help be reunited; for it is only this separation which gnaws at my heart, I mean, to be separated from you, *and to be living so very far off*. Otherwise, thank God, we

Maria Anna Mozart, the composer's mother, a detail from the family portrait by Johann Nepomuk della Croce. Though Leopold was very much the guiding spirit of the Mozart family, Maria Anna provided him and the children with unobtrusive and good-natured support; he was clearly fond of her, and genuinely moved by her death. It was a touching idea to include this framed picture of her in the family portrait painted more than two years later.

are well. We both kiss you and Wolfgang millions of times and implore you to take the very greatest care of your health.

I wrote the above yesterday, July 12th, and today, the 13th, this very moment, shortly before ten o'clock in the morning, I have received your distressing letter of July 3rd. You can imagine what we are both feeling like. We wept so bitterly that we could scarcely read the letter – and your sister! Great God in Thy mercy! Thy most holy will be done! My dear son! Though I am resigning myself as far as possible to the will of God, you will surely find it quite human and natural that my tears almost prevent me from writing. And after all, what conclusion am I to draw? Why none other than this, that this very moment as I write, she is probably gone – or that she has recovered, for you wrote to me on the 3rd, and today is the 13th. You say that after the blood-letting she felt quite well, but that a few days later she complained of shivering and feverishness. The last letter from both of you was dated June 12th and in it your mother said: '*I was bled yesterday*'. So that was on the 11th – and why was it done on a Saturday? – on a fast-day? Well, I assume that she had eaten some meat. She waited far too long to be bled. Knowing her as I do, I am aware that she likes to postpone everything from one day to the next, and especially in a strange place, where she would have first to make enquiries about a surgeon. Well, it has been done – and there is no help for it now. I have complete confidence in your filial love, and know that you have taken all possible care of your *devoted* mother, and if God still spares her, you will always do so; for she is a *good* mother and *you were the apple of her eye.* She was immensely attached to you, she was inordinately proud of you and (I know this better than you do) was absolutely bound up in your welfare. But if all our hopes are vain! If we have lost her! – Great God! *Then, indeed, you do need friends, honest friends!* Otherwise you will be ruined as far as your possessions are concerned – what with the funeral expenses, and so forth. Great Heavens! There are innumerable expenses about which you know absolutely nothing. People deceive, overcharge, delude a stranger, lure him into unnecessary extravagance and, if he has no honest friends, squeeze him dry. You can have no conception of it. If this misfortune has befallen you, ask Baron Grimm to let you bring all your mother's effects to him to keep, so that you may not have so many things to look after; or else lock up everything carefully, for, since for whole days at a time you are not at home, people might easily break into your room and rob you. God grant that all my precaution is unnecessary; but here you will recognize your father. My dear wife! my dear son! As she fell ill a few days after the blood-letting, she must have been suffering since June 16th or 17th. Surely you waited too long. She hoped to cure herself by resting in bed – by dieting – by treating herself. I know how it is. One hopes and postpones from day to day. Almighty God! We are in Thy hands . . .

I am writing this at half past three in the afternoon. I know now that my dear wife is in heaven. I write with tears in my eyes, but in complete submission to the will of God! As the church consecration took place at Holy Trinity yesterday, our usual shooting was postponed until today. I couldn't and didn't want to cancel it at such a late hour. We ate very little. Nannerl, who before lunch had wept copiously, had to vomit; she started a dreadful headache and afterwards lay down on her bed. Bullinger found us in the most distressing state, as did all the others. Without a word I gave him your letter to read; he acted his part very well and asked me what I thought. I replied that I was convinced that my dear wife had died already. He said that indeed he was inclined to think so himself; he urged me to take comfort, and being a true friend, he told me all that I had already *thought to myself.* I tried hard to be cheerful, and to resign myself to God's most holy will. We finished our shooting and all our friends went away feeling very sad. Bullinger stayed with me, and asked me quietly whether I thought that there was any hope for her in the condition which you had described. I replied that I was convinced not only that she was now dead but that she had died on the day you wrote to me, that I was submitting to the will of God and must remember that *I still had two children, who I hoped would continue to love me, seeing that I lived only for their sakes*; that I was so firmly persuaded that she was gone that I had even sent off a letter to you, reminding you and urging you to take care of her possessions and so forth. Whereupon he said: '*Yes, she is dead.*' As he said this, the scales fell from my eyes. So you had doubtless written the truth to Bullinger at the same time as I was reading your letter to me, which had really stunned me. At first I was too dejected to be able to collect my thoughts; and even now I do not know what to say. You may be quite easy in your mind about me; I shall play the man. But do not forget how tenderly loving was your mother – and you will only realize now how she cared for you – just as later on when I am gone you will love me more and more. If you love me, *as I do not doubt you do*, take care of your health. *On yours depends my life* and the future support of your excellent sister who loves you with all her heart. It is mysteriously sad when death severs a very happy marriage – you have to experience it before you can realize it. *Tell me everything in detail.* Perhaps she wasn't bled sufficiently? It is quite certain that she trusted too much to her strength and called in the doctor much too late. In the meantime the internal inflammation must have gained the upper hand. *Take care of your health!* If you do not, you will make us all unhappy! Nannerl doesn't know yet about Bullinger's letter. But I have prepared her so that she now suspects that her most beloved mother is dead. Write to me soon – tell me everything – what day she was buried – where? Great God! To think that I shall have to go to Paris to see her grave! We both embrace you with all our heart. I must close. The post is going.

Your honest and grievously distressed father

Mozart

Make sure that none of your possessions are lost.

Mozart to his Father

Monsieur mon trés cher Pére!

I hope you have safely received my last two letters. We will not talk any more about their chief contents. It is all over now; and were we to cover whole pages, we couldn't alter it! The principal object of this letter is to congratulate my dear sister on her name-day. But first of all, I must have a little chat with you. A fine style this,

Paris,
18 July 1778

isn't it? But, patience – I am not in the mood today to write more elegantly. You will have to be satisfied if you succeed in more or less understanding what I am trying to say. I think I told you already that M. Raaff had left Paris; but that he is my true and very special friend, on whose friendship I can absolutely rely, this I can't possibly have told you, for I myself didn't know that his affection for me was so deep. Now, to tell a tale properly, one ought to roll it off from the beginning. You must know, therefore, that Raaff lodged with M. Le Gros ... Raaff had never heard me play at Mannheim, except at the concert, where the noise and uproar was so great that nothing could be heard – and he himself has such a miserable clavier that I could not have done myself justice on it. Here, however, at Le Gros's the chopping-board is good; and I saw Raaff sitting opposite me, quite lost in thought. So, as you may imagine, I preluded in the manner of Fischietti, played off a galanterie sonata in the style and with the fire, spirit and precision of Haydn, and then played fugues with all the skill of a Lipp, Hülber and Aman. My fugal playing has won me everywhere the greatest reputation! Well, when I had finished playing (while Raaff kept on shouting 'Bravo' and showing by his expression his true and sincere delight) I dropped into conversation with Ritter and among other things said that I was not very happy here; and I added: 'The chief reason is, of course, the music. Besides, I can find no soulagement here, no recreation, no pleasant and sociable intercourse with anyone, especially with women, for most of them are prostitutes and the few who are not, have no savoir vivre.' Ritter could not deny that I was right. Raaff then said with a smile: 'Yes, I can quite believe it – for Herr Mozart is only *partly* here – that is, when it comes to admiring all the Parisian beauties. One half of him is elsewhere – where I have just come from.' This of course gave rise to much laughing and joking. In the end Raaff became quite serious and said: 'But you are right and I cannot blame you. She deserves it, for she is a charming, pretty, honourable girl and has excellent manners; besides, she is clever and is really very talented.' This gave me an excellent opportunity to recommend to him with all my heart my beloved Mlle Weber; but it was really not necessary for me to say much, as he was already very much taken with her. He promised, as soon as he returned to Mannheim, to give her lessons and to take an interest in her ...

After his mother's death Mozart stayed on in Paris for a further three months but to little avail, and at the beginning of October, after an absence of a year, he started for home – though even then he was unable to resist dragging his heels for another month in Mannheim (much to Leopold's fury). Back in Salzburg he took up the appointment of organist at the cathedral and settled into the old social routine, making up with a vigorous bout of compositional activity for the time that had been wasted in Mannheim and Paris. Then in the summer of 1780 came the commission

(left) 'Long-distance travel by carriage': detail from an Italian engraving of 1780. Mozart has amusing things to say about the miseries of travelling through Europe in the late 18th century, including a particularly painful experience on the road to Munich (see letter of 8 November 1780).

to write an opera seria for the carnival season in Munich. This was Mozart's biggest opportunity so far, both in itself and for where it might lead, and he seized it with enthusiasm. The subject, chosen by the Munich Court, was Idomeneo, rè di Creta, and Mozart asked the Court Chaplain of Salzburg, Gianbattista Varesco, to provide him with a libretto. Composition of the music was begun in Salzburg but at the beginning of November Mozart went to Munich and all further collaboration between the composer and his librettist was conducted by correspondence, with Leopold Mozart acting as the often rather crusty intermediary.

Mozart to his Father

Mon trés cher Pére!

    My arrival here was happy and pleasant – happy, because no mishap occurred during the journey; and pleasant, because we could hardly wait for the moment to reach our destination, on account of our drive, which though short was most uncomfortable. Indeed, I assure you that none of us managed to sleep for a moment the whole night through. Why, that carriage jolted the very souls out of our bodies – and the seats were as hard as stone! After we left Wasserburg I really believed

Munich,
8 November 1780

that I should never bring my behind to Munich intact. It became quite sore and no doubt was fiery red. For two whole stages I sat with my hands dug into the upholstery and my behind suspended in the air. But enough of this; it is all over now, though it will serve me as a warning rather to go on foot than to drive in a mail coach.

Now for Munich. We arrived here at one o'clock in the afternoon and on the very same evening I called on Count Seeau, for whom, as he was not at home, I left a note. On the following morning I went there with Becke, who sends his greetings to you all. Seeau has been moulded like wax by the Mannheim people. With regard to the libretto the Count says that Abbate Varesco need not copy it out again before sending it – for it is to be printed here – but I think that he ought to finish writing the text, and not forget *the little notes*, and send it to us with the synopsis as quickly as possible. As for the names of the singers, that is of no importance whatever, for these can be added most conveniently here. Some slight alterations will have to be made here and there, and the recitatives will have to be shortened a bit. But *everything will be printed*. I have just one request to make of the Abbate. Ilia's aria in Act II, Scene 2, should be altered slightly to suit what I require. 'Se il padre perdei. in te lo ritrovo'; this verse could not be better. But now comes what has always seemed unnatural to me – I mean, in an aria – and that is, *a spoken aside*. In a dialogue all these things are quite natural, for a few words can be spoken aside hurriedly; but in an aria where the words have to be repeated, it has a bad effect, and even if this were not the case, I should prefer an uninterrupted aria. The beginning may stand, if it suits him, for the poem is charming and, as it is absolutely natural and flowing and therefore as I have not got to contend with difficulties arising from the words, I can go on composing quite easily; for we have agreed to introduce here an aria andantino with obbligatos for four wind-instruments, that is, a flute, oboe, horn and bassoon. I beg you therefore to let me have the text as soon as possible. Now for a sorry story. I have not, it is true, the honour of being acquainted with the hero dal Prato; but from the description I have been given of him I should say that Ceccarelli is almost the better of the two; for often in the middle of an aria his breath gives out; and, mark you, he has never been on any stage – and Raaff is like a statue. Well, just picture to yourself the scene in Act I . . .

Leopold Mozart to his Son

Mon très cher Fils,

Salzburg,
11 November 1780

I am writing in great haste at half past nine in the evening, as I have had no time all day. Varesco brought me the libretto very late and Count Sepperl Überacker was with us from five o'clock until now.

I am returning the libretto and the draft, so that His Excellency Count Seeau may see that everything has been carried out to order. In about a week a complete copy of the text will follow by the mail coach, showing exactly how Abbate Varesco wants it to be printed. It will also include the necessary notes. Here is the aria, which is, I think, quite suitable. If not, let me know at once. What you say about the singers is really distressing. Well, your musical composition will have to make up for their deficiencies. I wish I could have heard Madame Mara. Do tell me how she sings. You can imagine that I am looking forward with childish delight to hearing that excellent orchestra. I only wish that I could get away soon. But I shall certainly not travel by mail coach, for I am rather careful of my two damson stones ...

Mozart to his Father

Mon très cher Père,

I write in the greatest haste, for I am not yet dressed and must be off to Count Seeau's. Cannabich, Quaglio and Le Grand, master of the ballet, are lunching there too in order to make the necessary arrangements for the opera ... *Munich, 13 November 1780*

The second duet is to be omitted altogether – and indeed with more profit than loss to the opera. For, when you read through the scenes, you will see that it obviously becomes limp and cold by the addition of an aria or a duet, and very gênant for the other actors who must stand by doing nothing; and, besides, the noble struggle between Ilia and Idamante would be too long and thus lose its whole force ...

Ex commissione of His Excellency I ought to reply in his name to Abbate Varesco; but I have no time and was not born to be a secretary. To Act I, Scene 8, Quaglio has made the same objection that we made originally – I mean, that it is not fitting that the king should be quite alone in the ship. If the Abbé thinks that he can be reasonably represented in the terrible storm, forsaken by everyone, without a ship, quite alone and exposed to the greatest peril, then let it stand; but please cut out the ship, for he cannot be alone in one; but if the other situation is adopted, a few generals, who are in his confidence, must land with him. Then he must address a few words to his people and desire them to leave him alone, which in his present melancholy situation is quite natural. A propos. Shall I soon have the aria for Madame Wendling?

Mara has not had the good fortune to please me. She has not the art to equal a Bastardella (for this is her peculiar style) – and has too much to touch the heart like a Weber – or any sensible singer.

PS. – My compliments to all our good friends. A propos. As translations are so badly done here, Count Seeau would like to have the opera translated in Salzburg. Only the arias need be in verse. He says that I ought to make a contract. In that case payments would be made simultaneously to the poet and to the translator. Send me a reply about this soon. Adieu. What about the family portrait? Is it a good likeness of you? Has the painter started on my sister yet? The first performance of the opera will not be until January 20th. Be so kind as to send me the scores of the two masses which I brought away with me – and also the mass in B♭ [K275] for Count Seeau will be telling the Elector something about them shortly. I should also like people to hear some of my compositions in this style. I have heard only one mass by Grua. Things like this one could easily turn out at the rate of half a dozen a day. If I had known that this castrato was so bad, I should certainly have recommended Ceccarelli!

Mon trés cher Pére!

Munich,
15 November 1780

I have received your letter or rather the whole parcel. Many thanks for the money order. So far I have not lunched once at home – and consequently have had no expenses save for friseur, barber and laundress – and breakfast. The aria is excellent now, but there is still one more alteration, for which Raaff is responsible. He is right, however, – and even if he were not, some courtesy ought to be shown to his grey hairs. He was with me yesterday. I ran through his first aria for him and he was very well pleased with it. Well – the man is old and can no longer show off in such an aria as that in Act II – 'Fuor del mar ho un mar nel seno'. So, as he has no aria in Act III and as his aria in Act I, owing to the expression of the words, cannot be as cantabile as he would like, he wishes to have a pretty one to sing (instead of the quartet) after his last speech, 'O Creta fortunata! O me felice!' Thus too a useless piece will be got rid of – and Act III will be far more effective. In the last scene of Act II Idomeneo has an aria or rather a sort of cavatina between the choruses. Here it will be *better* to have a mere recitative, well supported by the instruments. For in this scene which will be the finest in the whole opera (on account of the action and grouping which were settled recently with Le Grand), there will be so much noise and confusion on the stage that an aria at this particular point would cut a poor figure – and moreover there is the thunderstorm, which is not likely to subside during Herr Raaff's aria, is it? The effect, therefore, of a recitative between the choruses will be infinitely better. Lisel Wendling has also sung through her two arias half a dozen times and is delighted with them. I have it from a third party that the two Wendlings praised their arias very highly; and as for Raaff, he is my best and dearest friend!

But to my molto amato castrato dal Prato I shall have to teach the whole opera. He has no notion how to sing a cadenza effectively, and his voice is so uneven! He is only engaged for a year and at the end of that time, next September, Count Seeau will get somebody else. Ceccarelli might then have a chance – sérieusement.

I had almost forgotten my best news. Last Sunday after the service Count Seeau presented me en passant to His Highness the Elector, who was very gracious to me and said: '*I am glad to see you here again.*' On my replying that I would do my best to retain the good opinion of His Highness, he clapped me on the shoulder and said: '*Oh, I have no doubt whatever that all will go well.*' A piano piano, si va lontano ...

The tenor Anton Raaff (1714–97), much admired by Mozart and often mentioned in the letters. Raaff was still working at the age of 67 when Mozart wrote the role of Idomeneo for him. This watercolour shows him in costume for an unknown opera seria.

Mon trés cher Pére!

At last I am sending you the long-promised aria for Herr Schikaneder. During the first week I couldn't get it finished on account of the business for which, after all, I came here – and the other day Le Grand, master of the ballet, a terrible talker and seccatore, happened to be with me and by his chattering made me lose the mail coach. I hope that my sister is quite well. I have a cold at the moment, which in this weather is quite the fashion here. I hope and trust, however, that it will soon leave me, for the two light cuirassier regiments, cough and phlegm, are gradually disappearing. In your last letter you say repeatedly: 'Oh! my poor eyes! – I do not wish to write myself blind – half past seven in the evening and no spectacles.' But why do you write in the evening? And why without spectacles? That I cannot understand. I have not yet had an opportunity of speaking to Count Seeau, but I hope to

Munich,
22 November 1780

do so today and I shall send you an account of our conversation by the next post. For the moment everything will probably remain as it is. Herr Raaff came to see me yesterday morning and I gave him your regards, which pleased him immensely. He too sends you his greetings. He is indeed a worthy and thoroughly honest fellow! The day before yesterday dal Prato sang at the concert – most disgracefully. I bet you that fellow will never get through the rehearsals, still less the opera. Why, the rascal is rotten to the core. – Come in! Why, it's Herr Panzacchi, who has already paid me three visits and has just invited me to lunch on Sunday. I hope I shall not have the same experience as the two of us had with the coffee. He has enquired very meekly whether instead of 'se la sa' he may not sing 'se co la' – Well, why not 'ut re mi fa sol la'?

I am delighted whenever you send me long letters, but please do not write in the evening – and still less without spectacles. You must, however, forgive me if I do not send you much in return, for every minute is precious; and, as it is, I can generally only compose in the evenings, as the mornings are so dark; then I have to dress – and the merchant's servant at the Weiser sometimes lets in a troublesome visitor. When the castrato comes, I have to sing with him, for I have to teach him his whole part as if he were a child. He has not got a farthing's worth of method ...

Munich,
29 November 1780

The aria for Raaff which you have sent me pleases neither him nor myself. I shall not say anything about *era*, for in an aria of this kind that is always a mistake. Metastasio makes it sometimes, but very rarely, and, moreover, those particular arias are not his best; and is there any necessity for it? Besides, the aria is not at all what we wished it to be; I mean, it ought to express peace and contentment, and this it indicates only in the second part: for we have seen, heard and felt sufficiently throughout the whole opera all the misfortune which Idomeneo has had to endure; but he can certainly talk about his present condition. Nor do we need a second part – which is all the better ...

Tell me, don't you think that the speech of the subterranean voice is too long? Consider it carefully. Picture to yourself the theatre, and remember that the voice must be terrifying – must penetrate – that the audience must believe that it really exists. Well, how can this effect be produced if the speech is too long, for in this case the listeners will become more and more convinced that it means nothing. If the speech of the Ghost in Hamlet were not so long, it would be far more effective. It is quite easy to shorten the speech of the subterranean voice and it will gain thereby more than it will lose.

For the march in Act II, which is heard in the distance, I require mutes for the trumpets and horns, which it is impossible to get here. Will you send me one of each by the next mail coach, so that I may have them copied?

Mon trés chér Pére!

   The rehearsal went off extremely well. There were only six violins in all, but we *Munich,*
had the requisite wind-instruments. No listeners were admitted except Count *1 December 1780*
Seeau's sister and young Count Sensheim. This day week we are to have another
rehearsal, when we shall have twelve fiddlers for the first act (which I am having
copied for double forces in the meantime), and when the second act will be
rehearsed (like the first on the previous occasion). I cannot tell you how delighted
and surprised they all were. But indeed I never expected anything else, for I assure
you I went to that rehearsal with as easy a mind as if I were going to a lunch party
somewhere. Count Sensheim said to me: '*I assure you that though I expected a great
deal from you, I really did not expect that.*' The Cannabichs and all who frequent
their house are really true friends of mine. When I walked home with Cannabich
to his house after the rehearsal (for we still had much to talk over with the Count),
Madame Cannabich came out to meet us and embraced me, delighted that the
rehearsal had gone off so well. For Ramm and Lang had gone to her house, simply
beside themselves with joy. The good lady – a true friend of mine – who had been
alone in the house with her sick daughter Rosa, had been absorbed in a thousand
anxieties on my account. Ramm said to me – now when you meet him, you will
call him a true German – for he tells you to your face exactly what he thinks: '*I must
honestly confess that no music has ever made such an impression on me, and I can
assure you that I thought fifty times of your father and of what his delight will be
when he hears this opera.*'

   But enough of this. My cold has become somewhat worse owing to the rehearsal
– for, when honour and glory are at stake, you naturally get excited – however cool
you may be at first. I have used all the remedies you prescribed, but it is a slow
business and very inconvenient for me at the moment, for composing does not stop
a cold; and yet I must compose. I have begun to take fig-syrup and a little almond-
oil today, and already I feel some relief; and I have stayed indoors again for two days.

   Yesterday morning Mr. Raaff came to see me again in order to hear the aria in
Act II. The fellow is as infatuated with it as a young and ardent lover might be with
his fair one, for he sings it at night before going to sleep and in the morning when
he awakes. As I heard first from a reliable source and now from his own lips, he
said to Herr von Viereck, Chief Equerry, and to Herr von Castel: '*Hitherto both in
recitatives and arias I have always been accustomed to alter my parts to suit me,
but here everything remains as it was written, for I cannot find a note which does
not suit me, etc.*' Enfin, he is as happy as a king. At the same time he would like, as
I should, to alter slightly the aria which you have sent me. He too objects to the *era*
– and then – we should like at this point to have a peaceful quiet aria. Even if it
has only one part – so much the better; in every aria the second part must always

be kept for the middle section – and often indeed it gets in my way ...

PS. – Please send me the recipe for cooking sago – for a good friend. A thousand compliments from all – all.

Leopold Mozart to his Son

... I have just been to see Varesco. As your letter of December 1st arrived while I was out, your sister read it, looked up the passage in Metastasio, and sent the letter and the book after me to Varesco's. All that you have pointed out shall be done. You know that *I too thought the subterranean speech too long.* I have given Varesco my candid opinion and it will now be made as short as possible. We are delighted to hear that the rehearsal went so well. I have no doubt whatever nor am I the slightest bit anxious about your work, provided the production is good, I mean, *provided there are good people to perform it* – and that is the case in Munich. So I am not at all nervous; but when your music is performed by a mediocre orchestra, it will always be the loser, because it is composed with so much discernment for the various instruments and is far from being commonplace, as, on the whole, Italian music is. That your cold should have become worse after the rehearsal is only natural, for, owing to the concentration upon hearing and seeing, all the nerves of the head become excited and strained, and eagerness and attention extends this tension to the chest also ...

Mozart to his Father

Mon trés cher Pére!

The death of the Empress does not affect my opera in the least, for none of the theatres have been closed and plays are being performed as usual. The entire mourning is not to last longer than six weeks and my opera will not be performed before January 20th. I beg you to have my *black suit* thoroughly brushed, shaken out, done up as well as possible and sent to me by the next mail coach – for next week everyone will be in mourning – and I, who have always to be about, *must also weep* with the others ...

Leopold Mozart to his Son

... Here is the suit, such as it is. I had to have it patched quickly, for the whole taffeta lining of the waistcoat was in rags. I am writing this letter on Saturday, December 9th, at half past nine in the evening. Herr Esser gave a concert in the theatre today and actually made a profit of forty gulden. He will arrive in Munich by this diligence and will call on you at once. He is a jolly old fool of a fellow. But

he plays (when he plays *seriously*) with the *surest and most astounding execution.*
At the same time he has a *beautiful adagio*, which few good allegro-players possess.
But when he starts playing the fool, he plays on the G-string only and with the
greatest skill and technique. By striking his strings with a wooden pencil he performs whole pieces with amazing rapidity and precision. He plays the viola d'amore
charmingly. But what touched me and struck me at first as rather childish was his
whistling. He whistles recitatives and arias as competently as any singer and with
the most perfect expression, introducing portamento, flourishes, trills and so forth,
most admirably, and all the time accompanying himself pizzicato on the violin. He
came to see us every day *and drank like a fish.* This great talent of his brings him
in a good deal of money – *and yet he never has any cash.*

Addio. We both kiss you. I shall write to you again on Monday. Farewell. I am
your faithful father

MZT

You will find the two trumpet mutes packed with the suit.

... I enclose a note from Varesco and also the aria. Act I with the translation and
possibly Act II will arrive in Munich next week by the mail coach. I trust that you
are well. I advise you when composing to consider not only the musical, but also
the unmusical public. You must remember that to every ten real connoisseurs there
are a *hundred ignoramuses.* So do not neglect the so-called *popular* style, which
tickles *long ears.* What about the score? Are you not going to have it copied? You
must think over what you are going to do and *you must make some sensible arrangement.* The remuneration you are getting *is so small that you really cannot leave
your score behind.* Farewell. Give our greetings to all, just as all here send their
greetings to you. We kiss you millions of times and I am your honest old father

L. MZT

Do not hurry over Act III. You will certainly be ready in time.
All's well that ends well!

Salzburg,
11 December 1780

Mozart to his Father

Mon trés cher Pére!

I have received safely the last aria for Raaff (who sends greetings to you), the
two trumpet mutes, your letter of the 15th, and the pair of socks. The second
rehearsal went off as well as the first. The orchestra and the whole audience discovered to their delight that the second act was actually more expressive and original
than the first. Next Saturday both acts are to be rehearsed again. But this time the
rehearsal is to be held in a large hall at Court, and this I have long wished for,
because there is not nearly room enough at Count Seeau's. The Elector is to listen

Munich,
19 December 1780

incognito in an adjoining room. Well, as Cannabich said to me, 'We shall have to rehearse like the deuce.' At the last rehearsal he was dripping with perspiration . . .

A propos – now for the most important thing of all – for I must hurry. I hope to receive by the next mail coach the first act at least, together with the translation. The scene between father and son in Act I and the first scene in Act II between Idomeneo and Arbace are both too long. They would certainly bore the audience, particularly as in the first scene both the actors are bad, and in the second, one of them is; besides, they only contain a narrative of what the spectators have already seen with their own eyes. These scenes are being printed as they stand. But I should like the Abbate to indicate how they may be shortened – and as drastically as possible, – for otherwise I shall have to shorten them myself. These two scenes cannot remain as they are – I mean, when set to music . . .

Leopold Mozart to his Son

Salzburg,
22 December 1780

. . . I sent for Varesco at once, for I received your letter only at five o'clock this evening, and the mail coach leaves tomorrow morning. We have considered the first recitative in all its bearings and we both find no occasion to shorten it. It is translated from the French, according to the draft which was arranged. What is more, if you consult the draft, you will see that it was suggested that this recitative should be lengthened a little, so that father and son should not recognize one another too quickly . . . Or do you want to make father and son run up and recognize one another just as Harlequin and Brigella, who are disguised as servants in a foreign country, meet, recognize and embrace each other immediately? Remember that this is one of the *finest scenes in the whole opera*, nay, *the principal scene*, on which the entire remaining story depends. Further, this scene cannot weary the audience, *as it is in the first act.*

Nothing more can be cut in Act II, save a portion of Idomeneo's second speech. *Idomeneo.* '*Un sol consiglio or mi fa d'uopo. Ascolta. Tu sai quanto a' Troiani fu il mio brando fatal.*' Arbace. '*Tutto m' è noto, etc.*' Then the dialogue continues, and not a single word can be omitted without destroying the sense. Besides, the whole recitative cannot last long, because several passages must be spoken eagerly and rapidly. And if you were to cut it, you would only gain *half a minute*! Great gain, forsooth! Nor can this recitative weary a single soul, as it is the first scene in Act II . . . Everyone is patient during the first act of any opera and, further, the first recitative in a second act can never weary anyone. I think the whole thing is rather ridiculous. It is true that at a rehearsal where the eye has nothing to engage it, a recitative immediately becomes boring; but at the performance, where between the stage and the audience there are so many objects to entertain the eye, a recitative like this is over before the listeners are aware of it. You may tell the whole world that from me. However, if in spite of all, something has to be omitted, I insist that the passages shall be printed in full. Varesco knows nothing of what I have written to you . . .

The whole town is talking about the excellence of your opera. Baron Lehrbach spread the first report. The Court Chancellor's wife tells me that he told her that your opera was being praised to the skies. The second report was set going by Herr Becke's letter to Fiala, which the latter made everyone read. I should like Act III to produce the same effect I feel certain that it will, the more so as in this act great passions are expressed and the subterranean voice will undoubtedly astonish and terrify. Basta, I trust that people will say: *Finis coronat opus.* But do your best to keep the whole orchestra in good humour; flatter them, and, by praising them, keep them all well-disposed towards you. For I know your style of composition – it requires unusually close attention from the players of every type of instrument; and to keep the whole orchestra at such a pitch of industry and alertness for at least three hours is no joke. Each performer, even the most inferior viola-player, is deeply touched by personal praise and becomes much more zealous and attentive, while a little courtesy of this kind only costs you a word or two. However – you know all this yourself – I am just mentioning it, because rehearsals afford few opportunities to do this, and so it is forgotten; and when the opera is staged, one really needs the cordial friendship and the keenness of the whole orchestra. Their position is then quite different, and the attention of every single performer must be strained even further. You know that you cannot count on the goodwill of everyone, for there is always *an undercurrent of doubt and questioning.* People wondered whether Act II would be as original and excellent as Act I. As this doubt has now been removed, few will have any doubts as to Act III. But I will wager my head that there are some who are wondering whether *your music will produce the same effect in a theatre as it does in a room.* And here you really need the greatest keenness and goodwill on the part of the whole body of players . . .

Salzburg,
25 December 1780

. . . God be praised that His Highness is satisfied with the first two acts, or rather is thoroughly delighted. I daresay that when your opera is staged, you will have many more points to raise, particularly in Act III, where there is so much action.

I assume that you will choose very deep wind-instruments to accompany the subterranean voice. How would it be if after the slight subterranean rumble the instruments *sustained, or rather began to sustain, their notes piano and then made a crescendo such as might almost inspire terror, while after this and during the decrescendo the voice would begin to sing*? And there might be a terrifying crescendo at *every phrase uttered by the voice.* Owing to the rumble, which must be short, and

Salzburg,
29 December 1780

rather like the shock of a thunderbolt, which sends up the figure of Neptune, the attention of the audience is aroused; and this attention is intensified by the introduction of a quiet, prolonged and then swelling and very alarming wind-instrument passage, and finally becomes strained to the utmost when, behold! *a voice* is heard. Why, I seem to see and hear it.

It was a good thing to have your suit turned. Now that we are discussing clothes, *I suppose I can save myself the trouble of bringing my braided suit. You know that I do not care about dressing up.* Please let me know about this ...

Mozart to his Father

Mon trés cher Pére!

Munich,
3 January 1781

My head and my hands are so full of Act III that it would be no wonder if I were to turn into a third act myself. This act alone has cost me more trouble than a whole opera, for there is hardly a scene in it which is not extremely interesting. The accompaniment to the subterranean voice consists of five instruments only, that is, three trombones and two French horns, which are placed in the same quarter as that from which the voice proceeds. At this point the whole orchestra is silent. The dress rehearsal will take place *for certain* on January 20th and the first performance on the 22nd. All you will both require and all that you need bring with you is one black dress – and another, for everyday wear – when you are just visiting intimate friends, where there is no standing on ceremony – so that you may save your black one a little; and, if you like, a more elegant dress to wear at the ball and the académie masquée ...

Leopold Mozart to his Son

Mon très cher Fils!

Salzburg,
4 January 1781

I received your letter of December 30th at nine o'clock, just as I was going to the service. After Church I did my New Year *seccature* and then went to see Varesco at half past ten. He was horribly angry and said the most foolish things, as Italians or half-Italians do. He mentioned among other things that he had written a few days ago to Count Seeau asking him to see that there would be no misprints in the text; good! that he would like to have twelve copies; basta! that he hoped to receive a few more ducats in recognition of the fact that he had copied the text four times and subsequently had had to make a good many alterations: and that, if he had known beforehand, he would not have agreed to write the text for the small remuneration of twenty ducats. *As far as I am concerned, it was a good move.* But I immediately began to think that the godless Italian idea might occur to Varesco that *we had made a better bargain and were keeping the money* ... I listened to him with absolute calmness and when at last I got tired of his railing and his silly chatter,

I said to him: '*The only reply I want is whether or not I am to write today to say that next post-day, January 4th, another aria will be sent to Munich. For reply I must! The rest does not concern me in the very least.*' He then said: '*I will see whether anything occurs to me.*' So I went off to finish my New Year *seccature.* You can gather from the remarks he has jotted down beside the aria what else he said and how enraged he was . . .

Mozart to his Father

Mon trés cher Pére!

I have received your letter of the 11th – and your last one of the 13th, sent through Herr Fiala. Please forgive a short letter, but I must be off to the rehearsal this very moment (it is almost ten o'clock – in the morning, of course). For the first time we are having a rehearsal of recitatives today in the theatre. I have not been able to write until now, as my time has been taken up with those confounded dances. Laus Deo – I have got rid of them at last! But I can only send you my most important news. The rehearsal of Act III went off splendidly. It was considered much superior to the first two acts. But the libretto is too long and consequently the music also (an opinion which I have always held). Therefore Idamante's aria, '*No, la morte io non pavento*', is to be omitted; in any case it is out of place there. But those who have heard it with the music deplore this. The omission of Raaff's last aria too is even more regretted; but we must make a virtue of necessity. The speech of the oracle is still far too long and I have therefore shortened it; but Varesco need not know anything of this, because it will all be printed just as he wrote it . . .

Munich,
18 January 1781

A stove is out of the question, for it costs too much. I shall have another bed put in the room where the alcove is. We shall just have to manage as best we can.

Do not forget to bring my little watch with you. I hope we shall go over to Augsburg, where we can have the enamel repaired. I should like you to bring Schachtner's operetta [*Zaide*] too. There are some people who come to the Cannabichs, who might just as well hear a thing of this kind. Now I must be off to the rehearsal. Adieu. I kiss your hands a thousand times and embrace my sister with all my heart, and remain your obedient son

W. A. MZT

More news the next time – and still more when we meet. All sorts of messages from the Cannabichs.

After the performances of Idomeneo *Mozart overstayed his leave in Munich, and in March 1781 was summoned peremptorily to Vienna by the Archbishop of Salzburg, who had gone there on an extended visit with his entire Court and required the presence of his young employee to help in the entertainment of his guests. But relations between prelate and composer worsened rapidly and within three months Mozart at last found himself a free agent, alone and (to his father's evident apprehension) independent for the first time in his life. Though he didn't know it, he was never to live in Salzburg again.*

Mozart to his Father

Mon très cher Amy!

Yesterday, the 16th, I arrived here, thank God, all by myself in a post chaise – at nine o'clock in the morning – I was nearly forgetting to mention the hour. I travelled in the mail coach as far as Unterhaag – but by that time I was so sore in my behind and its surrounding parts that I could endure it no longer. So I was intending to proceed by the ordinaire, but Herr Escherich, a government official, had had enough of the mail coach too and gave me his company as far as Kemmelbach. There I was proposing to wait for the ordinaire, but the postmaster assured me that he could not possibly allow me to travel by it, as there was no head office there. So I was obliged to proceed *by extra post*, reached St. Pölten on Thursday, the 15th, at seven o'clock in the evening, as tired as a dog, slept until two in the morning and then drove on straight to Vienna. Where do you think I am writing this letter? In the Mesmers' garden in the Landstrasse. The old lady is not at home, but Fräulein Franzl, who is now Frau von Bosch, is here and asks me to send a thousand greetings to you and my sister. Well, upon my honour, I hardly recognized her, she has grown so plump and fat. She has three children, two young ladies and a young gentleman. The eldest young lady, who is called Nannerl, is four years old, but you would swear that she was six; the young gentleman is three, but you would swear that he was seven; and the infant of nine months you would take to be two years old, they are all so strong and robust. Now for the Archbishop. I have a charming room in the very same house where he is staying. Brunetti and Ceccarelli are lodging in another. *Che distinzione!* My neighbour is Herr von Kleinmayr – who loaded me on my arrival with all sorts of kindnesses. He is indeed a charming man. We lunch about twelve o'clock, unfortunately somewhat too early for me. Our party consists of the two valets, that is, the body and soul attendants of His Worship, the contrôleur, Herr Zetti, the confectioner, the two cooks, Ceccarelli, Brunetti and – my insignificant self. By the way, the two valets sit at the top of the table, but at least I have the honour of being placed above the cooks. Well, I almost believe myself back in Salzburg! A good deal of silly, coarse joking goes on at table, but no one cracks jokes with me, for I never say a word, or, *if I have to speak*, I always do so with the utmost gravity; and as soon as I have finished my lunch, I get up and go off. We do not meet for supper, but we each receive three ducats – which goes a long way! The Archbishop is so kind as to add to his lustre by his household, robs them of their chance of earning and pays them nothing. We had a concert yesterday at four o'clock, and at least twenty persons of the highest rank were present. Ceccarelli has already had to sing at Count Palffy's. Today we are to go to Prince Galitzin, who was at the Archbishop's yesterday. Well, I must wait and see whether I shall get anything. If I get nothing, I shall go to the Archbishop and tell him with absolute frankness that if he will not allow me to earn anything, then he must pay me, for I cannot live at my own expense . . .

. . . What you say about the Archbishop is to a certain extent perfectly true – I mean, as to the manner in which I tickle his ambition. But of what use is all this to me? I can't subsist on it. Believe me, I am right in saying that he acts as a *screen* to keep me from the notice of others. What distinction, pray, does he confer upon me? Herr von Kleinmayr and Bönike have a separate table with the illustrious Count Arco. It would be some distinction if I sat at that table, but there is none in sitting with the valets, who, when they are not occupying the best seats at table, have to light the chandeliers, open the doors and wait in the anteroom (*when I am within*) – and with the cooks too! Moreover, when we are summoned to a house where there is a concert, Herr Angerbauer has to watch outside until the Salzburg gentlemen arrive, when he sends a lackey to show them the way in. On hearing Brunetti tell this in the course of a conversation, I thought to myself, 'Just wait till I come along!' So the other day when we were to go to Prince Galitzin's . . . I went there alone on purpose, because I really feel ashamed to go anywhere with them. When I got upstairs, I found Angerbauer standing there to direct the lackey to show me in. But I took no notice, either of the valet or the lackey, but walked straight on through the rooms into the music room, for all the doors were open, – and went straight up to the Prince, paid him my respects and stood there talking to him. I had completely forgotten my friends Ceccarelli and Brunetti, for they were not to be seen. They were leaning against the wall behind the orchestra, not daring to come forward a single step. If a lady or a gentleman speaks to Ceccarelli, he always laughs: and if anyone at all addresses Brunetti, he colours and gives the dullest answers. Oh, I could cover whole sheets if I were to describe all the scenes which have taken place between the Archbishop and the two of them since I have been here and indeed before I came. . . . Prince Galitzin asked Ceccarelli to sing today. Next time it will be my turn to perform. I am going this evening with Herr von Klienmayr to Court Councillor Braun, a good friend of his, who is supposed to be one of the greatest enthusiasts for the clavier. I have lunched twice with Countess Thun and go there almost every day. She is the most charming and most lovable lady I have ever met; and I am very high in her favour. Her husband is still the same peculiar, but well-meaning and honourable gentleman. I have also lunched with Count Cobenzl. I owe

Vienna,
8 April 1781

this to his aunt, Countess von Rumbeck, sister of the Cobenzl in the Pagerie, who was at Salzburg with her husband. Well, my chief object here is to introduce myself to the Emperor in some becoming way, for I am absolutely determined that he shall *get to know me*. I should love to run through my opera for him and then play a lot of fugues, for that is what he likes. Oh, had I but known that I should be in Vienna

Countess Wilhelmine Thun, one of Mozart's favourite aristocratic patrons during his first years in Vienna: anonymous portrait in oils.

during Lent, I should have written a short oratorio and produced it in the theatre for my benefit, as they all do here. I could easily have written it beforehand, for I know all the voices. How gladly would I give a public concert, as is the custom here. But I know for certain that I should never get permission to do so – for just listen to this! You know that there is a society in Vienna which gives concerts for the benefit of the widows of musicians, at which every professional musician plays gratis. The orchestra is a hundred and eighty strong. No virtuoso who has any love for his neighbour, refuses to give his services, if the society asks him to do so. Besides, in this way he can win the favour both of the Emperor and of the public. Starzer was commissioned to invite me and I agreed at once, adding, however, that I must first obtain the consent of my Prince, which I had not the slightest doubt that he would give – as it was a matter of charity, or at any rate a good work, for which I should get no fee. *He would not permit me to take part.* All the nobility in Vienna have made a grievance of it. I am only sorry for the following reason. I should not have played a concerto, but (as the Emperor sits in the proscenium box) I should have extemporized and played a fugue and then the variations on 'je suis Lindor' on Countess Thun's beautiful Stein pianoforte, which she would have lent me. Wherever I have played this programme in public, I have always won the greatest applause – because the items set one another off so well, and because everyone has something to his taste. But pazienza! . . .

I could not finish this letter, because Herr von Kleinmayr fetched me in his carriage to go to a concert at Baron Braun's. So I can now add that the Archbishop has given me permission to play at the concert for the widows. For Starzer went to the concert at Galitzin's and he and all the nobility worried the Archbishop until he gave his consent. *I am so glad . . .*

28 March

. . . I told you about the applause in the theatre, but I must add that what delighted and surprised me most of all was the amazing silence – and also the cries of 'Bravo!' while I was playing. This is certainly honour enough in Vienna, where there are such numbers and numbers of good pianists. Today (for I am writing at eleven o'clock at night) we had a concert, where three of my compositions were performed

Vienna,
8 April 1781

An undated ticket for one of Mozart's concerts.

– new ones, of course; a rondo for a concerto for Brunetti [K373]; a sonata with violin accompaniment for myself [K379], which I composed last night between eleven and twelve (but in order to be able to finish it, I only wrote out the accompaniment for Brunetti and retained my own part in my head); and then a rondo for Ceccarelli [K374], which he had to repeat. I must now beg you to send me a letter as soon as possible and to give me your fatherly and most friendly advice on the following matter. It is said that we are to return to Salzburg in a fortnight. I can stay on here, and that too not to my loss, but to my advantage. So I am thinking of asking the Archbishop to allow me to remain in Vienna. Dearest father, I love you dearly; that you must realize from the fact that for your sake I renounce all my wishes and desires. For, were it not for you, I swear to you on my honour that I should not hesitate for a moment to leave the Archbishop's service. I should give a grand concert, take four pupils, and in a year I should have got on so well in Vienna that I could make at least a thousand thalers a year. I assure you that I often find it difficult to throw away my luck as I am doing. As you say, I am still young. True – but to waste one's youth in inactivity in such a beggarly place is really very sad – and it is such a loss. I should like to have your kind and fatherly advice about this, and very soon, – for I must tell him what I am going to do. But do have confidence in me, for I am more prudent now. Farewell. I kiss your hands a thousand times and embrace my sister with all my heart and am ever your most obedient

W. A. Mozart

Mon trés cher Pére!

Vienna,
9 May 1781

I am still seething with rage! And you, my dearest and most beloved father, are doubtless in the same condition. My patience has been so long tried that at last it has given out. I am no longer so unfortunate as to be in Salzburg service. Today is a happy day for me. Just listen.

Twice already that – I don't know what to call him – has said to my face the greatest *sottises* and *impertinences*, which I have not repeated to you, as I wished to spare your feelings, and for which I only refrained from taking my revenge on the spot because you, my most beloved father, were ever before my eyes. He called me a rascal and a dissolute fellow and told me to be off. And I – endured it all, although I felt that not only my honour but yours also was being attacked. But, as you would have it so, I was silent. Now listen to this. A week ago the footman came up unexpectedly and told me to clear out that very instant. All the others had been informed of the day of their departure, but not I. Well, I shoved everything into my trunk in haste, and old Madame Weber has been good enough to take me into her house, where I have a pretty room. Moreover, I am living with people who are obliging and who supply me with all the things which one often requires in a hurry and which one cannot have when one is living alone. I decided to travel home by the ordinaire on Wednesday, that is, today, May 9th. But as I could not collect the money still due to me within that time, I postponed my departure until Saturday. When I presented myself today, the valets informed me that the Archbishop wanted to give me a parcel to take charge of. I asked whether it was urgent. They told me, 'Yes, it is of the greatest importance.' 'Well,' said I, 'I am sorry that I cannot have the privilege of serving His Grace, for (on account of the reason mentioned above) I cannot leave before Saturday. I have left this house, and must live at my own expense. So it is evident that I cannot leave Vienna until I am in a position to do so. For surely no one will ask me to ruin myself.' Kleinmayr, Moll, Bönike and the two valets, all said that I was perfectly right. When I went in to the Archbishop – that reminds me, I must tell you first of all that Schlauka advised me to make the excuse that the ordinaire was already full, a reason which would carry more weight with him than if I gave him the true one, – well, when I entered the room, his first words were: – *Archbishop*: 'Well, young fellow, when are you going off?' *I*: 'I intended to go tonight, but all the seats were already engaged.' Then he rushed full steam ahead, without pausing for breath – I was the most dissolute fellow he knew – no one served him so badly as I did – I had better leave today or else he would write home and have my salary stopped. I couldn't get a word in edgeways, for he blazed away like a fire. I listened to it all very calmly. He lied to my face that my salary was five hundred gulden, called me a scoundrel, a rascal, a vagabond. Oh, I really cannot tell you all he said. At last my blood began to boil, I could no longer contain myself and I said, 'So Your Grace is not satisfied with me?' 'What, you dare to threaten me – you scoundrel? There is the door! Look out, for I will have nothing more to do with such a miserable wretch.' At last I said: 'Nor I with you!' 'Well, be off!' When leaving the room, I said, 'This is final. You shall have it tomorrow in writing.' Tell me now, most beloved father, did I not say the word too late rather than too soon? Just listen for a moment. My honour is more precious to me than anything else and I know that it is so to you also. Do not be the least bit anxious about me. I am so sure of my success in Vienna that I would have resigned even without the slightest reason; and now that I have a very good reason – and that too thrice over – I cannot make a virtue of it. Au contraire, I had twice played the coward and I could not do so a third time.

As long as the Archbishop remains here, I shall not give a concert. You are altogether mistaken if you think that I shall get a bad name with the Emperor and the nobility, for the Archbishop is detested here and most of all by the Emperor. In fact, he is furious because the Emperor did not invite him to Laxenburg. By the next post I shall send you a little money to show you that I am not starving. Now please be cheerful, for my good luck is just beginning, and I trust that my good luck

The aristocratic Archbishop Colloredo of Salzburg is now famous only for his quarrels with Mozart, but in his own time he was an all-powerful and often threatening influence in the young composer's life. Contemporary oil on canvas by an unknown artist.

will be yours also. Write to me in cypher that you are pleased – and indeed you may well be so – but in public rail at me as much as you like, so that none of the blame may fall on you. But if, in spite of this, the Archbishop should be the slightest bit impertinent to you, come at once with my sister to Vienna, for I give you my word of honour that there is enough for all three of us to live on. Still, I should prefer it if you could hold out for another year. Do not send any more letters to the Deutsches Haus, nor enclose them in their parcels – I want to hear nothing more about Salzburg. I hate the Archbishop to madness.

Adieu. I kiss your hands a thousand times and embrace my dear sister with all my heart and am ever your obedient son

W. A. Mozart

Just address your letters:

To be delivered Auf dem Peter, im Auge Gottes,

2nd Floor.

Please inform me soon of your approval, for that is the only thing which is still wanting to my present happiness. Adieu.

Mon trés cher Pére!

You will know from my last letter that I have asked the Prince for my discharge,
because he himself has told me to go. For already in the two previous audiences he
said to me: '*Clear out of this, if you will not serve me properly.*' He will deny it, of
course, but all the same it is as true as that God is in His Heaven. Is it any wonder
then if after being roused to fury by 'knave, scoundrel, rascal, dissolute fellow', and
other similar dignified expressions uttered by a Prince, I at last took '*Clear out of
this*' in its literal sense? On the following day I gave Count Arco a petition to present
to His Grace, and I returned my travelling expenses, which consisted of fifteen gulden, forty kreuzer for the diligence, and two ducats for my keep. He refused to take
either and assured me that I could not resign without your consent, my father. 'That
is your duty,' said he. I retorted that I knew my duty to my father as well as he did
and possibly better, and that I should be very sorry if I had to learn it first from
him. 'Very well,' he replied, 'if he is satisfied, you can ask for your discharge; if not,
you can ask for it all the same.' A pretty distinction! All the edifying things which
the Archbishop said to me during my three audiences, particularly during the last
one, all the subsequent remarks which this fine servant of God made to me, had
such an excellent effect on my health that in the evening I was obliged to leave the
opera in the middle of the first act and go home and lie down. For I was very feverish,
I was trembling in every limb, and I was staggering along the street like a drunkard.
I also stayed at home the following day, yesterday, and spent the morning in bed,
as I had taken tamarind water.

The Count has also been so kind as to write very flattering things about me to
his father, all of which you will probably have had to swallow by now. They will
certainly contain some astounding passages. But whoever writes a comedy and
wants to win applause, must exaggerate a little and not stick too closely to the truth.
Besides, you must remember how very anxious these gentlemen are to serve the
Archbishop.

Well, without losing my temper (for my health and my life are very precious to
me and I am only sorry when circumstances force me to get angry) I just want to
set down the chief accusation which was brought against me in respect of my service.
I did not know that I was a valet – and that was the last straw. I ought to have idled
away a couple of hours every morning in the antechamber. True, I was often told
that I ought to present myself, but I could never remember that this was part of my
duty, and I only turned up punctually whenever the Archbishop sent for me.

I will now confide to you very briefly my inflexible determination, but so that
the whole world may hear it. If I were offered a salary of 2000 gulden by the Archbishop of Salzburg and only 1000 gulden somewhere else, I should still take the
second offer. For instead of the extra 1000 gulden I should enjoy good health and

peace of mind. I trust, therefore, by all the fatherly love which you have lavished on me so richly from my childhood and for which I can never thank you enough (though indeed I can show it least of all in Salzburg), that, if you wish to see your son well and happy, you will say nothing to me about this affair and that you will bury it in the deepest oblivion. For one word about it would suffice to embitter me again and – if you will only admit it – to fill you too with bitterness.

Now farewell, and be glad that your son is no coward. I kiss your hands a thousand times, embrace my sister with all my heart and am ever your most obedient son

Wolfgang Amadè Mozart

Mon trés cher Pére!

Vienna,
12 May 1781

In the letter you received by post I spoke to you as if we were in the presence of the Archbishop, but now I am going to talk to you, my dearest father, as if we were quite alone. I shall say nothing whatever about all the injustice with which the Archbishop has treated me from the very beginning of his reign until now, of the incessant abuse, of all the *impertinences* and *sottises* which he has uttered to my face, of my undeniable right to leave him – for that cannot be disputed. I shall only speak of what would have induced me to leave him even without any cause of offence. I have here the finest and most useful acquaintances in the world. I am liked and respected by the greatest families. All possible honour is shown me and I am paid into the bargain. So why should I pine away in Salzburg for the sake of 400 gulden, linger on without remuneration or encouragement and be of no use to you in any way, when I can certainly help you here? What would be the end of it? Always the same. I should have to endure one insult after another or go away again. I need say no more, for you know it yourself. But this I must tell you, that everyone in Vienna has already heard my story. All the nobility are urging me not to let myself be made a fool of. Dearest father, people will come to you with fair words, but they are serpents and vipers. All base people are thus – disgustingly proud and haughty, yet always ready to crawl. How horrible! The two private valets have seen through the whole swinishness, and Schlauka in particular said to someone: 'As for me, I really cannot think that Mozart is wrong – in fact, I think he is quite right. I should like to have seen the Archbishop treat me in the same way. Why, he spoke to him as if he were some beggarly fellow. I heard him – infamous it was!' The Archbishop acknowledges that he has been unjust, but has he not had frequent occasion to acknowledge it? Has he reformed? Not a bit. So let us have done with him. If I had not been afraid of injuring you, things would have been on a very different footing long ago. But after all what can he do to you? – Nothing. Once you know that all is going well with me, you can easily dispense with the Archbishop's favour. He cannot deprive you of your salary, and besides you always do your duty. I pledge myself to succeed. Otherwise I should never have taken this step, although I must confess that after that insult, I should have gone off even if I had had to beg. For who will let himself be bullied, especially when he can do far better? So, if you are afraid, pretend to be angry with me, scold me roundly in your letters, provided that we two know how things really are between us. But do not let yourself be won over by flatteries – and be on your guard. Adieu. I kiss your hands a thousand times and embrace my dear sister with all my heart. By the next occasion I shall send you the portrait, the ribbons, the fichu and everything else. Adieu. I am ever your most obedient son

Wolfgang Amadè Mozart

Mon trés cher Pére!

I too do not know how to begin this letter, my dearest father, for I have not yet recovered from my astonishment and shall never be able to do so, if you continue to think and to write as you do. I must confess that there is not a single touch in your letter by which I recognize my father! I see a father, indeed, but not that most beloved and most loving father, who cares for his own honour and for that of his children – in short, not *my* father. But it must have been a dream. You are awake now and need no reply from me to your points in order to be fully convinced that – *now more than ever* – I can never abandon my resolve. Yet, because in certain passages my honour and my character are most cruelly assailed, I must reply to these points. You say that you can never approve of my having tendered my resignation while I was in Vienna. I should have thought that if I wished to do so (although at the time I did not, or I should have done so on the first occasion) the most sensible thing was to do it in a place where I had a good standing and the finest prospects in the world. It is possible that you will not approve this in the presence of the Archbishop, but to me you cannot but applaud my action. You say that the only way to save my honour is to abandon my resolve. How can you perpetrate such a contradiction! When you wrote this you surely did not bear in mind that such a recantation would prove me to be the basest fellow in the world. All Vienna knows that I have left the Archbishop, and all Vienna knows the reason! Everyone knows that it was because my honour was insulted – and, what is more, insulted three times. And am I publicly to prove the contrary? Am I to make myself out to be a cowardly sneak and the Archbishop a worthy prince? No one would like to do the former, and I least of all; and the latter God alone can accomplish, if it be His will to enlighten him. You say that I have never shown you any affection and therefore ought now to show it for the first time. Can you really say this? You add that I will never sacrifice any of my pleasures for your sake. But what pleasures have I here? The pleasure of taking trouble and pains to fill my purse? You seem to think

Vienna,
19 May 1781

that I am revelling in pleasures and amusements. Oh, how you deceive yourself indeed! ... All that I can say to you is this, that on your account – but solely on your account, my father – I am very sorry that I was driven to take this step, and that I wish that the Archbishop had acted more judiciously, if only in order that I might have been able to devote my whole life to you. To please you, my most beloved father, I would sacrifice my happiness, my health and my life. But my honour – *that* I prize, and you too must prize it, above everything. You may show this to Count Arco and to all Salzburg too. After that insult, that threefold insult, were the Archbishop to offer me 1200 gulden in person, I would not accept them. I am no skunk, no rascal; and, had it not been for you, I would not have waited for him to say to me for the third time, '*Clear out of this,*' without taking him at his word! What am I saying? Waited! Why, I should have said it, and not *he*! I am only surprised that the Archbishop would have behaved with so little discretion, particularly in a place like Vienna! Well, he will see that he has made a mistake. Prince Breuner and Count Arco need the Archbishop, but I do not; and if the worst comes to the worst and he forgets all the duties of a prince – of a *spiritual prince* – then come and join me in Vienna. You can get four hundred gulden anywhere. Just imagine how he would disgrace himself in the eyes of the Emperor, who already hates him, if he were to do that! My sister too would get on much better in Vienna than in Salzburg. There are many distinguished families here who hesitate to engage a male teacher, but would give handsome terms to a woman ...

Mon trés cher Pére!

Vienna,
9 June 1781

Well, Count Arco has made a nice mess of things! So that is the way to persuade people and to attract them! To refuse petitions from innate stupidity, not to say a word to your master from lack of courage and love of toadyism, to keep a fellow dangling about for four weeks, and finally, when he is obliged to present the petition in person, instead of *at least* granting him admittance, to throw him out of the room and give him a kick on his behind – that is the Count, who, according to your last letter, has my interest so much at heart – and that is the court where I ought to go on serving – the place where whoever wants to make a written application, instead of having its delivery facilitated, is treated in this fashion! The scene took place in the antechamber. So the only thing to do was to decamp and take to my heels – for, although Arco had already done so, I did not wish to show disrespect to the Prince's apartments. I have written three memoranda, which I have handed in five times; and each time they have been thrown back at me. I have carefully preserved them, and whoever wishes to read them may do so and convince himself that they do not contain the slightest personal remark. When at last I was handed back my memorandum in the evening through Herr von Kleinmayr (for that is his office), I was beside myself with rage, for the Archbishop's departure was fixed for the following day. I could not let him leave thus and, as I had heard from Arco (or so at least he had told me) that the Prince knew nothing about it, I realized how angry he would be with me for staying on so long and then at the very last moment appearing with a petition of this kind. I therefore wrote another memorandum, in which I explained to the Archbishop that it was now four weeks since I had drawn up a petition, but, finding myself for some unknown reason always put off, I was now obliged to present it to him in person, though at the very last moment. This memorandum procured me my dismissal from his service in the most pleasant way imaginable. For who knows whether the whole thing was not done at the command of the Archbishop himself? If Herr von Kleinmayr still wishes to maintain the character of an honest man, he can testify as can also the Archbishop's servants, that his command was carried out. So now I need not send in any petition, for the affair is at an end. I do not want to write anything more on the subject, and if the Archbishop were to offer me a salary of 1200 gulden, I would not accept it after such treatment. How easy it would have been to persuade me to remain! By kindness, but not by insolence and rudeness. I sent a message to Count Arco saying *that I had nothing more to say to him.* For he went for me so rudely when I first saw him and treated me as if I were a rogue, which he had no right to do. And – by Heaven! as I have already told you, I would not have gone to him the last time, if in his message he had not added that he had had a letter from you. Well, that will be the last time. What is it to him if I wish to get my discharge? And if he was really so well disposed towards me, he ought to have reasoned quietly with me – or have let things take their course, rather than throw such words about as 'clown' and 'knave' and hoof a fellow out of the room with a kick on his arse; but I am forgetting that this was probably done by order of our worthy Prince Archbishop . . .

Mon trés cher Pére!

Tomorrow the portrait and the ribbons for my sister will sail off to Salzburg. I do *Vienna,* not know whether the ribbons will be to her taste; but I assure her that they are in *16 June 1781* the latest fashion. If she would like to have some more or perhaps some which are not painted, she has only to let me know, and if there is anything else which she thinks can be got better in Vienna, she has only to write to me. I hope that she did not pay for the fichu, as it was paid for already. I forgot to mention this when writing, probably because I had so much to tell you about that accursed affair. I shall remit the money in the way you have directed.

Well, at last I call tell you something more about Vienna. Up to the present I have had to fill my letters with that swinish story. Thank God, it is over. The present season is, as you know, the worst for anyone who wants to make money. The most

The actor and playwright Gottlieb Stephanie (1741–1800): silhouette by J. H. Löschenkohl, 1786. Stephanie prepared the libretto for Die Entführung aus dem Serail *from a play by Bretzner. He was an influential figure and a good host, but not always an easy man to work with, as we see from Mozart's letters.*

distinguished families are in the country. So all I can do is to work hard in preparation for the winter, when I shall have less time to compose. As soon as the sonatas are finished [K376, 377 and 380], I shall look about for a short Italian cantata and set it to music, so that it may be produced at the theatre in Advent – for my benefit, of course. There is a little cunning in this, for then I can give it twice and make the same profit each time, since, when it is performed for the second time, I shall play something on a pianoforte. At present I have only one pupil, Countess Rumbeck, Cobenzl's cousin. I could have many more, it is true, if I chose to lower my terms, but by doing so, I should lose repute. My terms are six ducats for twelve lessons and even then I make it clearly understood that I am giving them as a favour. I would rather have three pupils who pay me well than six who pay badly. With this

one pupil I can just make *both ends meet*, and that is enough for the present. I simply mention this in order that you may not think me guilty of selfishness in sending you only thirty ducats. Believe me, I would gladly deprive myself of everything, if only I had it! But things are bound to improve. We must never let people know how we really stand financially.

Well, let us talk about the theatre. I think I mentioned the other day that before his departure Count Rosenberg commissioned Schröder to hunt up a libretto for me. It has now been found, and Stephanie junior, who is manager of the opera, has got it. Bergopzoomer, a really good friend of Schröder's and of mine, gave me the hint at once. So off I went to Stephanie, *en forme de visite*. For we thought it possible

Joseph II entertaining visitors at the royal residence of Schönbrunn in 1782: engraving (with detail) by Carl Schütz, 1783. Joseph had become sole ruler of the Habsburg territories after the (continued p. 107)

that his partiality for Umlauf might make him play me false. This suspicion proved, however, quite unfounded . . .

Well, I must now explain why we were suspicious of Stephanie. I regret to say that the fellow has the worst reputation in Vienna, for he is said to be rude, false and slanderous and to treat people most unfairly. But I pay no attention to these reports. There may be some truth in them, for everyone abuses him. On the other hand, he is in great favour with the Emperor. He was most friendly to me the very first time we met, and said: 'We are old friends already and I shall be delighted if it be in my power to render you any service.' I believe and hope too that he himself may write an opera libretto for me. Whether he has written his plays alone or with the help of others, whether he has plagiarized or created, he still understands the stage, and his plays are invariably popular . . .

Vienna,
1 August 1781

. . . Well, the day before yesterday Stephanie junior gave me a libretto to compose. I must confess that, however badly he may treat other people, about which I know nothing, he is an excellent friend to me. The libretto is quite good. The subject is Turkish and the title is: *Belmonte und Konstanze*, or *Die Verführung aus dem Serail*. I intend to write the overture, the chorus in Act I and the final chorus in the style of Turkish music. Mlle Cavalieri, Mlle Teiber, M. Fischer, M. Adamberger, M. Dauer and M. Walter are to sing in it. I am so delighted at having to compose this opera that I have already finished Cavalieri's first aria, Adamberger's aria and the trio which closes Act I. The time is short, it is true, for it is to be performed in the middle of September; but the circumstances connected with the date of performance and, in general, all my other prospects stimulate me to such a degree that I rush to my desk with the greatest eagerness and remain seated there with the greatest delight. The Grand Duke of Russia is coming here, and that is why Stephanie entreated me, if possible, to compose the opera in this short space of time . . .

Mon trés cher Pére!

I must write in haste, for I have only this very instant finished the Janissary chorus and it is past twelve o'clock and I have promised to drive out at two o'clock sharp with the Auernhammers and Mlle Cavalieri to Mingendorf near Laxenburg, where the camp now is. Adamberger, Mlle Cavalieri and Fischer are exceedingly pleased with their arias. I lunched yesterday with Countess Thun and am to do so again tomorrow. I played to her what I have finished composing and she told me afterwards that she would venture her life that what I have so far written cannot fail to please. But on this point I pay no attention whatever to *anybody's praise or blame* – I mean, until people have heard and seen the work *as a whole*. I simply follow *my own feelings*. All the same you may judge from this how pleased she must have been to express herself so emphatically . . .

Vienna,
8 August 1781

. . . We are now having one rehearsal after another in the theatre. The ballet-master Antoine has been summoned from Munich, and supers are being recruited throughout Vienna and all its suburbs. There is still a sorry remnant of Noverre's ballet, who, however, have not moved a leg for the last eight years and most of whom are like sticks. I think I mentioned the other day that Gluck's 'Iphigenie' is to be given in German and his 'Alceste' in Italian. If only one of the two were to be performed, I should not mind, but both – that is very annoying for me. I will tell you why. The translator of 'Iphigenie' into German is an excellent poet, and I would gladly have given him my Munich opera to translate. I would have altered the part of Idomeneo completely and changed it to a bass part for Fischer. In addition I would have made several other alterations and arranged it more in the French style. Mme Bernasconi, Adamberger and Fischer would have been delighted to sing it, but, as they now have two operas to study, and such exhausting ones, I am obliged to excuse them. Besides, a third opera would be too much . . .

Vienna,
12 September 1781

Mon trés cher Pére!

Forgive me for having made you pay an extra heavy postage fee the other day. But I happened to have nothing important to tell you and thought that it would afford you pleasure if I gave you some idea of my opera. As the original text began with a monologue, I asked Stephanie to make a little arietta out of it – and then to put in a duet instead of making the two chatter together after Osmin's short song.

Vienna,
26 September 1781

(continued from p. 104) *death of his mother, Maria Theresa, two years earlier. During his short reign he introduced liberal reforms including the relaxation of censorship, which promoted the development of cultural life, and the encouragement of trade and industry, which threw up a new generation of patrons. These reforms more or less coincided with Mozart's arrival in Vienna and affected his future profoundly.*

(right) Said to be the mistress of Salieri, who wrote several operas for her, the soprano Caterina Cavalieri (1760–1801) created the roles of Constanze in Die Entführung aus dem Serail *and Madame Silberklang in* Der Schauspieldirektor. *Silhouette by J. H. Löschenkohl.*

As we have given the part of Osmin to Herr Fischer, who certainly has an excellent bass voice (in spite of the fact that the Archbishop told me that he sang too low for a bass and that I assured him that he would sing higher next time), we must take advantage of it, particularly as he has the whole Viennese public on his side . . .

. . . I have sacrificed Constanze's aria a little to the flexible throat of Mlle Cavalieri, 'Trennung war mein banges Los und nun schwimmt mein Aug' in Tränen'. I have tried to express her feelings, as far as an Italian bravura aria will allow it. I have changed the 'Hui' to 'schnell', so it now runs thus – 'Doch wie schnell schwand meine Freude'. I really don't know what our German poets are thinking of. Even if they do not understand the theatre, or at all events operas, yet they should not make their characters talk as if they were addressing a herd of swine. Hui, sow!

Now for the trio at the close of Act I. Pedrillo has passed off his master as an

architect – to give him an opportunity of meeting his Constanze in the garden. Bassa Selim has taken him into his service. Osmin, the steward, knows nothing of this, and being a rude churl and a sworn foe to all strangers, is impertinent and refuses to let them into the garden. It opens quite abruptly – and because the words lend themselves to it, I have made it a fairly respectable piece of real three-part writing. Then the major key begins at once pianissimo – it must go very quickly – and wind up with a great deal of noise, which is always appropriate at the end of an act. The more noise the better, and the shorter the better, so that the audience may not have time to cool down with their applause.

I have sent you only fourteen bars of the overture, which is very short with alternate fortes and pianos, the Turkish music always coming in at the fortes. The overture modulates through different keys; and I doubt whether anyone, even if his previous night has been a sleepless one, could go to sleep over it. Now comes the rub! The first act was finished more than three weeks ago, as was also one aria in Act II and the drunken duet (*per i signori viennesi*) which consists entirely of *my Turkish tattoo*. But I cannot compose any more, because the whole story is being altered –

and, to tell the truth, at my own request. At the beginning of Act III there is a charming quintet or rather finale, but I should prefer to have it at the end of Act II. In order to make this practicable, great changes must be made, in fact an entirely new plot must be introduced – and Stephanie is up to the eyes in other work. So we must have a little patience. Everyone abuses Stephanie. It may be that in my case he is only very friendly to my face. But after all he is arranging the libretto for me – and, what is more, as I want it – exactly – and, by Heaven, I do not ask anything more of him ...

... Now as to the libretto of the opera. You are quite right so far as Stephanie's work is concerned. Still, the poetry is perfectly in keeping with the character of stupid, surly, malicious Osmin. I am well aware that the verse is not of the best, but it fitted in and it agreed so well with the musical ideas which already were buzzing in my head, that it could not fail to please me; and I would like to wager that when it is performed, no deficiencies will be found. As for the poetry which was there originally, I really have nothing to say against it. Belmonte's aria 'O wie ängstlich' could hardly be better written for music. Except for 'Hui' and 'Kummer ruht in meinem Schoss' (for sorrow – cannot rest), the aria too is not bad, particularly the first part. Besides, I should say that in an opera the poetry must be altogether the obedient daughter of the music. Why do Italian comic operas please everywhere – in spite of their miserable libretti – even in Paris, where I myself witnessed their success? Just because there the music reigns supreme and when one listens to it all else is forgotten. Why, an opera is sure of success when the plot is well worked out, the words written solely for the music and not shoved in here and there to suit some miserable rhyme (which, God knows, never enhances the value of any theatrical performance, be it what it may, but rather detracts from it) – I mean, words or even entire verses which ruin the composer's whole idea. Verses are indeed the most indispensable element for music – but rhymes – solely for the sake of rhyming – the most detrimental. Those high and mighty people who set to work in this pedantic fashion will always come to grief, both they and their music. The best thing of all is when a good composer, who understands the stage and is talented enough to make sound suggestions, meets an able poet, that true phoenix; in that case no fears need be entertained as to the applause even of the ignorant. Poets almost remind me of trumpeters with their professional tricks! If we composers were always to stick so faithfully to our rules (which were very good at a time when no one knew better), we should be concocting music as unpalatable as their libretti ...

Vienna,
13 October 1781

Mozart's wife Constanze in 1783, the year after her marriage to the composer. Biographers have traditionally regarded Constanze as a frivolous woman, but Mozart adored her and protested jealously when he suspected her of flirting with other men. This lithograph (after an anonymous oil portrait) was published in 1828 in the biography of Mozart written by Constanze's second husband, Georg Nissen.

Work on Die Entführung *continued to be held up, and the opera was not eventually performed until the following summer. But Mozart was beginning to make his way in Vienna, and a much-publicized keyboard contest with the Italian piano virtuoso Muzio Clementi, before the Emperor and a group of distinguished guests, helped to establish his name. Meanwhile, his last tussle with his father was over his marriage. Mozart's involvement with the Weber family (first cousins of the composer of* Der Freischütz) *went back to his first visit to Mannheim in 1778, when it had been the second daughter, Aloisia Weber, who had taken his fancy. But by now Aloisia was married to the actor, Joseph Lange, and Mozart, who had taken a room in the Webers' Viennese apartment at the time of his break with the Archbishop, fell in love with the third daughter, Constanze. He was obviously not sure of the reception which this development would receive from his father.*

Mozart to his Father

Vienna,
15 December 1781

... Dearest father! You demand an explanation of the words in the closing sentence of my last letter! Oh, how gladly would I have opened my heart to you long ago, but I was deterred by the reproaches you might have made to me for *thinking of such a thing at an unseasonable time* – although indeed thinking can never be un-seasonable. Meanwhile I am very anxious to secure here a small but *certain* income, which, together with what chance may provide, will enable me to live here quite comfortably – and then – to marry! You are horrified at the idea? But I entreat you, dearest, most beloved father, to listen to me. I have been obliged to reveal my intentions to you. You must, therefore, allow me to disclose to you my reasons, which, moreover, are very well founded. The voice of nature speaks as loud in me as in others, louder, perhaps, than in many a big strong lout of a fellow. I simply cannot live as most young men do in these days. In the first place, I have too much religion; in the second place, I have too great a love of my neighbour and too high a feeling of honour to seduce an innocent girl; and, in the third place, I have too much horror and disgust, too much dread and fear of diseases and too much care for my health to fool about with whores. So I can swear that I have never had relations of that sort with any woman. Besides, if such a thing had occurred, I should not have concealed it from you; for, after all, to err is natural enough in a man, and to err *once* would be mere weakness – although indeed I should not undertake to promise that if I had erred once in this way, I should stop short at one slip. However, I stake my life on the truth of what I have told you. I am well aware that this reason (power-ful as it is) is not urgent enough. But owing to my disposition, which is more inclined to a peaceful and domesticated existence than to revelry, I who from my youth up have never been accustomed to look after my own belongings, linen, clothes and so forth, cannot think of anything more necessary to me than a wife. I assure you that I am often obliged to spend unnecessarily, simply because I do not pay attention to things. I am absolutely convinced that I should manage better with a wife (on the same income which I have now) than I do by myself. And how many useless expenses would be avoided! True, other expenses would have to be met, but – one knows what they are and can be prepared for them – in short, one leads a well-ordered existence. A bachelor, in my opinion, is only half alive. Such are my views and I cannot help it. I have thought the matter over and reflected sufficiently, and I shall not change my mind. But who is the object of my love? Do not be horrified again, I entreat you. Surely not one of the Webers? Yes, one of the Webers – but not Josepha, nor Sophie, but Constanze, the middle one. In no other family have I ever come across such differences of character. The eldest is a lazy, gross perfidious woman, and as cunning as a fox. Mme Lange is a false, malicious person and a coquette. The youngest – is still too young to be anything in particular – she is just a good-natured, but feather-headed creature! May God protect her from seduction! But the middle one, my good, dear Constanze, is the martyr of the family and, probably for that very reason, is the kindest-hearted, the cleverest and, in short, the best of them all. She makes herself responsible for the whole household and yet in their opinion she does nothing right. Oh, my most beloved father, I could fill whole sheets with descriptions of all the scenes that I have witnessed in that house. If you want to read them, I shall do so in my next letter. But before I cease to plague you with my chatter, I must make you better acquainted with the character of my dear Constanze. She is not ugly, but at the same time far from beautiful. Her whole beauty consists in two little black eyes and a pretty figure. She has no wit, but she has enough common sense to enable her to fulfil her duties as a wife and mother. It is a downright lie that she is inclined to be extravagant. On the contrary, she is accustomed to be shabbily dressed, for the little that her mother has been able to do for her children, she has done for the two others, but never for Constanze. True, she would like to be neatly and cleanly dressed, but not smartly, and most things that a woman needs she is able to make for herself; and she dresses her own hair every day. Moreover she understands housekeeping and has the kindest heart in the world. I love her and she loves me with all her heart. Tell me whether I could wish myself a better wife?

One thing more I must tell you, which is that when I resigned the Archbishop's service, our love had not yet begun. It was born of her tender care and attentions when I was living in their house.

Accordingly, all that I desire is to have a small assured income (of which, thank God, I have good hopes), and then I shall never cease entreating you to allow me to save this poor girl – and to make myself and her – and, if I may say so, all of us very happy. For you surely are happy when I am? And you are to enjoy one half of *my fixed income*. My dearest father, I have opened my heart to you and explained my remarks. It is now my turn to beg you to explain yours in your last letter. You say that I cannot imagine that you were aware of a *proposal which had been made to me and to which I, at the time when you heard of it, had not yet replied*. I do not understand one word of this – I know of no such proposal. Please take pity on your son! I kiss your hands a thousand times and am ever your most obedient son

W. A. Mozart

Mon trés cher Pére!

Vienna,
22 December 1781

I am still full of rage and fury at the disgraceful lies of that arch-villain Winter – and yet I am calm and composed, because they do not affect me – and delighted and contented with my most inestimable, most dear and most beloved father. But I could never have expected anything else from your good sense, and your love and kindness to me. No doubt by this time you will have received my letter with the confession of my love and my intentions, and you will have gathered from it that I shall not be so foolish as to marry rashly in my twenty-sixth year without having some certain income – and that I have very well founded reasons for getting married as soon as possible – and that, from the description of her which I gave you, my girl will be a very suitable wife for me. For she is just as I have described her, not one whit better or worse …

…Well, let's come to the marriage contract, or rather to the written assurance of my honourable intentions towards the girl. You know, of course, that as the father is no longer alive (unhappily for the whole family as well as for my Constanze and myself) a guardian has taken his place. Certain busybodies and impudent gentle- men like Herr Winter must have shouted in the ears of this person (who doesn't know me at all) all sorts of stories about me – as, for example, that he should beware of me – that I have no settled income – that I was far too intimate with her – that I should probably jilt her – and that the girl would then be ruined, and so forth. All this made him smell a rat – for the mother who knows me and knows that I am honourable, let things take their course and said nothing to him about the mat- ter. For my whole association with her consisted in my lodging with the family and later in my going to their house every day. No one ever saw me with her outside the house. But the guardian kept on pestering the mother with his representations until she told me about them and asked me to speak to him myself, adding that he would come some day to her house. He came – and we had a talk – with the result (as I did not explain myself as clearly as he desired) that he told the mother to forbid me to associate with her daughter until I had come to a written agreement with him. The mother replied: 'Why, his whole association with her consists in his coming to my house, and – I cannot forbid him my house. He is too good a friend – and one to whom I owe a great deal. I am quite satisfied. I trust him. You must settle it with him yourself.' So he forbade me to have anything more to do with Constanze, unless I would give him a written undertaking. What other course was open to me? I had either to give him a written contract or – to desert the girl. What man who loves sincerely and honestly can forsake his beloved? Would not the mother, would not my loved one herself place the worst interpretation upon such conduct? That was my predicament. So I drew up a document to the effect *that I bound myself to marry Mlle Constanze Weber within the space of three years and that if it should prove impossible for me to do so owing to my changing my mind, she should be entitled to claim from me three hundred gulden a year.* Nothing in the world could have been easier for me to write. For I knew that I should never have to pay these three hundred gulden, because I should never forsake her, and that even should I be so unfortunate as to change my mind, I should only be too glad to get rid of her for three hundred gulden, while Constanze, as I knew her, would be too proud to let herself be sold. But what did the angelic girl do when the guardian was gone? She asked her mother for the document, and said to me: '*Dear Mozart! I need no written assurance from you. I believe what you say,*' and tore up

Mozart and his sister Nannerl playing a piano duet: a detail from the family portrait (1780–91) by Johann Nepomuk della Croce. Wolfgang and Nannerl were very close as children, and often played together in the Salzburg days, but soon after this portrait was completed Mozart removed permanently to Vienna, Nannerl married (in 1784), and opportunities for music-making became rare.

the paper. This action made my dear Constanze yet more precious to me, and the document having been destroyed and the guardian having given his *parole d'honn-eur* to keep the matter to himself, I was to a certain extent easy in my mind on your account, my most beloved father. For I had no fear but that ultimately you would give your consent to our marriage (since the girl has everything but money), because I know your sensible ideas on this subject. Will you forgive me? Indeed I hope so! Nor do I doubt it for a moment ...

Mozart to his Sister

Dearest Sister!

Vienna,
20 April 1782

My dear Constanze has at last summoned up courage to follow the impulse of her kind heart – and that is, to write to you, my dear sister! Should you be willing to favour her with a reply (and indeed I hope you will, so that I may see the sweet creature's delight reflected on her face), may I beg you to enclose your letter to me? I only mention this as a precaution and so that you may know that her mother and sisters are not aware that she has written to you. I send you herewith a prelude and a three-part fugue [K394]. The reason why I did not reply to your letter at once was that on account of the wearisome labour of writing these small notes, I could not finish the composition any sooner. And, even so, it is awkwardly done, for the prelude ought to come first and the fugue to follow. But I composed the fugue first and wrote it down while I was thinking out the prelude. I only hope that you will be able to read it, for it is written so very small; and I hope further that you will like it. Another time I will send you something better for the clavier. My dear Constanze is really the cause of this fugue's coming into the world. The Baron van Swieten, to whom I go every Sunday, gave me all the works of Handel and Sebastian Bach to take home with me (after I had played them to him). When Constanze heard the fugues, she absolutely fell in love with them. Now she will listen to nothing but fugues, and particularly (in this kind of composition) the works of Handel and Bach. Well, as she had often heard me play fugues out of my head, she asked me if I had ever written any down, and when I said I had not, she scolded me roundly for not record- ing some of my compositions in this most artistic and beautiful of all musical forms, and never ceased to entreat me until I wrote down a fugue for her. So that is its origin. I have purposely written above it *Andante Maestoso*, as it must not be played too fast. For if a fugue is not played slowly, the ear cannot clearly distinguish the theme when it comes in and consequently the effect is entirely missed. In time, and when I have a favourable opportunity, I intend to compose five more and then present them to the Baron van Swieten, whose collection of good music, though small in quantity, is great in quality. And for that very reason I beg you to keep your promise not to show this composition to a soul. Learn it by heart and play it. It is not so easy to pick up a fugue by ear. If Papa has not yet had those works by Eberlin copied, so much the better, for in the meantime I have got hold of them and now I see (for I had forgotten them) that they are unfortunately far too trivial to deserve a place beside Handel and Bach. With due respect for his four-part com- position I may say that his clavier fugues are nothing but long-drawn-out voluntar- ies. Now farewell. I am glad that the two caps suit you. I kiss you a thousand times and remain your sincere brother

W. A. Mozart

Tell Papa I kiss his hand. I received no letter today.

Constanze Weber to Nannerl Mozart

Most honoured and valued Friend!

I should never have been so bold as to follow the dictates of my heart and to write to you, most esteemed friend, had not your brother assured me that you would not be offended by this step which I am taking solely from an earnest longing to communicate, if only in writing, with a person who, though unknown to me, is yet very precious, as she bears the name of Mozart. Surely you will not be angry if I venture to tell you that though I have not the honour of knowing you personally I

Vienna,
20 April 1782

The Graben, one of the busiest squares in Vienna, where Mozart lived by himself 1781–2, and again with Constanze in 1784. Engraving by Carl Schütz, 1781.

esteem you most highly, as the sister of so excellent a brother, and that I love you and even venture to ask you for your friendship. Without undue pride I may say that I partly deserve it and shall endeavour to do so wholly! May I in exchange offer you mine, which, indeed, has long been yours in the secrecy of my heart? Ah! I trust you will accept it, and in this hope I remain, most honoured and valued friend, your most obedient servant and friend

Constanze Weber

Please tell your Papa that I kiss his hand.

Mozart attending Die Entführung aus dem Serail. *The occasion is probably a performance in May 1789 at the Royal National Theatre in Berlin, though it may perhaps be a rehearsal of the opera at the Burgtheater, Vienna, in 1782. Aquatint by Franz Hegl, 1833.*

Mozart to Constanze Weber

Dearest, most beloved Friend!

Surely you will still allow me to address you by this name? Surely you do not hate me so much that I may be your friend no longer, and you – no longer mine? And even if you will not be my friend any longer, yet you cannot forbid me to wish you well, my friend, since it has become very natural for me to do so. Do think over what you said to me today. In spite of all my entreaties you have thrown me over three times and told me to my face that you intend to have nothing more to do

*Vienna,
29 April 1782*

with me. I (to whom it means more than it does to you to lose the object of my love) am not so hot-tempered, so rash and so senseless as to accept my dismissal. I love you far too well to do so. I entreat you, therefore, to ponder and reflect upon the cause of all this unpleasantness, which arose from my being annoyed that you were so impudently inconsiderate as to say to your sisters – and, be it noted, in my presence – that you had let a *chapeau* [a young gallant] measure the calves of your legs. No woman who cares for her honour can do such a thing. It is quite a good maxim to do as one's company does. At the same time there are many other factors to be considered – as, for example, whether only intimate friends and acquaintances are present – whether I am a child or a *marriageable* girl – more particularly, whether I am already betrothed – but, above all, whether only people of my own social standing or my social inferiors – or, what is even more important, my social superiors are in the company? If it be true that the Baroness [von Waldstädten] herself allowed it to be done to her, the case is still quite different for she is already past her prime and cannot possibly attract any longer – and besides, she is inclined to be promiscuous with her favours. I hope, dearest friend, that, even if you do not wish to become my wife, you will never lead a life like hers. If it was quite impossible for you to resist the desire to take part in the game (although it is not always wise for a man to do so, and still less for a woman), then why in the name of Heaven did you not take the ribbon and measure your own calves *yourself* (as *all self-respecting women* have done on similar occasions in my presence) and not allow a *chapeau* to do so? – Why, I myself *in the presence of others* would never have done such a thing to you. I should have handed you the ribbon myself. Still less, then, should you have allowed it to be done to you by a stranger – a man about whom I know nothing. But it is all over now; and the least acknowledgment of your somewhat thoughtless behaviour on that occasion would have made everything all right again; and if you will not make a grievance of it, dearest friend, everything will still be all right. You realize now how much I love you. *I do not fly into a passion as you do.* I think, I reflect and I feel. *If you will but surrender to your feelings*, then I know that this very day I shall be able to say with absolute confidence that Constanze is the virtuous, honourable, prudent and loyal sweetheart of her honest and devoted

Mozart

Mozart to his Father

Mon trés cher Pére!

Vienna,
20 July 1782

I hope that you received safely my last letter informing you of the good reception of my opera. It was given yesterday for the second time. Can you really believe it, but yesterday there was an even stronger cabal against it than on the first evening! The whole first act was accompanied by hissing. But indeed they could not prevent the loud shouts of 'bravo' during the arias. I was relying on the closing trio, but, as ill-luck would have it, Fischer went wrong, which made Dauer (Pedrillo) go wrong too; and Adamberger alone could not sustain the trio, with the result that the whole effect was lost and that this time *it was not repeated*. I was in such a rage (and so was Adamberger) that I was simply beside myself and said at once that I would not let the opera be given again without having a short rehearsal for the singers. In the second act both duets were repeated as on the first night, and in addition Belmonte's rondo 'Wenn der Freude Tränen fliessen'. The theatre was almost more crowded than on the first night and on the preceding day no reserved seats were to be had, either in the stalls or in the third circle, and not a single box. My opera has brought in 1200 gulden in the two days. I send you herewith the original score and two copies of the libretto. You will see that I have cut out several passages. I knew that here the practice is for the score to be copied at once; but I first gave free rein to my ideas and then made my alterations and cuts at the last moment. The opera was performed just as you now have it; but here and there the parts for trumpets, drums, flutes, and clarinets, and the Turkish music are missing, because I could not get any music paper with so many lines. Those parts were written out on extra sheets, which the copyist has probably lost, for he could not find them. The first act, when I was sending it somewhere or other – I forget where, unfortunately fell in the mud, which explains why it is so dirty . . .

. . . Dearest, most beloved father, I implore you by all you hold dear in the world to give your consent to my marriage with my dear Constanze. Do not suppose that it is just for the sake of getting married. If that were the only reason, I would gladly wait. But I realize that it is absolutely necessary for my own honour and for that of my girl, and for the sake of my health and spirits. My heart is restless and my head confused; in such a condition how can one think and work to any good purpose? And why am I in this state? Well, because most people think that we are already married. Her mother gets very much annoyed when she hears these rumours, and, as for the poor girl and myself, we are tormented to death. This state of affairs can be remedied so easily. Believe me, it is just as easy to live in expensive Vienna as anywhere else. It all depends on economy and good management, which cannot be expected from a young fellow, particularly if he is in love. Whoever gets a wife like my Constanze will certainly be a happy man. We intend to live very modestly and quietly and yet we shall be happy. Do not be uneasy, for, if I were to fall ill today, which God forbid, I would wager that the leading nobles would stand by me manfully and the more so if I were married. I can say this with entire confidence. I know what Prince Kaunitz has said about me to the Emperor and to the Archduke Maximilian. Most beloved father, I am longing to have your consent. I feel sure that

Vienna,
27 July 1782

Leopold Mozart by an unknown artist, 1780. Mozart's relationship with his father had its stormy passages, the last of which raged around Wolfgang's intended marriage and, in particular, the promissory document he had been forced to sign because of the rumours about himself and Constanze that were circulating in Vienna. Leopold never really accepted Constanze, though his fierce pride in his son's achievements continued to the end of his life.

you will give it, for my honour and my peace of mind depend upon it. Do not postpone too long the joy of embracing your son and his wife. I kiss your hands a thousand times and am ever your

obedient son

W. A. Mozart

Mozart to the Baroness von Waldstädten

Most highly esteemed Baroness!

Vienna, shortly before 4 August 1782

Madame Weber's maid-servant has brought me my music, for which I have had to give her a written receipt. She has also told me something in confidence which, although I do not believe it could happen, since it would be a disgrace to the whole family, yet seems possible when one remembers Madame Weber's stupidity; and which consequently causes me anxiety. It appears that Sophie went to the maid-servant in tears and when the latter asked her what was the matter, she said: 'Do tell Mozart in secret to arrange for Constanze to go home, for my mother is absolutely determined to have her fetched by the police.' Are the police in Vienna allowed to go into any house? Perhaps the whole thing is only a trap to make her return home. But if it could be done, then the best plan I can think of is to marry Constanze tomorrow morning – or even today, if that is possible. For I should not like to expose my beloved one to this scandal – and there could not be one, if she were my wife. One thing more. Thorwart has been summoned to the Webers today. I entreat you, dear Baroness, to let me have your friendly advice and to assist us poor creatures. I shall be at home all day. I kiss your hands a thousand times and am your most grateful servant   W. A. Mozart

In the greatest haste. Constanze knows *nothing* of this as yet. Has Herr von Thorwart been to see you? Is it necessary for the two of us to visit him after lunch today?

Mozart to his Father

Mon trés cher Pére!

You are very much mistaken in your son if you can suppose him capable of acting dishonestly. My dear Constanze – now, thank God, at last my wife – knew my circumstances and heard from me long ago all that I had to expect from you. But her affection and her love for me were so great that she willingly and joyfully sacrificed her whole future to share my fate. I kiss your hands and thank you with all the tenderness which a son has ever felt for a father, for your kind consent and fatherly blessing. But indeed I could safely rely on it. For you know that I myself could not but see only too clearly all the objections that could be raised against such a step. At the same time you also know that I could not act otherwise without injury to my conscience and my honour. Consequently I could certainly rely on having your consent. So it was that having waited two post-days in vain for a reply and the ceremony having been fixed for a day by which I was certain to have received it, I was married by the blessing of God to my beloved Constanze. I was quite assured of your consent and was therefore comforted. The following day I received your two letters at once – Well, it is over! I only ask your forgiveness for my too hasty trust in your fatherly love. In this frank confession you have a fresh proof of my love of truth and hatred of a lie. Next post-day my dear wife will ask her dearest, most beloved Papa-in-law for his fatherly blessing and her beloved sister-in-law for the continuance of her most valued friendship. No one was present at the wedding save her mother and her youngest sister, Herr von Thorwart as guardian and witness for both of us, Herr von Cetto, district councillor, who gave away the bride, and Gilowsky as my best man. When we had been joined together, both my wife and I

Vienna,
7 August 1782

Christoph Willibald von Gluck (1714–87) was the greatest German opera composer before Mozart and the mentor of his rival, Salieri. Gluck paved the way for Mozart by subordinating vocal display to dramatic necessity. This portrait by Etienne Aubry was painted in 1772.

began to weep. All present, even the priest, were deeply touched and all wept to see how much our hearts were moved. Our whole wedding feast consisted of a supper given for us by the Baroness von Waldstädten, which indeed was more princely than baronial. My dear Constanze is now looking forward a hundred times more to a visit to Salzburg, and I wager – I wager – that you will rejoice in my happiness when you get to know her, that is, if you agree with me that a right-minded, honest, virtuous and amiable wife is a blessing to her husband.

I send you herewith a short march.[1] I only hope that all will reach you in good time, and be to your taste. The first Allegro must be played with great fire, the last – as fast as possible. My opera was given again yesterday – and that too at Gluck's request. He has been very complimentary to me about it. I am lunching with him tomorrow. You see by my writing how I must hurry. Adieu. My dear wife and I kiss your hands a thousand times and we both embrace our dear sister with all our hearts and I am ever your most obedient son

W. A. Mozart

1 K408, no. 2, a promised addition to K385, the 'Haffner' Symphony.

Mozart to the Baroness von Waldstädten

Most highly esteemed Baroness!

Vienna,
15 February 1783

Here I am in a fine dilemma! Herr von Trattner and I discussed the matter the other day and agreed to ask for an extension of a fortnight. As every merchant does this, unless he is the most disobliging man in the world, my mind was quite at ease and I hoped that by that time, if I were not in the position to pay the sum myself, I should be able to borrow it. Well, Herr von Trattner now informs me that the person in question absolutely refuses to wait and that if I do not pay the sum before tomorrow, he will *bring an action against me.* Only think, Your Ladyship, what an unpleasant business this would be for me! At the moment I cannot pay – not even half the sum! If I could have foreseen that the subscriptions for my concertos [K413–15] would come in so slowly, I should have raised the money on a longer time-limit. I entreat Your Ladyship for Heaven's sake to help me to keep my honour and my good name!

My poor little wife is slightly indisposed, so I cannot leave her; otherwise I should have come to you myself to ask in person for Your Ladyship's assistance. We kiss Your Ladyship's hands a thousand times and are both Your Ladyship's most obedient children

W. A. and C. Mozart

Mozart to his Father

Mon trés cher Pére!

Lorenzo da Ponte
(1749–1838):
anonymous
watercolour. Da
Ponte was the court
poet to Joseph II but
later migrated to the
USA where he held
the chair in Italian
Literature at
Columbia University
and wrote a
fascinating
autobiography. His
fame, however, rests
on his librettos for
Le nozze di Figaro,
Don Giovanni *and*
Così fan tutte.

...Well, the Italian opera buffa has started again here and is very popular. The buffo is particularly good – his name is Benucci. I have looked through at least a hundred libretti and more, but I have hardly a single one with which I am satisfied;

that is to say, so many alterations would have to be made here and there, that even if a poet would undertake to make them, it would be easier for him to write a completely new text – which it is always best to do.

Vienna,
7 May 1783

Our poet here is now a certain Abbate da Ponte. He has an enormous amount to do in revising pieces for the theatre and he has to write *per obbligo* an entirely new libretto for Salieri, which will take him two months. He has promised after that to write a new libretto for me. But who knows whether he will be able to keep his word – or will want to? For, as you are aware, these Italian gentlemen are very civil to your face. Enough, we know them! If he is in league with Salieri, I shall never get anything out of him. But indeed I should dearly love to show what I can do in an Italian opera! So I have been thinking that unless Varesco is still very much annoyed with us about the Munich opera, he might write me a new libretto for seven characters. Basta! You will know best if this can be arranged. In the meantime he could jot down a few ideas, and when I come to Salzburg we could then work them out together. The most essential thing is that on the whole the story should be really *comic*; and, if possible, he ought to introduce *two equally good female parts*, one of these to be *seria*, the other *mezzo carattere*, but both parts equal *in importance and excellence*. The third female *character*, however, may be entirely buffa, and so may all the male ones, if necessary. If you think that something can be got out of Varesco please discuss it with him soon. But you must not tell him that I am coming to Salzburg in July, or he will do no work; for I should very much like to have some of it while I am still in Vienna. Tell him too that his share will certainly amount to 400 or 500 gulden, for the custom here is that the poet gets the takings of the third performance.

Well, I must close, for I am not yet fully dressed. Meanwhile, farewell. My wife and I kiss your hands a thousand times and embrace our dear sister with all our hearts and are ever your most obedient children

W. A. Mozart

Vienna,
7 June 1783

... Well, I have a few words to say to my sister about Clementi's sonatas. Everyone who either hears them or plays them must feel that as compositions they are worthless. They contain no remarkable or striking passages except those in sixths and octaves. And I implore my sister not to practise those passages too much, so that she may not spoil her quiet, even touch and that her hand may not lose its natural lightness, flexibility and smooth rapidity. For after all what is to be gained by it? Supposing that you do play sixths and octaves with the utmost velocity (which no one can accomplish, not even Clementi) you only produce an atrocious chopping effect and nothing else whatever. Clementi is a *ciarlatano*, like all Italians. He writes *Presto* over a sonata or even *Prestissimo* and *Alla breve*, and plays it himself *Allegro*

Miniature portrait of Muzio Clementi (1752–1832), the virtuoso pianist and composer who engaged with Mozart in the famous piano contest staged by Joseph II. 'An excellent cembalo player,' wrote Mozart, 'but that is all … He has not a farthing's worth of taste or feeling; he is a mere mechanicus.' Clementi, at least officially, was rather nicer about Mozart: 'Until then I had never heard anyone play with such spirit and grace.'

in 4/4 time. I know this is the case, for I have heard him do so. What he really does well are his passages in thirds; but he sweated over them day and night in London. Apart from this, he can do nothing, absolutely nothing, for he has not the slightest expression or taste, still less, feeling …

Between 1782 and the beginning of 1785 Mozart gradually became more and more in demand as performer, teacher and composer: this was the period of the 'Haffner' and 'Linz' Symphonies, the first nine of the mature Piano Concertos written for his own Viennese performances, and the first of the great String Quartets later dedicated to Haydn. Nevertheless he was continually short of money, and from this period onward letters to various friends asking for financial help become a recurrent feature of his correspondence. But this was not the aspect of his son's life which Leopold Mozart saw when he paid a last visit to Vienna early in 1785.

Leopold Mozart to his Daughter

… We arrived at the Schulerstrasse No. 846, first floor, at one o'clock on Friday. That your brother has very fine quarters with all the necessary furniture you may gather from the fact that his rent is 460 gulden. On the same evening we drove to his first subscription concert, at which a great many members of the aristocracy were present. Each person pays a souverain d'or or three ducats for these Lenten concerts. Your brother is giving them at the Mehlgrube and only pays half a

Vienna, 16 February 1785

souverain d'or each time for the hall. The concert was magnificent and the orchestra played splendidly. In addition to the symphonies a female singer of the Italian theatre sang two arias. Then we had a new and very fine concerto [K466] by Wolfgang, which the copyist was still copying when we arrived, and the rondo of which your brother did not even have time to play through, as he had to supervise the copying. You can well imagine that I met many acquaintances there who all came up to speak to me. I was also introduced to several other people.

On Saturday evening Herr Joseph Haydn and the two Barons Tinti came to see us and the new quartets were performed, or rather, the three new ones [K458, 464 and 465] which Wolfgang has added to the other three which we have already. The new ones are somewhat easier, but at the same time excellent compositions. Haydn said to me: 'Before God and as an honest man I tell you that your son is the greatest composer known to me either in person or by name. He has taste and, what is more, the most profound knowledge of composition.'

On Sunday evening the Italian singer, Madame Laschi, who is leaving for Italy, gave a concert in the theatre, at which she sang two arias. A cello concerto was performed, a tenor and a bass each sang an aria and your brother played a glorious concerto, which he composed for Mlle Paradis for Paris. I was sitting only two boxes away from the very beautiful Princess of Wurtemberg and had the great pleasure of hearing so clearly all the interplay of the instruments that for sheer delight tears came into my eyes. When your brother left the platform the Emperor waved his hat

*Joseph Haydn
(1732–1809), the
composer from whom
the mature Mozart
learnt most, especially
about the composition
of string quartets.
Anonymous
miniature on ivory.*

and called out 'Bravo, Mozart!' And when he came on to play, there was a great deal of clapping.

We were not at the theatre yesterday, for every day there is a concert. This evening there is another one in the theatre, at which your brother is again playing a concerto. I shall bring back several of his new compositions. Little Carl is the picture of him. He seems very healthy, but now and then, of course, children have trouble with their teeth. On the whole the child is charming, for he is extremely friendly and laughs when spoken to. I have only seen him cry once and the next moment he started to laugh . . .

Mozart to Joseph Haydn[1]

To my dear friend Haydn.

A father who had decided to send out his sons into the great world, thought it his duty to entrust them to the protection and guidance of a man who was very celebrated at the time and who, moreover, happened to be his best friend.

Vienna,
1 September 1785

In like manner I send my six sons to you, most celebrated and very dear friend. They are, indeed, the fruit of a long and laborious study; but the hope which many friends have given me that this toil will be in some degree rewarded, encourages me and flatters me with the thought that these children may one day prove a source of consolation to me.

During your last stay in this capital you yourself, my very dear friend, expressed to me your approval of these compositions. Your good opinion encourages me to offer them to you and leads me to hope that you will not consider them wholly unworthy of your favour. Please then receive them kindly and be to them a father, guide and friend! From this moment I surrender to you all my rights over them. I entreat you, however, to be indulgent to those faults which may have escaped a father's partial eye, and, in spite of them, to continue your generous friendship towards one who so highly appreciates it. Meanwhile I remain with all my heart, dearest friend, your most sincere friend

W. A. Mozart

Mozart to Franz Anton Hoffmeister

Dearest Hoffmeister!

I turn to you in my distress and beg you to help me out with some money, which I need very badly at the moment. Further, I entreat you to endeavour to procure for me as soon as possible the thing you know about. Forgive me for constantly worrying you, but as you know me and are aware how anxious I am that your

Vienna,
20 November 1785

1 A dedication, in Italian, published in Artaria's first edition of the six string quartets K387, 421, 428, 458, 464 and 465, which Mozart had composed during the years 1782 to 1785.

business should succeed, I am convinced that you will not take my importunity amiss and that you will help me as readily as I shall help you.

MZT

By the beginning of 1787 Mozart had embarked on his last great creative period. The success of Le nozze di Figaro *in Vienna eight months earlier had just been repeated in Prague, and a new opera (*Don Giovanni*) commissioned for the following season in the Bohemian capital. The last symphonies, concertos and chamber works,* Cosí fan tutte, Die Zauberflöte, La clemenza di Tito *and the Requiem were still to come. But his father's death put an end to the flood of correspondence between the two men which gives so lively a picture of Mozart's working life in earlier years, and during his last four years his letters are mainly concerned with his financial difficulties, asking for one loan after another from his Freemason friends (he had become a Mason himself in 1784), or to his wife in Baden where she went to take cures in each of the three years before his death.*

Nikolaus Joseph, Baron von Jacquin, the famous botanist who became professor of chemistry at Vienna University: lithograph by Joseph Lanzedelly after a drawing by V. G. Kininger. Mozart was very close to the Jacquin family (who were Masons) during his last years, especially to the Baron's second son, Gottfried, and daughter Franziska, one of his best piano pupils.

Mozart to Baron Gottfried von Jacquin, Vienna

Dearest Friend!

*Prague,
15 January 1787*

At last I have found a moment to write to you. I resolved immediately after my arrival to write four letters to Vienna, but in vain! I was only able to manage one (to my mother-in-law) and then only half of it. My wife and Hofer had to finish it.

Immediately after our arrival at noon on Thursday, the 11th, we had a dreadful rush to get ready for lunch at one o'clock. After the meal old Count Thun entertained us with some music, performed by his own people, which lasted about an hour and a half. This kind of *real entertainment* I could enjoy every day. At six o'clock I drove with Count Canal to the so-called Breitfeld ball, where the cream of the beauties of Prague is wont to gather. Why – *you* ought to have been there, my friend! I fancy I see you running, or rather, limping after all those pretty girls and women! I neither danced nor flirted with any of them, the former, because I was too tired, and the latter owing to my natural bashfulness. I looked on, however, with the greatest pleasure while all these people flew about in sheer delight to the music of my 'Figaro', arranged for contredanses and German dances. For here they talk about nothing but 'Figaro'. Nothing is played, sung or whistled but 'Figaro'. No opera is drawing like 'Figaro'. Nothing, nothing but 'Figaro'. Certainly a great honour for me! Well, to return to my order of the day. As I got home very late from the ball and moreover was tired and sleepy after my journey, nothing in the world could be more natural than that I should sleep it out next morning; which was just what I did. So the whole of the next morning was spent *sine linea*. After lunch the Count's music must always be listened to, and as on that very day an excellent pianoforte had been put in my room, you may readily suppose that I did not leave it unused and untouched for the whole evening; and that as a matter of course we performed amongst ourselves a little *Quatuor in caritatis camera* ('und das schöne Bandl hammera') and in this way the whole evening was again spent *sine linea*; and so it actually was. Well, you must scold not me but Morpheus, for that deity is very attentive to us in Prague. What the cause may have been I know not; at any rate we slept it out. Still, we managed to be at Father Unger's at eleven o'clock and made a *thorough* inspection of the Imperial Library and the General Theological Seminary. When we had almost stared our eyes out, we thought that we heard a little stomach-aria in our insides and that it would be just as well to drive to Count Canal's for lunch. The evening surprised us sooner than you might perhaps believe. Well, it was soon time to go to the opera. We heard 'Le gare generose' [by Giovanni Paisiello]. In regard to the performance of this opera I can give no definite opinion because I talked a lot; but that quite contrary to my usual custom I chattered so much may have been due to … Well, never mind! that evening too was frittered away *al solito*. Today I have at last been so fortunate as to find a moment to enquire after the health of your dear parents and the whole Jacquin family. I hope and trust with all my heart that you are all as well as we are. I must frankly admit that, although I meet with all possible courtesies and honours here and although Prague is indeed a very beautiful and pleasant place, I long most ardently to be back in Vienna; and believe me, the chief cause of this homesickness is certainly *your* family. When I remember that after

The Hannibal-Platz (now Makart-Platz) in Salzburg, with the house in which Leopold Mozart lived from 1773 until his death in 1787. Engraving after Pezolt, c. 1830.

my return I shall enjoy only for a short while the pleasure of your valued society and shall then have to forgo this happiness for such a long time, perhaps for ever, then indeed I realize the extent of the friendship and regard which I cherish for your whole family. Now farewell, dearest friend, dearest Hinkiti Honky! That is your name, so that you know. We all invented names for ourselves on the journey. Here they are. I am Punkititi. My wife is Schabla Pumfa. Hofer is Rozka-Pumpa. Stadler is Natschibinitschibi. My servant Joseph is Sagadaratà. My dog Gauckerl is Schamanuzky. Madame Quallenberg is Runzifunzi. Mlle Crux. PS. Ramlo is Schurimuri. Freistädtler is Gaulimauli. Be so kind as to tell him his name. Well, adieu . . .

Mozart to his Father

Vienna,
4 April 1787

. . . This very moment I have received a piece of news which greatly distresses me, the more so as I gathered from your last letter that, thank God, you were very well indeed. But now I hear that you are really ill. I need hardly tell you how greatly I am longing to receive some reassuring news from yourself. And I still expect it; although I have now made a habit of being prepared in all affairs of life for the worst. As death, when we come to consider it closely, is the true goal of our existence, I have formed during the last few years such close relations with this best and truest friend of mankind, that his image is not only no longer terrifying to me, but is indeed very soothing and consoling! And I thank my God for graciously granting me the opportunity (you know what I mean) of learning that death is the *key* which unlocks the door to our true happiness. I never lie down at night without reflecting that – young as I am – I may not live to see another day. Yet no one of all my acquaintances could say that in company I am morose or disgruntled. For this blessing I daily thank my Creator and wish with all my heart that each one of my fellow-creatures could enjoy it. In the letter which Madame Storace took away with her, I expressed my views to you on this point, in connexion with the sad death of my dearest and most beloved friend, the Count von Hatzfeld. He was just thirty-one, my own age. I do not feel sorry for him, but I pity most sincerely both myself and all who knew him as well as I did. I hope and trust that while I am writing this, you are feeling better. But if, contrary to all expectation, you are not recovering, I implore you by ... not to hide it from me, but to tell me the whole truth or get someone to write it to me, so that as quickly as is humanly possible I may come to your arms. I entreat you by all that is sacred – to both of us. Nevertheless I trust that I shall soon have a reassuring letter from you; and cherishing this pleasant hope, I and my wife and our little Carl kiss your hands a thousand times and I am ever

your most obedient son

W. A. Mozart

Mozart to Baron Gottfried von Jacquin

Dearest Friend!

Please tell Herr Exner to come at nine o'clock tomorrow morning to bleed my wife. *Vienna?, end of May 1787*

I send you herewith your Amynt and the sacred song. Please be so good as to give the sonata to your sister with my compliments and tell her to tackle it at once, for it is rather difficult. Adieu. Your true friend

Mozart

I inform you that on returning home today I received the sad news of my most beloved father's death. You can imagine the state I am in.

Mozart to his Sister

Dearest Sister!

You can easily imagine, as our loss is equally great, how pained I was by the sad news of the sudden death of our dearest father. Since at the moment it is impossible for me to leave Vienna (which I would the more gladly do to have the pleasure of embracing you) and since it would be hardly worth my while to do so for the sake *Vienna, 2 June 1787* of our late father's estate, I must confess that I too am entirely of your opinion about having a public auction. But before it takes place I should like to see the inventory, so as to be able to choose some personal effects. But if, as Herr d'Yppold has written to tell me, there is a dispositio paterna inter liberos, then, of course, I must be informed of this dispositio beforehand, so as to be able to make further arrangements; – hence I am now expecting an accurate copy of it and after a rapid perusal of its contents I shall let you have my opinion at once – Please see that the enclosed letter is handed to our kind and sincere friend Herr d'Yppold. As he has already proved his friendship to our family on so many occasions, I trust that he will again be a friend to me also and act for me in any necessary events. Farewell, dearest sister! I am ever your faithful brother

W. A. Mozart

PS. – My wife wishes to be remembered to you and your husband, and so do I.

Mozart to Baron Gottfried von Jacquin, Vienna

Dearest, most beloved Friend!

Prague,
4 November 1787

I hope you received my letter. My opera 'Don Giovanni' had its first performance on October 29th and was received with the greatest applause. It was performed yesterday for the fourth time, for my benefit. I am thinking of leaving here on the 12th or 13th. When I return, you shall have the aria at once, remember, *between ourselves.* How I wish that my good friends, particularly you and Bridi, were here just for one evening in order to share my pleasure! But perhaps my opera will be performed in Vienna after all! I hope so. People here are doing their best to persuade me to remain on for a couple of months and write another one. But I cannot accept this proposal, however flattering it may be …

Mozart to Michael Puchberg

Most honourable Brother of the Order,

Dearest, most beloved Friend!

Vienna,
before 17 June 1788

The conviction that you are *indeed my friend* and that you know me to be *a man of honour* encourages me to open my heart to you completely and to make you the following request. In accordance with my natural frankness I shall go straight to the point without affectation.

If you have sufficient regard and friendship for me to assist me for a year or two with one or two thousand gulden, at a suitable rate of interest, you will help me enormously! You yourself will surely admit *the sense and truth* of my statement when I say that it is difficult, nay impossible, to live when one has to wait for various odd sums. If one has not at least a *minimum of capital* behind one, it is impossible to keep one's affairs in order. *Nothing* can be done with nothing. If you will do me this kindness then, *primo*, as I shall have some money to go on with, I can meet necessary expenses *whenever they occur*, and therefore *more easily*, whereas now I have to *postpone* payments and then often *at the most awkward time* have to spend *all I receive at one go*; *secondo*, I can work with a mind more free from care and *with a lighter heart*, and thus *earn more*. As to security I do not suppose that you will have any doubts. You know more or less how I stand and you know *my principles*. You need not be anxious about the subscription: I am now extending the time by a few months. I have hopes of finding more patrons *abroad* than *here*.

I have now opened my *whole* heart to you in a matter which is of the utmost importance to me; that is, I have acted as a *true brother*. But it is only with a *true brother* that one can be *perfectly* frank. And now I look forward eagerly to your reply, which I do hope will be *favourable*. I do not know, but I take you to be a *man* who, provided he can do so, will like *myself* certainly assist a friend, if he be a *true* friend, or his brother, if he be *indeed a brother*. If you should find it inconvenient to part with so large a sum at once, then I beg you to lend me until tomorrow *at least a couple of hundred gulden*, for my landlord in the Landstrasse has been so importunate that in order to avoid an unpleasant incident I have had to pay him on the spot, and this has made things very awkward for me! We are sleeping tonight, for the first time, in our new quarters, where we shall remain both summer and winter. On the whole the change is all the same to me, in fact I prefer it. As it is, I have very little to do in town and, as I am not exposed to so many visitors, I shall have more time for work. If I have to go to town on business, which will certainly not be very often, any fiacre will take me there for ten kreuzer. Moreover our rooms are cheaper and during the spring, summer and autumn *more pleasant*, as I have a garden too. The address is Währingergasse, bei den Drei Sternen, No. 135. Pray regard this letter as a real proof of my complete confidence in you and remain ever my friend and brother as I shall be until the grave, your true, most devoted friend and brother

W. A. Mozart[1]

PS. – When are we to have a little musical party at your house again? I have composed a new trio! [K542]

Dearest Friend and B.O.,

Owing to great difficulties and complications my affairs have become so involved that is of the utmost importance to raise some money on these two pawnbroker's

(right) No book setting out to give an impression of Mozart as he was in life can afford to be without the unfinished portrait painted in about 1790 by his brother-in-law, Joseph Lange – the last important picture of the composer, and the one regarded by Constanze Mozart as the best likeness.

Vienna, beginning of July, 1788

1 Puchberg noted on this letter, 'sent 200 gulden on 17 June 1788'.

tickets. In the name of our friendship I implore you to do me this favour; but you must do it immediately. Forgive my importunity, but you know my situation. Ah! If only you had done what I asked you! Do it even now – then everything will be as I desire.

Ever your

Mozart

Mozart to Franz Hofdemel

Dearest Friend!

I am taking the liberty of asking you without any hesitation for a favour. I should be very much obliged to you if you could and would lend me a hundred gulden until the 20th of next month. On that day I receive the quarterly instalment of my salary and shall then repay the loan with thanks. I have relied too much on a sum of a hundred ducats due to me from abroad. Up to the present I have not yet received it, although I am expecting it daily. Meanwhile I have left myself too short of cash, so that *at the moment* I greatly need some ready money and have therefore appealed to your goodness, for I am absolutely convinced of your friendship.

Well, we shall soon be able to call one another by a *more delightful name!* For your novitiate is very nearly at an end!

*Vienna,
end of March 1789*

Mozart

Mozart to his Wife

Dearest, most beloved little Wife!

We expected to reach Dresden after dinner on Saturday, but we did not arrive until yesterday, Sunday, at two o'clock in the afternoon, because the roads were so bad. All the same I went yesterday to the Neumanns, where Madame Duschek is staying, in order to deliver her husband's letter. Her room is on the third floor beside the corridor and from it you can see anyone who is coming to the house. When I arrived at the door, Herr Neumann was already there and asked me to whom he had the honour to speak. 'That I shall tell you in a moment,' I replied, 'but please be so kind as to call Madame Duschek, so that my joke may not be spoilt.' But at the same moment Madame Duschek stood before me for she had recognized me from the window and had said at once: 'Why here comes someone who is very like Mozart.' Well, we were all delighted. There was a large party, consisting entirely of ugly women, who by their charm, however, made up for their lack of beauty. The Prince [Carl Lichnowsky] and I are going to breakfast there today; we shall then see Naumann and then the chapel. Tomorrow or the day after we shall leave for Leipzig. After receiving this letter you must write to Berlin, Poste Restante. I trust that you got my letter from Prague. All the Neumanns and the

*Dresden,
13 April 1789
at seven o'clock
in the morning*

Duscheks send their greetings to you and also to my brother-in-law Lange and his wife.

Dearest little wife, if only I had a letter from you! If I were to tell you all the things I do with your dear portrait, I think that you would often laugh. For instance, when I take it out of its case, I say 'Good-day, Stanzerl! – Good-day, little rascal, pussy-pussy, little turned-up noise, little bagatelle, Schluck and Druck', and when I put it away again, I let it slip in very slowly, saying all the time, 'Nu – Nu – Nu – Nu!' with the peculiar *emphasis* which this word so full of meaning demands, and then just at the last, quickly, 'Good night, little mouse, sleep well'. Well, I suppose I have been writing something very foolish (to the world at all events); but to us who love each other so dearly, it is not foolish at all. Today is the sixth day since I left you and by Heaven! it seems a year. I expect you will have some difficulty here and there in reading my letter, because I am writing in a hurry and therefore rather badly. Adieu, my only love! The carriage is waiting. This time I do not say: 'Hurrah – the carriage has come at last', but *'male'*. Farewell, and love me for ever as I love you. I kiss you a million times most lovingly and am ever your husband who loves you tenderly

W. A. Mozart

PS. – How is our Carl behaving? Well, I hope. Kiss him for me. All sorts of kind messages to Herr and Frau von Puchberg. Remember, you must not regulate the length of your letters by that of mine. Mine are rather short, but only because I am in a hurry. If I were not, I should cover a whole sheet. But you have more leisure. Adieu.

Dresden,
16 April 1789

... Dear little wife, I have a number of requests to make.

(1) I beg you not to be melancholy,

(2) *to take care of your health* and *to beware of* the spring breezes,

(3) not to go out walking alone – and preferably not to *go out walking* at all,

(4) to feel absolutely assured of my love. Up to the present I have not written a single letter to you without placing your dear portrait before me.

(5) I beg you in your conduct not only to be careful of *your honour* and *mine*, but also to consider *appearances*. Do not be angry with me for asking this. You ought to love me even more for thus valuing your honour.

(6) and lastly I beg you to send me more details in your letters. I should very much like to know whether our brother-in-law Hofer came to see us the day after my departure? Whether he comes very often, as he promised me he would? Whether the Langes come sometimes? Whether progress is being made with the portrait? What sort of life you are leading? All these things are naturally of great interest to me ...

Dearest, most beloved little Wife of my Heart!

Well, I trust that you will by now have received some letters from me, for they can't all have been lost. This time I can't write very much to you, as I have to pay some calls and I am only sending you this to announce my arrival. I shall probably be able to leave by the 25th; at least I shall do my best to do so. But I shall let you know definitely before then. I shall quite certainly get away by the 27th. Oh, how glad I shall be to be with you again, my darling! But the first thing I shall do is to take you by your front curls; for how on earth could you think, or even imagine, that I had forgotten you? How could I possibly do so? For even *supposing* such a thing, you will get on the very first night a thorough spanking on your dear little kissable arse, and this you may count upon.

Adieu.

> Ever your only friend and your husband
> who loves you with all his heart   W. A. Mozart

Berlin,
19 May 1789

Mozart to Michael Puchberg

Dearest Friend and Brother!

Since the time when you rendered me that great and friendly service, I have been living in such *misery*, that for very grief not only have I not been able to go out, but I could not even write.

At the moment she is easier, and if *she had not contracted bed-sores*, which make her condition most wretched, she would be able to sleep. The only fear is that the bone may be affected. She is extraordinarily resigned and awaits recovery or death with true philosophic calm. My tears flow as I write. Come and see us, most beloved friend, if you can; and, *if you can*, give me your advice and help *in the matter you know of*.   Mozart

Vienna,
second half of July,
1789

Mozart to his Wife at Baden

Dearest little Wife!

I was delighted to get your dear letter – and I trust that you received yesterday my second one together with the infusion, the electuaries and the ants' eggs. I shall sail off to you at five o'clock tomorrow morning. Were it not for the joy of seeing you again and embracing you, I should not drive out to Baden just yet, for 'Figaro' is going to be performed very soon, and as I have some alterations to make, my presence will be required at the rehearsals. I shall probably have to be back here by the 19th. But to stay here until the 19th *without you* would be quite impossible. Dear little wife! I want to talk to you quite frankly. You have no reason whatever to be unhappy. You have a husband who loves you and does all he possibly can for you. As for your foot, you must just be patient and it will surely get well again. I am glad

Vienna,
first half of August,
1789

indeed when you have some fun – of course I am – but I do wish that you would not sometimes make yourself so cheap. In my opinion you are too free and easy with N.N. [name erased] ... and it was the same with N.N., when he was still at Baden. Now please remember that N.N. are not half so familiar with other women, whom they perhaps know more intimately, as they are with you. Why, N.N. who is usually a well-conducted fellow and particularly respectful to women, must have been misled by your behaviour into writing the most disgusting and most impertinent sottises which he put into his letter. A woman must always make herself respected, or else people will begin to talk about her. My love! Forgive me for being so frank, but my peace of mind demands it as well as our mutual happiness. Remember that you yourself once admitted to me that you were inclined to *comply too easily*. You know the consequences of that. Remember too the promise you gave to me. Oh, God, do try, my love! Be merry and happy and charming to me. Do not torment yourself and me with unnecessary jealousy. Believe in my love, for surely you have proofs of it, and you will see how happy we shall be. Rest assured that it is only by her prudent behaviour that a wife can enchain her husband. Adieu. Tomorrow I shall kiss you most tenderly.   Mozart

Detail of an anonymous portrait of Joseph II, probably painted in 1790, the year of the Emperor's death. Joseph's liberal intentions, though partly undermined by his own irritable and autocratic character, had been of immense benefit to Viennese society and culture, and he had been one of Mozart's earliest – and most loyal – patrons.

Mozart to Archduke Francis[1]

Your Royal Highness,

I make so bold as to beg your Royal Highness very respectfully to use your most gracious influence with His Majesty the King with regard to my most humble

Vienna, during the first half of May, 1790

1 This is the unfinished draft of a petition to the Archduke Francis to use his influence with his father, King Leopold II, who had succeeded to the throne on 13 March 1790, and was crowned Holy Roman Emperor on 9 October.

petition to His Majesty. Prompted by a desire for fame, by a love of work and by a conviction of my wide knowledge, I venture to apply for the post of second Kapell-meister, particularly as Salieri, that very gifted Kapellmeister, has never devoted himself to church music, whereas from my youth up I have made myself completely familiar with this style. The slight reputation which I have acquired in the world by my pianoforte playing, has encouraged me to ask His Majesty for the favour of being entrusted with the musical education of the Royal Family. In the sure convic-tion that I have applied to the most worthy mediators who, moreover, are particu-larly gracious to me, I am full of confidence and . . .

The Rauhensteingasse in Vienna showing (left) the house in which Mozart died. Constanze had moved into this house in September 1790, shortly after Mozart left for the coronation of Leopold II in Frankfurt. Early 19th-century watercolour by J. Wohlmuth.

Mozart to his Wife at Baden

Dearest little Wife!

    I trust that you have received my letter. Well, I must scold you a little, my love! Even if it is not possible for you to get a letter from me, you could write all the same; for must all your letters be *replies* to mine? I was most certainly expecting a letter from my dear little wife – but unfortunately I was mistaken. Well, you must make amends and I advise you to do so, otherwise I shall never, never forgive you. Yesterday I was at the second part of 'Cosa rara', but I did not like it as much as 'Die Antons'. If you return to Vienna on Saturday, you will be able to spend Sunday morning here. We have been invited to a service and to lunch at Schwechat. Adieu – Take care of your health. A propos. N.N. (you know whom I mean) is a cad. He

Vienna?, 2 June 1790

is very pleasant to my face, but he runs down 'Figaro' in public – and has treated me most abominably in the matters you know of – *I know it for certain.*

Your husband, who loves you with all his heart,

Mozart

Dearest, most beloved little Wife!

I simply cannot describe my delight at receiving your last letter of the 6th, which told me that you are well and in good health, and that, very sensibly, you are not taking baths every day. Heavens! How delighted I should have been if you had come

Vienna,
7 June 1791

By turns actor, singer, playwright and theatre manager, Emanuel Schikaneder (1751–1812) wrote the libretto for Die Zauberflöte *in which he also sang the role of Papageno when the opera was premièred in his theatre in a Vienna suburb. Engraving by Philipp Richter.*

to me with the Wildburgs! Indeed I was wild with myself for not telling you to drive into town – but I was afraid of the expense. Yet it would have been *charmant* if you had done so. At five o'clock tomorrow morning, we are all driving out, three carriagefuls of us, and so between nine and ten I expect to find in your arms all the joy which only a man can feel who loves his wife as I do! It is only a pity that I can't take with me either the clavier or the bird! That is why I would rather have gone out alone; but, as it is, I can't get out of the arrangement without offending the company.

I lunched yesterday with Süssmayr at the 'Ungarische Krone', as I still had business in town at one o'clock, – as S— has to lunch early and Mme S—, who wanted me very much to lunch with them one of these days, had an engagement at Schönbrunn. Today I am lunching with Schikaneder, for you know, you too were invited.

So far I have had no letter from Mme Duschek; but I shall enquire again today. I can't find out anything about your dress, as I have not seen the Wildburgs since. If it is at all possible, I shall certainly bring your hat with me. Adieu, my little sweetheart. I simply cannot tell you how I am looking forward to tomorrow. Ever your

Mozart

Ma trés chere Epouse!

Criés avec moi contre mon mauvais sort! Mlle Kirchgessner ne donne pas son academie lundi! Par consequent j'aurais pu vous posseder, ma chère, tout ce jour de dimanche. Mercredi je viendrai sûrement. *Vienna, 11 June 1791*

I must hurry, as it is already a quarter to seven – and the coach leaves at seven. When you are bathing, do take care not to slip and never stay in alone. If I were you I should occasionally omit a day in order not to do the cure too violently. I trust that someone slept with you last night. I cannot tell you what I would not give to be with you at Baden instead of being stuck here. From sheer boredom I composed today an aria for my opera [*Die Zauberflöte*]. I got up as early as half past four. Wonderful to relate, I have got back my watch – but – as I have no key, I have unfortunately not been able to wind it. What a nuisance! Schlumbla! That is a word to ponder on. Well, I wound *our big clock* instead. Adieu – my love! I am lunching today with Puchberg. I kiss you a thousand times and say with you in thought: 'Death and despair were his reward!'

Ever your loving husband

W. A. Mozart

See that Carl behaves himself. Give him kisses from me.

Take an electuary if you are constipated – not otherwise. Take care of yourself in the morning and evening, if it is chilly.

Ma trés chere Épouse!

I have this moment received your letter, which has given me extraordinary pleasure. I am now longing for a second one to tell me how the baths are affecting you. I too am sorry not to have been present yesterday at your fine concert, not on account of the music, but because I should have been so happy to be with you. I gave . . . a surprise today. First of all I went to the Rehbergs. Well, Frau Rehberg sent one of her daughters upstairs to tell him that a dear old friend had come from Rome and had searched all the houses in the town without being able to find him. He sent down a message to say, would I please wait for a few minutes. Meanwhile the poor fellow put on his Sunday best, his finest clothes, and turned up with his *Vienna, 25 June 1791* hair most elaborately dressed. You can imagine how we made fun of him. I can never resist making a fool of someone – if it is not . . ., then it must be . . . or Snai. And where did I sleep? At home, of course. And I slept very well, save that the mice kept me most excellent company. Why, I had a first-rate argument with them. I was up before five o'clock. A propos, I advise you not to go to Mass tomorrow. Those peasant louts are too cheeky for my taste. True, you have a rough *compagnon*, but the peasants don't respect him, *perdunt respectum*, as they see at once that he is a silly ass – Snai!

I shall give a verbal reply to Süssmayr. I would rather not waste paper on him.

Tell Krügel or Klüsel that you would like to have better food. Perhaps, when you are passing, you could speak to him yourself. That would be even better. He is a good fellow in other ways and respects me.

Tomorrow I shall join the procession to the Josefstadt, holding a candle in my hand! – Snai!

Do not forget my warnings about the morning and evening air and about bathing too long. My kind regards to Count and Countess Wagensperg. Adieu. I kiss you one thousand times in thought and am ever

your

Mozart

PS. – Perhaps after all it would be well to give Carl a little rhubarb. Why did you not send me that long letter? Here is a letter for him – I should like to have an answer. Catch – Catch – bis – bis – bs – bs – kisses are flying about for you – bs – why, another one is staggering after the rest!

I have this moment received your second letter. Beware of the baths! And do sleep more – and not so irregularly, or I shall worry – I am a little anxious as it is. Adieu.

Mozart to Michael Puchberg

Dearest, most beloved Friend!

Vienna,
25 June 1791

Most honourable Brother!

Business has prevented me from having the pleasure of calling on you today. I have a request to make. My wife writes to say that she can see that, although they are not expecting it, the people with whom she is living would be glad to receive some payment for her board and lodging and she begs me to send her some money. I had intended to settle everything when it was time for her to leave and I now find myself in very great embarrassment. I should not like to expose her to any unpleasantness; yet at the moment I cannot leave myself short of money. If you, most beloved friend, can assist me with a small sum, which I can send to her at once, you will oblige me exceedingly. I require the loan only for a few days, when you will receive 2000 gulden in my name, from which you can then refund yourself.

Ever your   Mozart[1]

Mozart to his Wife at Baden

Ma trés chere Epouse!

I trust that you are very well. I have just remembered that you have *very seldom* been upset during pregnancy. Perhaps the baths are having a too laxative effect? I should not wait for *certain proofs*, which would be too unpleasant. My advice is that you should stop them now! Then I should feel quite easy in my mind. Today is the day when you are not supposed to take one and yet I wager that that little wife of mine has been to the baths? *Seriously* – I had much rather you would prolong your cure well into the autumn. I hope that you got my first little note.

Vienna,
2 July 1791

Please tell that idiotic fellow Süssmayr to send me my score of the first act, from the introduction to the finale, so that I may orchestrate it. It would be a good thing if he could put it together today and dispatch it by the first coach tomorrow, for I should then have it at noon. I have just had a visit from a couple of Englishmen who refused to leave Vienna without making my acquaintance. But of course the real truth is that they wanted to meet that great fellow Süssmayr and only came to see me in order to find out where he lived, as they had heard that I was fortunate enough to enjoy his favour. I told them to go to the 'Ungarische Krone' and to wait there until he should return from Baden! Snai! They want to engage him to clean the lamps. I am longing most ardently for news of you. It is half past twelve already and I have heard nothing. I shall wait a little longer before sealing my letter … Nothing has come, so I must close it! Farewell, dearest, most beloved little wife! Take care of your health, for as long as you are well and are kind to me, I don't care a fig if everything else goes wrong. Follow the advice I gave you at the beginning of this letter and farewell. Adieu – a thousand kisses for you and a thousand boxes on the ear for Lacci Bacci. Ever your   Mozart

Dearest, most beloved little Wife of my heart!

I received your letter together with Montecucoli's and am delighted to hear that you are well and in good spirits. I thought as much. If you take the baths twice in succession, you will be thoroughly spanked when I come out to you again! Thanks for the finale you sent and my clothes, but I cannot understand why you did not put in a letter. I searched all the pockets in the coat and trousers. Well, perhaps the post-woman is still carrying it about in her pocket! I am only delighted that you

Vienna,
3 July 1791
Sunday

---

1 Puchberg noted on this letter, 'sent *eodem die* 25 gulden'.

are in good health, my dear little wife. I rely on your following my advice. If you do, I can feel a little calmer! As for my health, I feel pretty well. I trust that my affairs will improve as rapidly as possible. Until they are settled I cannot be quite easy in my mind. But I hope to be so soon.

I trust that Süssmayr will not forget to copy out at once what I left for him; and I am counting on receiving today those portions of my score for which I asked. I see from . . .'s Latin letter that neither of you is drinking any wine. I don't like that. Have a word with your supervisor, who no doubt will only be too delighted to give you some on my account. It is a wholesome wine and not expensive, whereas the water is horrid. I lunched yesterday at Schikaneder's with the Lieutenant-Colonel, who is also taking the Antony baths. Today I am lunching with Puchberg. Adieu, little sweetheart. Dear Stanzi Marini, I must close in haste, for I have just heard one o'clock strike; and you know that Puchberg likes to lunch early. Adieu. Ever your

Mozart

Lots of kisses for Carl – and whippings for . . .[1]

Dearest, most beloved little Wife!

I have this moment returned from the opera, which was as full as ever. As usual the duet 'Mann und Weib' and Papageno's glockenspiel in Act I had to be repeated and also the trio of the boys in Act II. But what always gives me most pleasure is the *silent approval*! You can see how this opera is becoming more and more esteemed. Now for an account of my own doings. Immediately after your departure I played two games of billiards with Herr von Mozart, the fellow who wrote the opera which is running at Schikaneder's theatre; then I sold my nag for fourteen ducats; then I told Joseph to get Primus to fetch me some black coffee, with which I smoked a splendid pipe of tobacco; and then I orchestrated almost the whole of Stadler's rondo [from K622]. Meanwhile I have had a letter which Stadler has sent me from Prague. All the Duscheks are well. I really think that she cannot have received a single one of your letters – and yet I can hardly believe it. Well, they have all heard already about the splendid reception of my German opera. And the strangest thing of all is that on the very evening when my new opera was performed for the first time with such success, 'Tito' was given in Prague for the last time with tremendous applause. Bedini sang better than ever. The little duet in A major which the two maidens sing was repeated; and had not the audience wished to spare Madame Marchetti, a repetition of the rondo would have been very welcome. Cries of 'Bravo' were shouted at Stodla from the parterre and even from the orchestra – 'What a miracle for Bohemia!' he writes, 'but indeed I *did my very best*.' Stodla

---

1 Probably Süssmayr.

writes too that Süssmayr . . . but I now see that he is an ass – . . ., I mean, not Stodla, who is only a bit of an ass – but . . ., why, he is a full-blown ass. At half past five I left my room and took my favourite walk by the Glacis to the theatre. But what do I see? What do I smell? Why, here is Don Primus with the cutlets! Che gusto! Now I am eating to your health! It is just striking eleven. Perhaps you are already asleep? St! St! St! I won't wake you.

Saturday, the 8th. You should have seen me at supper yesterday! I couldn't find the old tablecloth, so I fished out one as white as a snowdrop, and put in front of me the double candlestick with wax candles. According to Stadler's letter the Italians are done for in Vienna. Further, Madame Duschek must have got *one* letter from you, for he says: 'The lady was very well pleased with Mathies' postscript. She said: "I like the ASS, or A-S-S, as he is".' Do urge . . . to write something for . . ., for he has begged me very earnestly to see to this. As I write, no doubt you will be having a good swim. The friseur came punctually at six o'clock. At half past five Primus had lit the fire and he then woke me up at a quarter to six. Why must it rain just now? I did so much hope that you would have lovely weather. Do keep very warm, so that you may not catch a cold. I hope that these baths will help you to keep well

Die Zauberflöte, Act I, scene 8: Tamino, Papageno and the Three Ladies. A coloured engraving by Joseph and Peter Schaffer, published in Brno in 1795 but dating from about 1793 and perhaps recording the performance of the opera in Brno in that year.

The frontispiece from the libretto of Die Zauberflöte, *engraved by Alberti in 1791.*

during the winter. For only the desire to see you in good health made me urge you to go to Baden. I already feel lonely without you. I knew I should. If I had had nothing to do, I should have gone off at once to spend the week with you, but I have *no facilities for working at Baden*, and I am anxious, as far as possible, to avoid all risk of *money difficulties*. For the most pleasant thing of all is to have a mind at peace. To achieve this, however, one must work hard; and I like hard work. Give . . . a few sound boxes on the ear from me, and I ask . . ., whom I kiss a thousand times, to give him a couple too. For Heaven's sake do not let him starve in this respect. The last thing in the world I could wish would be his reproach that you had not treated or looked after him properly. Rather give him too many blows than too few. It would be a good thing if you were to leave a bump on his nose, or knock out an eye, or inflict some other visible injury, so that the fellow may never be able to deny that he has got something from you.

Adieu, dear little wife! The coach is just going. I trust that I shall have a letter from you today and in this sweet hope I kiss you a thousand times and am ever

your loving husband

W. A. Mozart

Dearest, most beloved little Wife,

I was exceedingly delighted and overjoyed to find your letter on my return from
the opera. Although Saturday, as it is post-day, is always a bad night, the opera was
performed to a full house and with the usual applause and repetition of numbers.
It will be given again tomorrow, but there will be no performance on Monday. So
Süssmayr may bring Stoll in on *Tuesday* when it will be given again *for the first
time*. I say *for the first time*, because it will probably be performed again several
times in succession. I have just swallowed a delicious slice of sturgeon which Don
Primus (who is my faithful valet) has brought me; and as I have a rather voracious
appetite today, I have sent him off again to fetch some more if he can. So during
this interval I shall go on writing to you. This morning I worked so hard at my
composition that I went on until half past one. So I dashed off in great haste to
Hofer, simply in order not to lunch alone, where I found Mamma too. After lunch
I went home at once and composed again until it was time to go to the opera.
Leutgeb begged me to take him a second time and I did so. I am taking *Mamma*
tomorrow. Hofer has already given her the libretto to read. In her case what will
probably happen will be that she will *see* the opera, but not *hear* it. The ... had a
box this evening ... applauded *everything* most heartily. But he, the know-all,
showed himself to be such a thorough *Bavarian* that I could not remain or I should
have had to call him an ass. Unfortunately I was there just when the second act
began, that is, at the solemn scene. He laughed at everything. At first I was patient
enough to draw his attention to a few passages. But he laughed at everything. Well,
I could stand it no longer. I called him a Papageno and cleared out. But I don't
think that the idiot understood my remark. So I went into another box where *Flamm*
and his wife happened to be. There everything was very pleasant and I stayed to
the end. But during Papageno's aria with the glockenspiel I went behind the scenes,
as I felt a sort of impulse today to play it myself. Well, just for fun, at the point
where Schikaneder has a pause, I played an arpeggio. He was startled, looked behind
the wings and saw me. When he had his next pause, I played no arpeggio. This time
he stopped and refused to go on. I guessed what he was thinking and again played
a chord. He then struck the glockenspiel and said '*Shut up*'. Whereupon everyone
laughed. I am inclined to think that this joke taught many of the audience for the
first time that Papageno does not play the instrument himself. By the way, you have
no idea how charming the music sounds when you hear it from a box close to the
orchestra – it sounds much better than from the gallery. As soon as you return –
you must try this for yourself.

Sunday, at seven o'clock in the morning. I have slept very well and hope that you
too have done the same. I have just enjoyed thoroughly my half of a capon which
friend Primus has brought back with him. I am going to the service at the Piarists

*Vienna,
8–9 October 1791
Saturday night at
half past ten o'clock*

at ten o'clock, for Leutgeb has told me that I can then have a word with the Director; and I shall stay to lunch.

Primus told me last night that a great many people in Baden are ill. Is this true? Do take care and don't trust the weather. Well, Primus has just returned with the tiresome news that the coach left today before seven o'clock and that there won't be another one until the afternoon. So all my writing at night and in the early morning has been to no purpose and you will not get my letter until this evening, which is very annoying. I shall certainly come out next Sunday, when we shall all visit the Casino and come home together on Monday. Lechleitner was again at the opera. Though he is no connoisseur, he is at any rate a genuine lover of music, which N.N. is not. He is really a nonentity and much prefers a dinée. Farewell, my love – I kiss you millions of times and am ever your

Mozart

PS. – Kiss Sophie for me. I send Süssmayr a few good *nose-pulls* and a proper *hair-tug* and Stoll a thousand greetings. Adieu. The hour is striking – Farewell – We shall meet again.

NB. – You probably sent the two pairs of yellow winter stockings for the boots to the laundry, for Joseph and I have hunted for them in vain! *Adieu.*

Dearest, most beloved little Wife,

Vienna,
14 October 1791

Hofer drove out with me yesterday, Thursday the 13th, to see our Carl.[1] We lunched there and then we all drove back to Vienna. At six o'clock I called in the carriage for Salieri and Madame Cavalieri – and drove them to my box. Then I drove back quickly to fetch Mamma and Carl, whom I had left at Hofer's. You can hardly imagine how charming they were and how much they liked not only my music, but the libretto and everything. They both said that it was an *operone*, worthy to be performed for the grandest festival and before the greatest monarch, and that they would often go to see it, as they had never seen a more beautiful or delightful show. Salieri listened and watched most attentively and from the overture to the last chorus there was not a single number that did not call forth from him a bravo! or bello! It seemed as if they could not thank me enough for my kindness. They had intended in any case to go to the opera yesterday. But they would have had to be in their places by four o'clock. As it was, they saw and heard everything in comfort in my box. When it was over I drove them home and then had supper at Hofer's with Carl. Then I drove him home and we both slept soundly. Carl was absolutely delighted at being taken to the opera. He is looking splendid. As far as health is

1 Carl Mozart was at school in Perchtoldsdorf, a suburb of Vienna.

concerned, he could not be in a better place, but everything else there is wretched, alas! All they can do is to turn out a good peasant into the world. But enough of this. As his serious studies (God help them!) do not begin until Monday, I have arranged to keep him until after lunch on Sunday. I told them that you would like to see him. So tomorrow, Saturday, I shall drive out with Carl to see you. You can then keep him, or I shall take him back to Heeger's after lunch. Think it over. A month can hardly do him much harm. In the meantime the arrangement with the Piarists, which is now under discussion, may come to something. On the whole, Carl is no worse; but at the same time he is not one whit better than he was. He still has his old bad manners; he never stops chattering just as he used to do in the past; and he is, if anything, *less inclined to learn than before*, for out there [at Perchtoldsdorf] all he does is to wander about in the garden for five hours in the morning and five hours in the afternoon, as he has himself confessed. In short, the children do nothing but eat, drink, sleep and go for walks. Leutgeb and Hofer are with me at the moment. The former is staying to supper with me. I have sent out my faithful comrade Primus to fetch some food from the Bürgerspital. I am quite satisfied with the fellow. He has only let me down once, when I was obliged to sleep at Hofer's, which annoyed me intensely, as they sleep far too long there. I am happiest at home, for I am accustomed to my own hours. This one occasion put me in a very bad humour. Yesterday the whole day was taken up with that trip to Bernstorf, so I could not write to you. But that you have not written to me for two days, is really unforgivable. I hope that I shall certainly have a letter from you today, and that tomorrow I shall talk to you and embrace you with all my heart.

Farewell. Ever your

Mozart

I kiss Sophie a thousand times. Do what you like with N.N. Adieu.

Mozart died on 5 December 1791. Among those who attended him in his last illness was Constanze's youngest sister, Sophie Haibel, who many years later wrote the following account in a letter to Constanze's second husband, Georg Nissen, then collecting material for his biography of Mozart.

Now I must tell you about Mozart's last days. Well, Mozart became fonder and fonder of our dear departed mother and she of him. Indeed he often came running along in great haste to the Wieden (where she and I were lodging at the Goldner Pflug), carrying under his arm a little bag containing coffee and sugar, which he would hand to our good mother, saying, 'Here, mother dear, now you can have a little "Jause".' She used to be as delighted as a child. He did this very often. In short, Mozart in the end never came to see us without bringing something.

Diakovar,
7 April 1825

The suburban setting of St. Marx, where Mozart's remains were interred in the local cemetery: coloured engraving (1792) by Johann Ziegler.

Now when Mozart fell ill, we both made him a night-jacket which he could put on frontways, since on account of his swollen condition he was unable to turn in bed. Then, as we didn't know how seriously ill he was, we also made him a quilted dressing-gown (though indeed his dear wife, my sister, had given us the materials for both garments), so that when he got up he should have everything he needed. We often visited him and he was really delighted with the dressing-gown. I used to go into town every day to see him. Well, one Saturday when I was with him, Mozart said to me: 'Dear Sophie, do tell Mamma that I am fairly well and that I shall be able to go and congratulate her in the octave of her name-day.' Who could have been more delighted than I to bring such cheerful news to my mother, when she could barely expect the news? I hurried home therefore to comfort her, the more so as he himself really seemed to be bright and happy. The following day was a

Sunday. I was young then and rather vain, I confess, and liked to dress up. But I never cared to go out walking from our suburb into town in my fine clothes, and I had no money for a drive. So I said to our good mother: 'Dear Mamma, I'm not going to see Mozart today. He was so well yesterday that surely he will be even better today, and one day more or less won't make much difference.' Well, my mother said: 'Listen to this. Make me a cup of coffee and then I'll tell you what you ought to do.' She was rather inclined to keep me at home; and indeed my sister knows how much I had to be with her. I went into the kitchen. The fire was out. I had to light the lamp and make a fire. All the time I was thinking of Mozart. I had made the coffee and the lamp was still burning. Then I noticed how wasteful I had been with my lamp, I mean, that I had burned so much wax. It was still burning brightly. I stared into the flame and thought to myself, 'How I should love to know how Mozart is.' While I was thinking and gazing at the flame, it went out, as completely as if the lamp had never been burning. Not a spark remained on the big wick and yet there wasn't the slightest draught – that I can swear to. A horrible feeling came over me. I ran to our mother and told her all. She said, 'Well, take off your fine clothes and go into town and bring me back news of him at once. But be sure not to delay.' I hurried along as fast as I could. Alas, how frightened I was when my sister, who was almost despairing and yet trying to keep calm, came out to me, saying: 'Thank God that you have come, dear Sophie. Last night he was so ill that I thought he would not be alive this morning. Do stay with me today, for if he has another bad turn, he will pass away tonight. Go in to him for a little while and see how he is.' I tried to control myself and went to his bedside. He immediately called me to him and said: 'Ah, dear Sophie, how glad I am that you have come. You must stay here tonight and see me die.' I tried hard to be brave and to persuade him to the contrary. But to all my attempts he only replied: 'Why, I have already the taste of death on my tongue.' And, 'if you do not stay, who will support my dearest Constanze if you don't stay here?' 'Yes, yes, dear Mozart,' I assured him, 'but I must first go back to our mother and tell her that you would like me to stay with you today. Otherwise she will think that some misfortune has befallen you.' 'Yes, do so,' said Mozart, 'but be sure and come back soon.' Good God, how distressed I felt! My poor sister followed me to the door and begged me for Heaven's sake to go to the priests at St. Peter's and implore one of them to come to Mozart – a chance call, as it were. I did so, but for a long time they refused to come and I had a great deal of trouble to persuade one of those clerical brutes to go to him. Then I ran off to my mother who was anxiously awaiting me. It was already dark. Poor soul, how shocked she was! I persuaded her to go and spend the night with her eldest daughter, the late Josepha Hofer. I then ran back as fast as I could to my distracted sister. Süssmayr was at Mozart's bedside. The well-known Requiem lay on the quilt and Mozart was explaining to him how, in his opinion, he ought to finish it, when he was gone. Further, he urged his wife to keep his death a secret until she should have informed Albrechtsberger, for the post should be his before God and the world. A long search was made for Dr. Closset, who was found at the theatre, but who had to wait for the end of the play. He came and ordered *cold* poultices to be placed on Mozart's burning head, which, however, affected him to such an extent that he became unconscious and remained so until he died. His last movement was an attempt to express with his mouth the drum passages in the Requiem. That I can still hear. Müller from the Art Gallery came and took a cast of his pale, dead face. Words fail me, dearest brother, to describe how his devoted wife in her utter misery threw herself on her knees and implored the Almighty for His aid. She simply could not tear herself away from Mozart, however much I begged her to do so. If it was possible to increase her sorrow, this was done on the day after that dreadful night, when crowds of people passed by and wept and wailed for him. All my life I have never seen Mozart in a temper, still less, angry.

The approach to Schönbrunn, main official residence of the Habsburg emperors. Mozart performed Der Schauspieldirektor *in the Orangerie here in 1786. Engraving by Carl Schütz, 1783.*

Music Notes

The works included on the CDs that accompany this volume have been selected to complement those accompanying the first volume on Mozart *in the Everyman series.*

CD1   *Der Schauspieldirektor* (The Impresario), Overture

Between the age of eleven and the year of his death, Mozart produced overtures or introductions for nineteen theatrical works, of which none is more concise or more sparkling than the one he wrote for the curious little theatrical extravaganza *Der Schauspieldirektor* in 1786. Written at the command of the Emperor Joseph II for a fête he was giving at the Schönbrunn Palace for his sister Marie Christine and her husband the Duke of Saxe-Teschen, this was performed, after a spectacular banquet, at one end of the Orangerie, and followed (after the chairs had all been turned round) by a performance of Salieri's *Prima la musica, e poi le parole* (First the music, then the words) at the other end.

    Salieri's contribution appears to have been received with greater applause, but then Salieri was the official composer with a string of operatic successes to his credit in Vienna, and the libretto he used on this occasion not only provided him with the text for a fully composed short opera but was also exceptionally well-written –

so well, in fact, that it turned up again 150 years later as the starting-point for Richard Strauss's last opera, *Capriccio*. By contrast, Mozart was still making his name in Vienna and had only produced one opera there, *Die Entführung aus dem Serail*. His text (by the librettist of *Die Entführung*, Gottlieb Stephanie) was really no more than a spoken comedy with musical numbers: it dealt, at considerable length, with the backstage squabbles of rival actresses and singers over precedence and pay, and included auditions of scenes from three spoken plays as well as an aria each for the two rival sopranos, a trio in which they are only kept from one another's throats by the efforts of the tenor, and a closing ensemble that also provides a semi-singing part for the impresario himself.

All the music is charming, sometimes more than that, and ideally suited to its purpose, with the result that many attempts have been made over the years to reduce Stephanie's text to manageable proportions – with varying success. But the Overture which precedes the play is one of Mozart's mature best, a beautifully economical symphonic structure with a fizzing C major opening and a particularly beguiling second theme in contrast. It is not difficult to feel the approach of *Figaro* only three months later.

Canzonetta, 'Ridente la calma' (K152)

Mozart is not particularly thought of as a song writer, though the Köchel catalogue lists no fewer than thirty-five songs and other short pieces for solo voice and piano. Not much seems to be known about the little canzonetta included here: it was probably written at Salzburg in 1775, after Mozart and his father had returned from their various Italian journeys, at about the time of the performance of *La finta giardiniera* in Munich. It was no doubt intended for a local singer or friend of the Mozart family, and has probably never been better sung than in this performance by Elisabeth Schwarzkopf, recorded in 1955.

Serenade for Thirteen Wind Instruments in B flat major (K361)

The Serenade in B flat was long thought to be one of the last works Mozart wrote for Salzburg before leaving the service of Archbishop Colloredo in May 1781. That would put it between *Idomeneo* (K366) and *Die Entführung aus dem Serail* (K384), and there seem to be hints of both operas, in the exquisite melody of the Adagio, recalling *Idomeneo*, and the Turkish music of the finale which is pure *Entführung*. The traditional dating is now disputed, however, and all we know for certain is that the work came into existence before 1784. Nevertheless, the operatic comparisons are still relevant. Like most of Mozart's purely instrumental compositions, the

Serenade, while written idiomatically for the instruments involved, often suggests vocal parts, and the music has the colour and dramatic immediacy we are used to in his operas.

It is scored for two oboes, two clarinets, two basset horns, four French horns, two bassoons and double bass, the last instrument sometimes replaced by a double bassoon. The omission of flutes and the weighting of French horns and bassoons gives the work a firm and, at times, even dark texture, sharpened by oboes and infused with a marvellously liquid quality by clarinets and basset horns, often playing in thirds and sixths in a manner reminiscent of yet another opera, *Così fan tutte*. Virtuosity is required from all the players, but the clarinets have an especially important role, so perhaps it isn't surprising that four of the seven movements, including the opening Allegro, the first Minuet, the Adagio and the

A silhouette of Count Wallerstein's wind band from about 1785. As usual with such ensembles, the band is supplemented with a string bass. This is the sort of ensemble for which K361 was composed.

Rondo finale, were performed at a benefit concert for Mozart's friend and colleague, the clarinettist Anton Stadler, on 23 March 1784; those are the movements reproduced here.

The most celebrated of Mozart's many serenades is the *Eine kleine Nachtmusik* (K525) and, as the title of that work suggests, the genre was originally conceived as a kind of night – or rather evening – entertainment. In the later eighteenth century it became virtually interchangeable with the divertimento and the cassation, all forms meant to accompany other activities or written for special occasions, such as the wedding which gave its name to the 'Haffner' Serenade. These pieces were often scored for wind instruments to make the sound carry further when performed out of doors. We can therefore imagine K361 being played at an afternoon party, or in an aristocratic garden on a summer evening, while guests talk and mingle.

At least, we might imagine such a situation, if it weren't for the fact that the extraordinary quality of this work makes it hard to believe that anyone would treat it as mere background music. Many of Mozart's serenades are suitable for that purpose, but not K361. With seven movements, and lasting more than forty-five minutes, it is a work on the largest scale, but the length is less important than the symphonic proportions and expressive power of each section.

Formally, the serenade comes somewhere between the symphony and the suite. While more than a series of dance movements, it is normally less than a fully-fledged sonata structure. In K361, however, Mozart combines elements of both. After a slow introduction, alternating grand chords and syncopated melodic phrases, the vigorous opening Allegro molto appears to follow conventional form – i.e., statement of themes, development and recapitulation – but with an unexpected twist, in that Mozart continues to develop the themes in the recapitulation and adds a fine coda to wind up the movement.

The following Minuet with two Trios is more like a typical serenade movement, though even here the sinuous chromatic lines and shifting harmonies raise it far above the conventional level. Especially charming is the first Trio, scored for clarinets and basset horns only, dancing a rustic minuet of their own. But once again Mozart produces a surprise, this time in the second Trio, turning what at first appears to be no more than an accompaniment figure in running triplets into the basis for a miniature symphonic development.

It is in the third movement, however, that the work reaches sublime heights – a point acknowledged in Peter Schaffer's play *Amadeus* where this music accompanies Salieri's realization that he can never compete with a composer who is divinely inspired. Whatever one thinks of the fictional Salieri's deduction, there is no doubt that this Adagio for oboe, clarinet and basset horn over throbbing accompaniment represents a high point in Mozart's music, recalling not only *Idomeneo* but also the famous trio in *Così*. As so often in Mozart, one can only wonder at the intensity he generates from the simplest materials: the opening statement of the common chord, the repeated notes of the accompaniment, a melody which consists of little more than a decorated scale.

The Rondo (Allegro molto) which concludes the work could hardly be in sharper contrast to the sustained beauty of the Adagio, using spiky melodic fragments, frequently repeated, and abrupt dynamic contrasts to fine comic effect. The writing for bassoons is especially striking in this movement, exploiting their humorous potential to the full.

Sonata in D major for Two Pianos (K448)

Mozart composed a considerable amount of music for four hands at one keyboard – notably the magnificent F major Sonata (K497) which is really a piano symphony – but he also wrote fine works for two players at two keyboards, including the delightful Concerto in E flat (K365) and this Sonata in D.

As it happens, the two-piano sonata has an amusing genesis which can be followed in the composer's letters. In the summer of 1781, Mozart moved from Salzburg to Vienna. He was working on his opera, *Die Entführung*, and living in the house of the Weber family where he fell in love with Constanze Weber. When Mozart's father, Leopold, disapproving of his entanglement with the Webers, insisted that he leave their house, Wolfgang complied and found himself lodgings – overrun, as he said, by rats and mice. But even there, he found it hard to stay out of trouble with women. Although already deeply involved with Constanze, he was pursued by a young pupil, Josepha von Auernhammer, the daughter of a city councillor.

According to Mozart, Josepha looked like a devil but played like an angel, so it was just as well that (as she was careful to tell him) she had decided not to marry but to make a musical career. Unfortunately for her, he soon realized that this confidence was merely a ploy to lull any suspicions he might have about her intentions towards himself, writing to his father on 22 August that 'She is not satisfied if I spend two hours a day with her; I am to sit there all day long – and she acts such gentility! – But more than that: she is *serieusement* enamoured of me.'

By 12 September he was frantic because 'Fräulein von Auernhammer is worrying me to death about the two double concertos ...' and using these as an excuse to pursue him. We don't know how Mozart finally extricated himself from this awkward situation: perhaps news of his engagement to Constanze did the trick. But at least we can be grateful to Josepha for prompting the wonderful Sonata in D, a work Mozart wrote to play with her. One wonders whether he felt that, under the circumstances, two pianos were safer than four hands at one keyboard. Whatever the reason for his choice of scoring, the technical brilliance of this sonata – and the high musical quality – suggest that Fräulein von Auernhammer was indeed an accomplished pianist, if not in Mozart's own class. They gave the first performance on 23 November 1781, with the composer taking second piano.

The work is not well-known, probably because two-piano recitals, like two-piano pieces, are as rare now as they were in Mozart's time. Whether K448 was prompted by anything other than his relationship with Josepha we do not know, though it seems likely that the composer heard Johann Christian Bach's op. 15 duets which were published in Paris in 1778, while he was staying in the city. The older man was certainly a major influence on Mozart. It is fascinating to think that Bach, in turn, may have taken his cue from the two-keyboard arrangements of Italian concertos by his own father, Johann Sebastian.

However tenuous the historical connection, there is a more substantial comparison to be made between Mozart's sonata and J. S. Bach's multiple-keyboard works, in that both composers show complete mastery of what is generally acknowledged to be a difficult medium. The problem is a textural one: how to balance the parts and avoid the clutter of sound produced by two identical instruments. Needless to say, Mozart solves it, apparently without effort, and the texture is limpid to a degree. One attractive feature of his solution is the way he engages the two pianos in dialogue, echoing and replying to each other's statement of the themes in different registers.

D major is traditionally the key for brilliant music, and the first movement of this sonata is a virtuoso piece for both players. The first theme is constructed from little more than scales and arpeggios in Mozart's liveliest style – the movement is well labelled Allegro con spirito. The second more lyrical theme not only makes a telling contrast, it also provides fertile material for development. The central Andante is an operatic cantabile of the sort familiar from the solo piano sonatas, in which a simple melody is elaborately decorated as the two piano parts weave round one another. The ending is particularly fine. The work concludes with a Rondo (Allegro molto), in many ways the most impressive movement, with an especially beautiful second theme.

Idomeneo, rè di Creta Act III, scenes 1 to 3

Idomeneo is the first of Mozart's operas that is regularly performed today. It is very much a young man's opera, of a kind that he was never to repeat, written at a moment when far-reaching changes were taking place in the operatic world. By the middle of the eighteenth century, Italian opera (serious Italian opera anyhow) had settled into a formal rut, with severely classical subjects, plots that stretched credulity to its limits, and a rigid framework of musical forms and conventions that existed mainly to allow a maximum of vocal display for the singers – particularly the castratos, the Hollywood stars of their day. In France, on the other hand, opera had followed a rather different course. Here what came first was the text: the music served more to accompany and enrich than to dominate it, and opera was a theatrical rather than a musical experience.

By the second half of the century this situation was showing signs of change, and the figure who emerged at the centre of this change was Gluck, a German by birth who lived most of his life in Vienna, writing Italian operas at the beginning of his career and French operas at the end. From *Orfeo* and, more particularly, *Alceste* onwards, Gluck's theatrical works had been specifically designed to reform many of the worst excesses of the Italian *opera seria* tradition, and to produce a form of music drama more in accordance with common sense and dramatic veracity. *Orfeo* and *Alceste* had their first performances in Vienna in 1762 and 1767 respectively. At this time Mozart was still a child, but he must have known both operas, and we know that later in 1781 he attended nearly all the rehearsals for the Vienna production of

Iphigénie en Tauride. So when he was commissioned to write an opera for the carnival season at Munich at the beginning of that year he was already determined to produce something very different from the run-of-the-mill opera seria that the Munich public was probably expecting.

Idomeneo is the one work of Mozart for which we have a substantial group of letters describing the process of its composition. Mozart's librettist was the Salzburg court chaplain Gianbattista Varesco, and to begin with it was possible for the two men to work together personally. But early in November 1780 Mozart left Salzburg for Munich, where he completed the composition of his score, and all further collaboration with Varesco had to be conducted by letter through Mozart's father – whose frequent advice and comments add much to the liveliness of the correspondence.

Varesco was a man of limited imagination and a high opinion of his own literary merit: the text he provided was wordy and far too long, and the impatient composer was constantly demanding cuts and dramatic tightenings (his observations on the ghost scene in *Hamlet* are fascinating) in order to lay bare the fundamental strength of an albeit unoriginal plot. You can feel his irritation growing every time convention is allowed to endanger the musical or theatrical effect he is looking for. He draws upon all the artistic resources at his disposal, and his score, shot through with melody, has a wonderful richness of orchestral detail. The twenty-four-year-old Mozart was clearly determined that nothing should stand in the way of the youthful thrust and energy with which he was revitalizing the skeleton of opera seria.

The source of the story was a French lyric tragedy by Antoine Danchet, originally set to music by André Campra in 1712. Idomeneo, King of Crete, is shipwrecked as he returns home from a victorious war against Troy, and saves his life by making a vow to Neptune that he will sacrifice to the gods the first person he meets when he reaches dry land. This turns out to be his own son, Idamante, and the whole of the rest of the opera revolves around Idomeneo's efforts to avoid the plain but dreadful implications of his vow. The hidden love of the exiled Trojan princess, Ilia, for Idamante, the jealousy of her rival, the Greek princess Elettra; the terror of the Cretan people at the sea monster sent by Neptune – all are overshadowed by the doom that threatens Idomeneo and his son.

The King hopes to circumvent fate by the simple expedient of sending Idamante away from Crete. In the exquisitely beautiful aria that opens Act III, Ilia sings of her love for Idamante, and when he himself appears and tells her that he intends to kill the sea monster or die in the attempt she confesses her feelings for him. But Idomeneo still insists that Idamante's departure is the only way of placating Neptune, and in the great quartet that follows the four principals reflect on the suffering this course will bring upon them all. Mozart himself thought this the best piece in the opera, but the original singer of the role of Idomeneo was not so sure.

Raaff alone thinks it will produce no effect whatever. He said to me when we were by ourselves: 'Non c' è da spianar la voce' (it gives me no scope). As if in a quartet the words should not be spoken much more than sung. That kind of thing he does not understand at all. All I said was: 'My very dear friend, if I knew of one single note which ought to be altered in this quartet, I would alter it at once. But so far there is nothing in my opera with which I am so pleased as with this quartet; and when you have once heard it sung as a whole, you will talk very differently. I have taken great pains to serve you well in your two arias; I shall do the same with your third one – and shall hope to succeed. But as far as trios and quartets are concerned, the composer must have a free hand.' Whereupon he said that he was satisfied.

And indeed only three days later Mozart reported to his father: 'Raaff is delighted that he was mistaken about the quartet and no longer doubts its effect.' It is an astonishing piece. In its masterly interweaving of the various musical and emotional strands involved, it represents the high point of Mozart's ensemble writing to this date, and the last words of Idamante *'Andrò ramingo e solo'* (I go, wandering and alone) touch the heart as few other moments in Mozart's music.

Idomeneo was not often performed after Mozart's death, and very seldom outside the German-speaking countries. In the last half-century, revivals have become more frequent, among the most important of them being the Glyndebourne production under the baton of Fritz Busch in 1951, which used the Vienna version of the opera for which Mozart changed the original castrato part of Idamante to a tenor. The recording from which this excerpt is taken is based on that performance, with three of the original soloists – Richard Lewis as a great Idomeneo, Léopold Simoneau a honey-toned Idamante and Sena Jurinac an unforgettably appealing Ilia – and that great Mozartean John Pritchard conducting.

CD2 *Die Entführung aus dem Serail*
(The Abduction from the Seraglio) Act I, nos. 3 to 5

Die Entführung is a very different matter from *Idomeneo*. In the first place it is a comedy, an essentially popular piece far from the aristocratic world of Italian opera seria, and in the second it is a German comedy – written expressly for the National Singspiel at the Burgtheater, which Joseph II had brought in to replace the traditional Italian company in the hope of encouraging German opera. The librettist was Gottlieb Stephanie, the director of the National Singspiel, and his text an adaptation of a libretto by the Leipzig playwright Christoph Bretzner (who published a protest against this infringement of his rights by 'a certain individual, Mozart by name, in Vienna'). In fact the libretto is not a very distinguished one, either from a literary or a dramatic point of view. It is the dramatic weakness which perhaps

*Ludwig Fischer
(1745–1825), a great
friend of Mozart's,
was said to be the
best bass in Germany.
He was the first
Osmin, and was also
the first man to sing
the role of Count
Almaviva in
England, in 1812.
Lithograph by
Ferdinand von
Lütgendorff.*

most militates against its success, since the poverty of the verse does not seem to have affected Mozart at all – indeed, this much longed-for opportunity to write again for the theatre released a surge of creative energy, and the music simply poured out of him.

It was therefore all the more frustrating that the first performance, originally billed as part of the celebrations for a visit to Vienna of the Grand Duke Paul of Russia, should have been so frequently postponed. When it eventually took place in July 1782 it was a tremendous success, and the opera did much to lay the foundations of Mozart's reputation in Germany. Later, however, it came to be overshadowed by *Figaro, Don Giovanni, Così fan tutte* and *The Magic Flute*, and as a result is less often performed – which is a pity because, although it may not be a consistent dramatic masterpiece, it has the vitality and freshness of youth and contains a great deal of enchanting music.

The plot is of a fairly standard 'exotic' opera type, and concerns the attempts of a Spanish nobleman, Belmonte, to rescue his betrothed, Constanze, who has been captured by pirates and is now immured in the palace of the Pasha Selim. Mozart, as always, was very much aware that the success of his first opera in Vienna would depend heavily on his singers. Chief among these was the great *buffo* bass Ludwig Fischer, and for him Mozart and Stephanie created the role of the ill-tempered overseer Osmin. In a letter to his father of 26 September 1781 Mozart gives us what is, apart from the *Idomeneo* correspondence, one of the very few glimpses we are ever allowed into his creative thinking.

As we have given the part of Osmin to Herr Fischer, who certainly has an excellent bass voice (in spite of the fact that the Archbishop told me that he sang too low for a bass and that I assured him that he would sing higher next time), we must take advantage of it, particularly as he has the whole Viennese public on his side. But in the original libretto Osmin has only (one) short song and nothing else to sing, except in the trio and the finale; so he has been given an aria in Act I, and he is to have another in Act II. I have explained to Stephanie the words I require for the aria – indeed I had finished composing most of the music for it before Stephanie knew anything whatever about it ... Osmin's rage is rendered comical by the use of the Turkish music. In working out the aria I have (in spite of our Salzburg Midas) allowed Fischer's beautiful deep notes to glow. The passage 'Drum beim Barte des Propheten' is indeed in the same tempo, but with quick notes; and as Osmin's rage gradually increases, there comes (just when the aria seems to be at an end) the allegro assai, *which is in a totally different metre and in a different key; this is bound to be very effective. For just as a man in such a towering rage oversteps all the bounds of order, moderation and propriety and completely forgets himself, so must the music too forget itself. But since passions, whether violent or not, must never be expressed to the point of exciting disgust, and as music, even in the most terrible situations, must never offend the ear, but must please the listener, or in other words must never cease to be* music, *so I have not chosen a key foreign to F (in which the aria is written) but one related to it – not the nearest, D minor, but the more remote A minor.*

This is the aria that opens the excerpt from *Die Entführung* included here. When Osmin has finished his outburst of fury against intruding foreigners and their dandi-fied ways, he storms off and leaves the stage to Belmonte for a heartfelt expression of love for Constanze.

Let me now turn to Belmonte's aria in A major ... Would you like to know how I have expressed it – and even indicated his throbbing heart? By the two violins playing in octaves. This is the favourite aria of all those who have heard it, and it is mine also. I wrote it expressly to suit Adamberger's voice. You see the trembling – the faltering – you see how his throbbing breast begins to swell; this I have expressed by a crescendo. You hear the whispering and the sighing – which I have indicated by the first violins with mutes and a flute playing in unison.

As Belmonte finishes his aria, Pasha Selim himself is announced. He enters to a splendid burst of that characteristic Turkish music which was a *sine qua non* in any eighteenth-century theatrical work with a vaguely oriental background, and which

Mozart had often shown himself fond of (the famous Rondo alla turca in the A major Piano Sonata is an example). Mozart was perfectly aware of its purpose: 'the Janissary chorus is, as such, all that can be desired, that is, short, lively and written to please the Viennese' – but it is none the worse for that, and can be an exhilarating *tour de force* under the baton of a conductor like Sir Thomas Beecham.

Fantasia in D minor for Piano (K397)

This delightful piece must be familiar to every piano pupil, but there is rather more to it than youthful performers may realize. To begin with, what are we to make of the form? Of course, we expect a fantasy to be formally free, but this example can seem almost unbalanced, with the slow opening section more than twice as long as the brief finale. Then there is the stylistic puzzle of passionate and impressive slow music which is contrasted so abruptly with the cool formality of what follows – a contrast which makes the greatest demands on performers.

The solution to both problems is perhaps to regard this piece as an improvisation. Like most composers in the eighteenth century, Mozart could invent music at will and he was often called upon to do so at parties and impromptu concerts. Here, the solemn opening arpeggios rising from the bass – a popular way of beginning improvisations – suggest the composer collecting his thoughts, while the tender and even tragic melody which follows, interrupted by stabbing chords and rapid scales, evokes high drama. Indeed, we might think of this piece as a tiny opera without voices. The third repetition of the melody ushers in a miniature finale in D major which resolves the mysterious conflict of the opening. If the music is over all too soon, that is surely a reflection on the prodigality and beauty of Mozart's invention.

String Quartet no. 19 ('Dissonance') in C major (K465)

Joseph Haydn spent the winter of 1784 at Prince Esterházy's town house in Vienna. Mozart was then living in the city, only a short distance away. There was a strong mutual admiration between the two composers and the younger man was often invited to play at Prince Esterházy's musical evenings. In return, Haydn visited his friend's house where the two of them made up a string quartet with the composers Dittersdorf and Vanhal, Mozart playing viola. It was at one of these parties that Haydn met Leopold in the spring of 1785 and paid his famous tribute: 'Before God and as an honest man I tell you that your son is the greatest composer known to me either in person or by name. He has taste and, what is more, the most profound knowledge of composition.' These words may have been prompted in part by the

A painting by Julius
Schmid of Haydn
playing the violin in
a string quartet.

fact that Mozart had just completed his Quartets in B flat major (K458), A major (K464), and C major (K465), finishing the C major in mid-January 1785. No doubt the evenings with Haydn, Vanhal and Dittersdorf had focused his attention on the medium: these three men wrote more than two hundred string quartets between them! But it was Haydn who towered above the others in Mozart's estimation, so it isn't surprising that, when he gathered his three new quartets together with three existing works, in the autumn of 1785, he dedicated the set of six to Haydn (this dedication may be found on p. 126).

We may well wonder whether Haydn's reference to Mozart's 'profound knowledge of composition' was suggested by the many passages of chromatic harmony in these very quartets, not least the extraordinary introduction to K465 which is a stunning example of the composer's harmonic daring, technical skill and dramatic audacity. At the time of publication it was thought so outrageous that a fellow composer, Sarti, wrote a short treatise against it. Even today the opening bars are disorienting, and listeners will hardly find the effect diminished by repeated hearings. Furthermore, recent scholarship has made it clear that this effect is neither trivial nor casual. Examination of the manuscripts shows that, despite the speed with which they were completed, these quartets were the fruit of long thought and labour – as Mozart points out in his dedication.

The music of the introduction begins with a repeated low C on the cello, as if to establish the key beyond doubt, but the entries of the other players immediately overthrow that tonality, before they gradually find their way back to it. This contrast between certainty and doubt makes it all the more intriguing that the introduction itself precedes a movement which could hardly be more firmly grounded in C major. Its chromatic harmony, in other words, is less daring than the stark contrast between introduction and movement proper, a feature which suggests that the composer was seeing how far he could go in this respect. The contrast between an introduction and the movement which follows it is not unusual in itself, of course: there is a similar feature in Symphony no. 39, discussed below, and it can be argued that such contrast is the whole point of using an introduction. But whereas the Symphony's introduction begins with an unmistakable affirmation of E flat major in majestic chords, the opening of the 'Dissonance' Quartet is far more disturbing.

When the Allegro does arrive, it proves to be a sturdy, lively movement with more than a passing rememblance to several Haydn quartet movements, not least because it is virtually monothematic. Indeed, economy of material is a feature of this work. Much of the slow movement is built on one four-note figure, repeatedly passed between cello and first violin. The Minuet echoes the chromatic dislocations of the dissonant introduction, but these are controlled by a firm structure and a vigorous pulse, while the brilliant finale makes a fitting conclusion to a remarkable work.

Symphony no. 39 in E flat major (K543)

This is the first of three symphonies Mozart completed in the summer of 1788 within the incredible space of six weeks – incredible because each is quite different from the others. The last Symphony, no. 41 in C major (K551, the 'Jupiter'), is broad and brilliant in character, with a remarkable fugue in the last movement. No. 40 in G minor (K550) is tense, anguished and even tragic. K543, by contrast, is one of Mozart's sunniest and most spacious late works, its scoring enriched (unlike the other two) by important clarinet parts. All three symphonies are conceived on a large scale, and – in that sense only – look forward to Beethoven. The interesting musical puzzle here, however, is not the anticipation of Beethoven but the role of Haydn.

The complex interplay of mutual influence between Mozart and Haydn has led scholars to wonder whether these symphonies were written with the older composer's six 'Paris' Symphonies in mind. Published in December 1787, three of these works are in the keys of E flat (84), G minor (83) and C major (82). A direct relationship would be hard to prove, but there are certainly fascinating comparisons to be made. The dignified introduction to the first movement, the main theme of the slow movement and the headlong finale of K543, for example, are all reminiscent of Haydn's symphonic manner. But as with the string quartet, what counts for more than particular links or parallels is the general example Haydn provided for Mozart, as a symphonist who perpetually explored new possibilities.

K543 is rare among Mozart's mature symphonies in beginning with a slow introduction in duple time, its dotted rhythms and stately chords recalling the manner of the early eighteenth-century overture. The movement which follows is an energetic Allegro in triple time, but the broad main theme teases the ear with its phrasing and syncopations, making it hard to tell at first whether it is to be measured in fours or threes. Mozart also shortens the normal sixteen-bar phrase by one bar, thus throwing the music slightly off balance. The consequent uncertainty is playful rather than disturbing, and it is soon dissipated by the vigorous forward impetus of the movement, but it underlines the skill and subtlety at work beneath the music's untroubled surface.

The second movement is a marvellous Andante, rich in thematic material, which Mozart, with his customary economy, nevertheless derives largely from a rising dotted motif heard in the first bar, and a series of repeated notes. The third movement, though nominally a Minuet, is really more like a lively country dance, with its thumping chords and galumphing arpeggios. Mozart was writing such dances in large numbers during 1788, so desperate was he for money: at the very time he was composing the three last Symphonies he began sending his pitiful begging letters to Michael Puchberg. This is not something you would guess from the finale of K543, in which a single perky theme twists and turns through increasingly remote keys, ending on a teasing downbeat.

CD3   *Don Giovanni* Act I, nos. 6 to 12

After the immense success of *The Marriage of Figaro* in Prague in December 1786, Mozart was invited to visit the Bohemian capital and returned to Vienna with a commission for a new opera. His librettist was once again Lorenzo da Ponte, but whereas in *Figaro* da Ponte had treated an up-to-date, sharp-witted, politically risqué subject and turned it into brilliant domestic comedy, for his next opera he fell back on an age-old Spanish myth which had recently been given operatic treatment by a relatively unknown composer, Giuseppe Gazzaniga. *Don Giovanni Tenorio* (in one act only) was first performed in Venice in January 1787, only a month or two before Mozart started work on his own opera. We don't know how much Mozart knew about Gazzaniga's music (his opera was never performed in Vienna), but da Ponte certainly knew the text and modelled his own version on it quite shamelessly – though of course the single act needed considerable filling out to provide the three acts required for Prague.

So Mozart's *Don Giovanni* started life as an *opera buffa* in the Italian tradition, and in one sense that is what it remained. But later in life da Ponte claimed that Mozart had really wanted to write a serious opera at this point in his career, and had to be persuaded to allow the comic element to remain. Certainly it is true that he found opportunities to include, particularly in the arias and ensembles associated with Donna Anna and her lover Don Ottavio, music of a tragic intensity and purity of form that he had not been able to write since *Idomeneo*, and which he was never again to achieve in quite the same measure. The result is a curious mixture, moving freely from farce to high drama; from the simple pleasures of peasant life through the amazing display of theatrical virtuosity in the ball scene to the overwhelmingly powerful denouement as Don Giovanni is dragged down to hell. And even then the whole thing is sent up in a final scene of deliberate, everyday jollity. The comic lies so close to the tragic that the two can often combine within the same musical structure, thereby heightening its effect. Da Ponte's text sets a uniquely complex operatic problem, resolved with a mastery and spontaneity that no one but Mozart could have conceived.

Don Giovanni is an opera so vast in emotional range that it is virtually impossible to give an impression of it in any short excerpt. The passage here included from Act I attempts a portrait of Don Giovanni himself in relation to some of the main characters in the opera. It opens with Don Giovanni's laugh of triumph as he finally succeeds in separating the peasant girl Zerlina from her comrades – and more particularly from her bridegroom, Masetto. The recitative that follows, though only declaimed to harpsichord accompaniment in the 'dry' style of traditional opera buffa, allows a good interpreter of the role plenty of opportunity to begin his seduction of Zerlina, which is completed in the famous duet that follows (*Là ci darem la mano*). But Don Giovanni doesn't quite get his prey away in time: as he is escaping with her to his little garden-house, he is interrupted by Donna Elvira, an earlier conquest whom he had promised to marry and then abandoned. She denounces him to Zerlina in a short but energetic aria (*Ah fuggi il traditor*) and, when the high-born Donna Anna and her fiancé Don Ottavio appear on the scene, warns them against him too. In the magnificent quartet which follows (*Non ti fidar, o misera*), Don Giovanni tries to persuade the new arrivals that Donna Elvira, poor woman, is mad, but as he slips away Donna Anna recognizes him as the villain who had attempted to rape her and then murdered her father. In a tremendous outburst (*Or sai chi l'onore*) she implores Don Ottavio to join her in vengeance (a real departure into heroic opera, this one), and he responds in a calm aria of great tenderness (*Dalla sua pace* – in fact added by Mozart for the performance of the opera in

Vienna). The noble lovers leave the stage, and Don Giovanni returns with his servant and general factotum Leporello, to whom he gives his instructions for a party that he is proposing to offer Zerlina and her peasant companions. It is clear from the recitative that Leporello understands perfectly well the reason for the party, and the part which Don Giovanni intends Zerlina to play in it, and Don Giovanni bursts into a triumphant aria of ravenous anticipation (*Fin ch'han dal vino*).

Clarinet Quintet in A major (K581)

It is easy to see why Mozart's Clarinet Quintet is among his most popular works. The clarinet always elicited from him music of extraordinary charm and warmth. As so often, the composer's inventive powers were stimulated by a particular player, in this case the Austrian clarinettist Anton Stadler (1753–1812). It is probable that Mozart met Stadler in Salzburg where he was a member of the court orchestra until he moved to Vienna in 1787. But Stadler was clearly more than an ordinary orchestral player: he was also a virtuoso on the basset horn (or alto clarinet), which Mozart used in the Requiem and *The Magic Flute*, and he played a role in the technical development of the clarinet, extending the range of the instrument downward by four semitones. The clarinet and basset horn obbligatos in *La clemenza di Tito* were written for Stadler to play – and other works, including K453 and K361, show signs of his influence.

The two men became such good friends that, in the baby-language he used with his wife, Mozart gave Stadler the nickname of Natschibinitschibi. Sadly, this changed to Redcurrant Face in later years, after Mozart lent Stadler money which his friend failed to repay, despite the composer's desperate straits. When Mozart died, 800 gulden owed to his estate by Stadler and another friend had to be written off – and this despite the fact that Mozart finished his last piece for Stadler, the ravishing Concerto in A (K622), only two months before his death.

Altogether, Mozart wrote three major works for Stadler, or at least with him in mind: the Concerto, the Quintet – completed just a year earlier in September 1790 – and a Trio for Clarinet, Viola and Piano (K498). All three are wonderfully mellow, and in the Trio especially the combination of clarinet and viola gives a thrillingly rich sound. The Quintet, though actually richer in scoring, has a lighter, more luminous texture: it is, indeed, one of Mozart's most radiant works.

On paper, the beginning of the first movement looks ordinary, even dull, as the strings enunciate a four-square phrase. But the entry of the clarinet on a series of simply rising and falling arpeggios instantly transforms the piece from the plain to the ravishing. This opening – and indeed the whole work – is an astonishing example of Mozart's ability to turn the simplest materials into magic, partly by

Mozart's original wish for a serious opera after Le nozze di Figaro *was to some extent satisfied by the more sombre aspects of* Don Giovanni, *which were in any case eagerly taken up by early designers. Here is a watercolour set design by Joseph Quaglio for the graveyard scene in Act II, as performed at Mannheim in 1789.*

virtue of his perfect sense of balance, proportion and contrast, combined with an unfailing understanding of instrumental colour – and partly for reasons which are quite beyond analysis.

The Larghetto second movement might be an aria from *Così* but for the fact that it explores the clarinet's full range, making occasional use of the *chalumeau* or lower notes of the instrument, perhaps as a compliment to Stadler. After a Minuet with two Trios, the last movement, an Allegretto with variations, provides plenty of opportunity for display but, as elsewhere, the clarinet, though dominant, never overpowers the strings. Ever the practical musician, Mozart makes sure that each player has his turn to shine: no one is relegated to mere accompaniment.

The Requiem (Introit, Kyrie and Sequence to bar 8 of Lacrymosa)

The story of the Mozart Requiem is so well-known that it might be thought hardly necessary to repeat it here. The trouble is, it is rather too well-known, and the romantic accretions of the last couple of centuries (particularly, perhaps, the last decade) justify a plain restatement of the facts – which are remarkable enough in any case.

The work was commissioned in the summer of 1791 by a stranger who arrived unannounced on Mozart's doorstep, acting as messenger for a person who wished to remain anonymous but offered a fee that Mozart felt unable to refuse. By this time the composer was ill, in debt and desperately overworked: he couldn't begin on the Requiem at once because he had still to write *La clemenza di Tito* for Prague by September and complete *The Magic Flute* for Vienna by the end of the same month; only after finishing the clarinet concerto for his friend Stadler in October was he free to devote himself wholly to the new commission. But by now the mysterious stranger, from whom he had received further visits, had begun to assume an ominous significance in Mozart's disordered mind, and he became obsessed with the idea that he was writing the Requiem for his own death. As his health deteriorated – he was now subject to hysterical attacks – he worked more and more feverishly at his score, eventually calling in his pupil Franz Süssmayr to help with the composition and copying. Even so, he was unable to get beyond the first eight bars of the Lacrymosa before he himself died on 5 December, 1791. His widow Constanze, in desperate financial straits, was determined not to lose the money for the commission. So she persuaded Süssmayr, to whom Mozart had already given hints and instructions on how the work was to be completed, to finish the score and deliver it to its anonymous owner.

The truth about this curious story did not finally emerge until 1964, when it was discovered that the mysterious stranger was nothing more sinister than the agent of a certain Count Franz Walsegg, an aristocrat and amateur musician who was in the habit of commissioning works from other composers and passing them off as his own. His wife having died in February 1791, he decided to provide her with a Requiem by the same procedure – and it has to be said that he showed a very proper respect for her memory in choosing Mozart as its author. The work was first performed in Vienna on 2 January 1793, at a concert for Constanze's benefit, and Count Walsegg did not direct his own performance until December of the same year. In both cases the Süssmayr completion was used, and it is in this form that it has mostly been given, and achieved its massive reputation, during the two hundred years since then. There have always been a number of eminent musicians and scholars, however, who felt that Süssmayr's work was not ideal and that alternative completions ought to be attempted. Sometimes these were based on contemporary material (particularly that of Joseph Eybler, whom Constanze had in fact originally chosen for the job in preference to Süssmayr), sometimes on more recent attempts at original reconstruction.

The version used on CD3 was made in 1984 by Duncan Druce, and is played on period instruments to get as close as possible to the tone colour which Mozart himself would have expected to hear. Druce has been much more far-reaching in his reconstruction than many of his predecessors, incorporating comparatively little of Süssmayr's material and courageously adding a full-scale 'Amen' chorus at the end of the Lacrymosa, which it is known that Mozart intended and for which he left a sketch that Süssmayr failed to use. In the earlier part of the work, however (that is, the Introit, Kyrie, Dies irae, Tuba mirum, Rex tremendae majestatis, Recordare, Confutatis and the first eight bars of the Lacrymosa), Mozart either managed to complete his score or else left enough music composed to make his intentions clear. In these movements there is obviously less need for editorial intervention, and in the excerpt included on this disc we have preferred to end Mozart's last work at the point at which he appears to have ended it himself.

Further Reading and Listening

There are clearly two priorities for anyone who has enjoyed reading this book. The first is a good short life of Mozart, to fill out the background to the letters reproduced in it, and for this the obvious choice is Andrew Steptoe's *Mozart* volume in the Everyman–EMI Companion series – particularly since it comes with three CDs which offer a selection of music that complements the discs included here. And second, the complete text of the letters themselves, originally published in 1938 as *The Letters of Mozart and his Family*, edited and translated by Emily Anderson, and now in its third edition with annotations and supplementary information updated by Stanley Sadie and Fiona Smart (Macmillan, 1985).

For the rest, the very full suggestions for further reading made by Professor Steptoe are as valid here as they are for his own volume. Given the essentially intimate and human content of the letters, it is perhaps worth emphasizing the two books by H. C. Robbins Landon, *1791: Mozart's Last Year* and *Mozart: The Golden Years* (Thames and Hudson, 1988 and 1989 respectively), which are particularly strong on the personal and social background to Mozart's life during its final decade. A third volume by the same author, *Mozart and Vienna* (Thames and Hudson, 1991), uses a similar approach to the city which was the focus of Mozart's activity at so many periods in his career. All three make copious use of contemporary documents, and these can be supplemented by the few original sources that are available in modern editions, for example the racy and rather unreliable *Memoirs of Lorenzo da Ponte* (translated by Elisabeth Abbott, New York 1929, reprinted 1967), and the equally lively *Reminiscences of Michael Kelly*, the Irish tenor who created the roles of Don Curzio and Don Basilio in *Le nozze di Figaro* (London 1826, reprinted 1968 and, edited R. Fiske, 1975). The latter, in particular, gives a vivid impression of music and manners in the Vienna of his day. Finally, an attractive and unusual personal record: *A Mozart Pilgrimage, Being the Travel Diaries of Vincent & Mary Novello in the year 1829* (transcribed and edited by Nerina Medici di Marignano and Rosemary Hughes, London 1955), which contains descriptions of meetings with Mozart's widow, sister-in-law and sister, as well as other people who had known the composer during his lifetime, some thirty-eight years after his death.

*   *   *

With such an immense range of music to choose from it is difficult to know where to begin. As mentioned above, the selection on the discs that come with the present volume has been devised to complement the discs which accompany Andrew Steptoe's book, and anyone seeking a complete overall impression of Mozart's output might do well to begin there. Another starting-point might be to hear in full some of the operatic (and choral) works of which it has only been possible to include isolated scenes or movements in the time available – in which case don't forget *Così fan tutte*, the only major comic opera not represented, in some ways Mozart's most perfect theatrical masterpiece and one which perhaps has particular social relevance today. (The final opera seria, *La clemenza di Tito*, contains ravishingly beautiful music in a very much more serious and formal dramatic framework.)

Of the instrumental works, the last symphonies must have pride of place, from no. 38 (the 'Prague' Symphony) to no. 41, the 'Jupiter', generally acknowledged to be the crown of Mozart's orchestral music – and not forgetting the G minor Symphony (no. 40) which remains a work of stunning originality and perfection in spite of the humiliating uses to which its opening theme has been put on every electronic device from telephone answering tape to alarm clock. But of all orchestral forms it is the piano concerto which Mozart made most particularly his own: almost any of the later ones (say from K450 onwards) count among the greatest examples of the genre, and as early as K271 there are unmistakeable signs of new mastery at work. The other concertos include five for violin (slighter works, from the earlier, Salzburg days), four for horn (tuneful and lively), and one for clarinet, Mozart's last instrumental composition and a hauntingly beautiful farewell to the instrument for which he wrote so well.

Among the chamber works, don't neglect the two piano quartets, neither of which has found a place in these selections, especially perhaps the first in G minor (K478), a mature masterpiece fully worthy to stand beside the late symphony and string quintet in that key. The string quintets themselves (the last four, anyhow) offer another wonderful avenue of exploration, the quartets too (especially the remaining five of the six dedicated to Haydn), while, for those who enjoy the Serenade for thirteen wind instruments in the present selection, there are two further wind serenades in E flat and C minor (K375 and 388, both for eight instruments), the second of which, in particular, is a very much more serious work than the title Serenade suggests. Finally, there are innumerable treasures among what might at first sight appear to be slighter works – for example the exquisite Rondo in A minor for piano solo (K511), the late violin sonatas (K454 onwards) or, after a lifetime of charming but often rather slender serenades, cassations and divertimenti, the unexpected Divertimento in E flat for string trio, K563, which brings this usually lightweight form to a level of inspiration and originality that places it unquestionably beside the very greatest chamber music that Mozart ever wrote.

DATE	LIFE AND WORKS	MUSICAL CONTEXT	HISTORICAL BACKGROUND
1756	Birth of Wolfgang Amadeus Mozart at Salzburg, 27 January, second of two surviving children of Leopold and Maria Anna Mozart (baptised Joannes Chrysostomus Wolfgangus Theophilus, 28 January). Publication of Leopold Mozart's *Violinschule*.	Gluck 42; Haydn 24; Clementi 4.	Alliances of Austria with France, and Britain with Prussia. Seven Years' War begins.
1757		Death of Domenico Scarlatti (72).	Birth of William Blake.
1758/9		Haydn's first symphonies.	
1759		Death of Handel (74).	Voltaire: *Candide*. Birth of Schiller.
1760	Mozart learns to play some of the pieces in his sister Nannerl's music book.	Rameau's last *comédie ballet*, *Les Paladins*. Piccinni: *La buona figliuola* (Rome).	Accession of George III in England.
1761	First compositions written down by his father.	Haydn enters the service of the Esterházy family and moves to Eisenstadt.	Rousseau: *La Nouvelle Héloïse*.
1762	Visits to Munich and Vienna with his sister and father, where Mozart plays at fashionable occasions.	Gluck: *Orfeo ed Euridice* (Vienna). J. C. Bach moves to London.	Rousseau: *Du contrat social*; *Émile*. Ossian: *Fingal*. Accession of Catherine the Great of Russia.
1763	First visit to Paris with his sister and father. Plays at Versailles.		End of Seven Years' War.
1764	Leaves Paris for London. Plays at court of George III. First symphony composed.	Death of Rameau (81).	
1765	Leaves London for The Hague.		Joseph II becomes Holy Roman Emperor, and co-ruler with Maria Theresa of the Habsburg territories. Archduke Leopold becomes ruler of Tuscany.
1766	Visits Amsterdam and returns to Paris. Thence to Munich via Switzerland and back to Salzburg.	Haydn moves to Eszterháza.	Lessing: *Laokoon*.
1767	Second family visit to Vienna. Mozart and his sister severely ill with smallpox.	Gluck: *Alceste* (Vienna). Paisiello's first big success, *L'idolo cinese* (Naples).	Sterne completes *Tristram Shandy*.
1768	Composes *La finta semplice*, and *Bastien und Bastienne* which is performed in Vienna.		Captain Cook's voyages in the Pacific (to 1779).
1769	Family returns to Salzburg. Composes first mass (*Missa brevis*). Leaves for Italy with his father.		Birth of Napoleon Bonaparte. James Watt patents the steam engine.
1770	Visits Milan, Bologna, Florence and Rome, where he writes down the music of Allegri's *Miserere* from memory. Composes first string quartet. *Mitridate, rè di Ponto* performed in Milan with great success.	Birth of Beethoven in Bonn.	Marie Antoinette marries French Dauphin. Holbach: *Le Système de la Nature*. Goethe begins *Faust*. Birth of Hegel, Hölderlin, Wordsworth.

DATE	LIFE AND WORKS	MUSICAL CONTEXT	HISTORICAL BACKGROUND
1771	Visits Turin and Venice, then returns to Salzburg. Back in Milan for the performance of *Ascanio in Alba*.	Grétry: *Zémire et Azor* (Fontainebleau).	Birth of Walter Scott.
1772	Composes music for the enthronement of the new archbishop of Salzburg. Composes 6 symphonies, 3 divertimenti, 6 string quartets. Third visit to Milan for first performance of *Lucio Silla*.	Haydn: 'Farewell' Symphony; St Nicholas Mass; String Quartets op. 20.	First Partition of Poland.
1773	Returns to Salzburg. The Mozarts move house. Visits Vienna, but fails to get court appointment. Composes first piano concerto.		Pope Clement XIV dissolves Jesuit order. Boston Tea Party.
1774	Finishes 5 symphonies (begun in 1773), including K201; composes Bassoon Concerto, 2 masses, first string quintet. Leaves with his father for Munich.	Gluck: *Iphigénie en Aulide* (Paris). Haydn: Symphonies 54–7.	Death of Louis XV of France; accession of Louis XVI. Goethe: *Die Leiden des jungen Werthers*. Joseph II's *Allgemeine Schulordnung*: universal system of education to be created.
1775	*La finta giardiniera* performed in Munich. Returns to Salzburg. Four violin concertos composed, and *Il rè pastore*.		American War of Independence begins. Pugachev rebellion crushed in Russia. Beaumarchais: *Le Barbier de Séville*.
1776	*Serenata notturna*, 'Haffner' Serenade and 4 masses composed.		American Declaration of Independence. Vol. 1 of Gibbon's *The Decline and Fall of the Roman Empire*. Adam Smith: *The Wealth of Nations*.
1777	Piano Concerto in E♭ (K271) composed. Relations with the archbishop's court deteriorate. Mozart leaves with his mother for Paris, travelling via Munich, Augsburg and Mannheim.		Sheridan: *The School for Scandal*.
1777/9		Rivalry between Gluck and Piccinni in Paris.	
1778	In Mannheim falls in love with Aloisia Weber. Under pressure from his father in Salzburg continues journey to Paris, where the current preoccupation with Gluck and Piccinni militates against his success. 'Paris' Symphony performed. Death of his mother in Paris. Returns to Mannheim and Munich.	Cimarosa's first big success, *L'Italiana in Londra* (Rome).	War of the Bavarian Succession (to 1779). Death of Voltaire, Rousseau.
1779	Arrives back in Salzburg. Composes *Sinfonia concertante* for violin and viola, concerto for 2 pianos, the 'Coronation' Mass.	Gluck: *Iphigénie en Tauride* (Paris). After his last opera, *Echo et Narcisse*, Gluck leaves Paris for the last time and returns to Vienna.	

DATE	LIFE AND WORKS	MUSICAL CONTEXT	HISTORICAL BACKGROUND
1780	Performance of incidental music for *Thamos, König in Ägypten*. Receives commission for *Idomeneo*. Travels to Munich to finish the composition.		Death of the Empress Maria Theresa.
1781	Performance of *Idomeneo* in Munich. Summoned to Vienna by the archbishop. Resigns his post at the archbishop's court. Lodges with the Webers in Vienna and falls in love with Constanze. Composes 6 violin and piano sonatas. Begins work on *Die Entführung aus dem Serail*. Piano contest with Clementi. Meets Haydn.	Gluck's *Iphigénie en Tauride* performed in Vienna.	Austro–Russian alliance against Ottoman Empire. Joseph II introduces religious toleration and freedom of the press. Serfdom and guilds abolished. Kant: *The Critique of Pure Reason*. Schiller: *Die Räuber*. Death of Lessing.
1782	First concert in Vienna. *Entführung* performed by command of Joseph II. Marries Constanze Weber against his father's wishes. Composes 'Haffner' Symphony, first 3 mature piano concertos.	Death of J. C. Bach in London (47). Birth of Paganini. Haydn: *Orlando Paladino* (his most successful opera during his lifetime). Paisiello: *Il barbiere di Siviglia* (St Petersburg).	Pope Pius VI visits Vienna. Montgolfier's first hot-air balloon. Laclos: *Les liaisons dangereuses*.
1783	First son born, and dies after two months. Unfinished Mass in C minor performed. Visit to Salzburg to introduce Constanze to his father, and to Linz where he writes the 'Linz' Symphony (K425).	Haydn's last opera for Eszterháza, *Armida*. Piccinni: *Didon* (Paris). Beethoven's first publication (a set of variations for piano).	Peace of Versailles. British recognize American independence. Joseph II enforces German language in Bohemia.
1784	Meets Paisiello, plays at the Esterházy musical evenings with Haydn conducting. Second son, Carl Thomas, born. 6 piano concertos composed, also Quintet for Piano and Wind K452. Becomes a Freemason.	Paisiello: *Il rè Teodoro in Venezia* (Vienna). Grétry: *Richard Coeur-de-Lion* (Paris).	Beaumarchais: *Le Mariage de Figaro*. Herder: *Ideas towards the Philosophy of Mankind* (to 1791). Death of Diderot, Samuel Johnson.
1785	Plays quartets with Haydn, Dittersdorf and Vanhal. Publication of 6 string quartets dedicated to Haydn, who meets Mozart's father (on a visit to Vienna). Composes 3 more piano concertos, the G minor Piano Quartet, and begins work on *Le nozze di Figaro*.		
1786	Production of *Figaro* in Vienna. Third son born, and dies after one month. Composes a good deal of chamber music, 3 piano concertos (including K488), the 'Prague' Symphony.	Birth of Weber. Martín y Soler: *Una cosa rara* (Vienna).	Death of Frederick the Great of Prussia; accession of Frederick William II.

DATE	LIFE AND WORKS	MUSICAL CONTEXT	HISTORICAL BACKGROUND
1787	Visits Prague, where an opera is commissioned. Back in Vienna composes *Don Giovanni*, produced in Prague on a second visit. Appointed chamber musician and court composer by Joseph II. Death of Leopold Mozart in Salzburg. First daughter born.	Death of Gluck (73). Beethoven visits Vienna and plays to Mozart. Gazzaniga: *Don Giovanni Tenorio* (Venice). Salieri: *Tarare* (Paris).	Schiller: *Don Carlos*.
1788	*Don Giovanni* performed in Vienna. Piano Concerto K537 and last 3 symphonies composed, also 3 piano trios and String Trio K563. Daughter dies.	Death of C. P. E. Bach (74).	Austria enters Russia's war with Turkey (to 1791). Birth of Byron.
1788/9		Haydn: Symphonies 90–92.	
1789	Visits Dresden, Leipzig and Berlin, where he is presented to Frederick William II of Prussia to whom he later dedicates a string quartet. Constanze ill and goes to Baden. Clarinet Quintet composed, and *Così fan tutte* commissioned. Second daughter born and dies.	Paisiello: *Nina, ossia La pazza per amore* (Naples).	French Revolution. Storming of the Bastille. Proclamation of *liberté, égalité, fraternité*. Revolution in the Austrian Netherlands (suppressed 1790). Austrians take Belgrade and Bucharest. Washington first US president. Mutiny on HMS *Bounty*.
1790	Production of *Così fan tutte*. Stays in Baden with Constanze. Visits Frankfurt for the coronation of Leopold II. Visits Mainz, Mannheim and Munich, where he plays at a concert in honour of the king of Naples. Composes quartets and String Quintet K593.	Haydn gives up his post at Eszterháza and takes up permanent residence in Vienna. Salieri retires as director of the Court Opera.	Hungarian revolt. Death of Joseph II; accession of his brother, Leopold II.
1791	Composes last piano concerto, last string quintet, *Ave verum corpus*. Constanze in Baden again. Son, Franz Xaver Wolfgang, born. Composition of *Die Zauberflöte*, commission for the Requiem and for *La clemenza di Tito*. Goes to Prague for composition and production of *Clemenza*. Returns to Vienna, composes Clarinet Concerto and directs first performance of *Die Zauberflöte*. Health rapidly deteriorating, works feverishly on the Requiem which he leaves unfinished at his death on 5 December.	Birth of Meyerbeer. Haydn's first visit to London: Symphonies 95 and 96.	Proclamation of new constitution in France; Legislative Assembly. Boswell: *Life of Samuel Johnson*.
1792		Beethoven arrives in Vienna to study with Haydn. Cimarosa: *Il matrimonio segreto* (Vienna). Birth of Rossini.	Death of Emperor Leopold II. French declare war on Austria. France declared a republic. Thomas Paine: *The Rights of Man*. Birth of Shelley. Death of Joshua Reynolds.

The Publishers gratefully acknowledge permission given by the following to reproduce illustrations and photographs:
Museum Carolino Augusteum, Salzburg vi, 97, 129; AKG London 3 (Nannerl Mozart: Internationale Stiftung Mozarteum, Salzburg; Wolfgang Mozart: Internationale Stiftung Mozarteum, Salzburg/Erich Lessing) & 11 & 12 (The Treasury, Vienna) & 13 & 26 (Internationale Stiftung Mozarteum, Salzburg) & 65 (British Museum, London) & 68 & 71 & 74 & 104–5 (Staatl. Kupferstichkabinett, Dresden) & 113 (Internationale Stiftung Mozarteum, Salzburg) & 115 (Historisches Museum der Stadt Wien) & 116 & 124 & 133 (Internationale Stiftung Mozarteum, Salzburg/Erich Lessing) & 138 (Internationale Stiftung Mozarteum, Salzburg) & 144 (Internationale Stiftung Mozarteum, Salzburg/Erich Lessing) & 145 & 152 & 161 [*Die Entführung* costumes] & 169 (Deutsches Theatermuseum, Munich); © Internationale Stiftung Mozarteum, Salzburg 2, 4, 94, 109, 119; British Library, London 5 (BURNEY.532.b), 7 (461.k.25); © Sterling and Francine Clark Art Institute, Williamstown, Massachusetts, USA 19; From the Blair Castle Collection, Perthshire 21; Staatliche Museen, Kassel 23; Museo Bibliografico Musicale, Bologna/SCALA 29; Archiv der Gesellschaft der Musikfreunde, Vienna 38, 125; Germanisches Nationalmuseum, Nuremberg 43, 44; Reiss-Museum Mannheim, Kunst- und Stadtgeschichtliche Sammlungen 51; The British School at Rome Library 78; Deutsches Theatermuseum, Munich 82; Bildarchiv der Österreichen Nationalbibliothek, Vienna 93, 107, 127, 161 [Ludwig Fischer]; Musée du Louvre, Paris/Lauros-Giraudon 121; Private Collection 122, 137; Historisches Museum der Stadt Wien 103, 139, 164; Graphische Sammlung Albertina, Vienna 149; Fürstlich Oettingen-Wallerstein'sche Bibliothek und Kunstsammlung, Schloss Harburg 155.